THE BOOK OF
20-Minute
Workouts

THE BOOK OF

20-Minute Workouts

Pilates, Yoga, Resistance Band, Swiss Ball, Core Training, and much more

SALAMANDER

Produced by Salamander Books
An imprint of the Anova Books Company Ltd,
151 Freston Road, London W10 6TH, U.K.

ISBN: 1-84065-562-3

1 2 3 4 5 09 08 07 06

Printed in China

All photography © Anova Image Library

The exercise programs described in this book are based on well-established practices proven to be
effective for over-all health and fitness, but they are not a substitute for personalized advice
from a qualified practitioner. Always consult with a qualified health care professional in matters
relating to your health before beginning this or any exercise program. This is especially important
if you are pregnant or nursing, if you are elderly, or if you have any chronic or recurring medical
condition. As with any exercise program, if at any point during your workout you begin to feel
faint, dizzy, or have physical discomfort, you should stop immediately and consult a physician.

The purpose of this book is to educate and is sold with the understanding that the author and
the publisher shall have neither liability nor responsibility for any injury caused or alleged to be
caused directly or indirectly by the information contained in this book.

Contents

Introduction

Exercise is good for you. Providing it's not done to excess exercise can bring any number of rewards—improved health, extra flexibility, greater muscle tone, weight loss, more energy, and, most important of all, less stress.

This book aims to give readers a basic introduction to a wide variety of popular fitness programs; whether based round an equipment piece, such as the Resistance Band or Swiss Ball; around a fitness philosophy, such as Pilates or Yoga; or around an exercise regime, such as Core Training or Stretching & Toning.

The exercises are all designed for healthy and fit beginners and most can be attempted by a variety of ages from young to senior. However, the cardinal rule when starting any new fitness program—if you believe it may affect an old injury or weakness—is to consult your medical practitioner. Pain is nature's way of telling you to stop something, and though it will be emphasised throughout the book, if a stretch or an exercise hurts, stop at once. The expression, "no pain, no gain" does *not* apply. Also, unless you have plans on becoming an elite athlete, it is wise to leave 48 hours between training sessions, particularly when tackling the exercise programs for the first time. To start off with, three times a week should be more than enough to increase your levels of fitness and flexibility, and make a noticeable difference to your life.

How to use this book

Covering so many disciplines within the same book means that there is a slight variation of approach in each section. Some programs, such as Yoga and Core Training, give an explanation of a number of different postures/exercises before ending with a sequence of those that fit into a balanced 20-minute workout. You will also find extra exercises which can either be added to or substituted in your routine as you become familiar with the program and want to develop particular muscle groups.

Other sections, such as Pilates and Massage, explain their 20-minute sequences as they go along. However with two Pilates programs to chose from, exercises can be swapped between the two to provide a variation.

Though massage as an exercise routine is the least calorie-burning of the disciplines, it is important in that it can un-knot tensed up muscles and help you relax.

Reducing stress

The stress response is designed to get your muscles ready to fight or flee. It's no surprise, then, that muscle tension is one of the cardinal signs of stress. If you can eliminate that muscle tension through stretching or aerobic exercise then you'll often find that the psychological stress vanishes with it.

Stretching loosens up your muscles to relax your mind and help prevent aches, pains, and stiffness. It's an easy way to cut down on stress while you're sitting at a desk, standing in line, watching the kids, or doing almost anything. You might think that aerobic exercise, which makes the muscles tighten and work, would have the opposite effect. However, aerobic activities turn out to be great stress relievers, too, in part because they let you burn off muscle tension the way nature intended.

Increasing movement range

If you had to distil what this book can do for you into two basic goals it would be:
1) Increase your range of movements and
2) Improve your muscle strength in many valuable areas.

The nice thing about easy stretching is that it hardly requires any special skill, equipment, or clothing. With appropriate modifications, it can be done by just about anyone, anywhere. Since stretching is performed slowly and methodically, it's easily combined with slow, deep, even breathing. Using this combination, you can activate the relaxation response at the same time that you're releasing tension from your muscles, delivering a one-two punch to knock out stress.

Of course, stretching, like anything else, can be taken to an extreme. There's a big difference between the intense flexibility exercises practiced by ballerinas or yoga instructors, and the simple, gentle stretching you do first thing in the morning when you're just getting out of bed. What we're talking about here falls more into the latter category. While it may help you maintain your natural flexibility, gentle stretching won't drastically improve your range of motion. However, it can loosen up tight muscles and tendons so that you feel more comfortable and less stiff.

This kind of easy stretching is quite safe, but you should still use common sense and restraint. Don't push beyond your own limits. If a stretch hurts, you've gone too far, and you need to ease up immediately. Take your time. The secret to releasing tension from your muscles is to hold a mild stretch for 10 to 30 seconds. For best results, you should repeat each stretch a few times. If you're doing a stretch correctly, it should get easier as the seconds tick away and your muscles gradually loosen up. If it gets more uncomfortable the longer you stretch, you're straining too hard and missing the point.

Aerobic exercise

Aerobic exercise—also known as endurance or cardiovascular exercise—refers to activities that increase your heart rate and breathing for an extended period of time. Examples include brisk walking, running, hiking, stair-climbing, bicycling, swimming, and many of the exercises that follow. Exercise increases blood flow to the brain, releases hormones, and stimulates the nervous system. It can trigger the release of chemicals in the brain that produce a feeling of euphoria lasting for up to two hours afterward. The effect has been nicknamed the "runner's high," but it can follow any sort of vigorous workout. Besides instilling a sense of well-being, this natural high can alleviate anxiety and depression.

New research also suggests that exercise may have a positive effect on the area of the brain that plays a key role in learning and memory. This is the same area in which long-term stress seems to cause the destruction of brain cells. In contrast, aerobic exercise seems to lead to the proliferation of brain cells in the region. More research is still needed to show whether the same holds true for humans running around a track. However, since scientists have recently found that human brains continue to make new cells even in adulthood, it seems plausible that regular exercise might help people pump up their brainpower.

The type of aerobic exercise that's right for you depends on your physical health and personal preferences. In general, though, organizations such as the American College of Sports Medicine and the U.S. Centers for Disease Control and Prevention recommend that most adults engage in moderate-intensity physical activities for at least 30 minutes on five or more days of the week. With a few sensible precautions, the benefits of exercise are open to nearly everyone, including people of all ages, fitness levels, and physical abilities.

Anaerobic exercise

Other forms of exercise can help reduce your pent-up tension, increase your stamina and, in particular, improve your muscle tone. Strength exercise—also known as resistance training or weight training, refers to exercises that build up muscles through the power of resistance, an opposing force against which the muscles must strain. The resistance can be supplied by dumbbells or barbells, suspensory weight machines that you would find in gyms, or in the case of this book, the resistance band (or tube).

At one time, such exercises were mainly the domain of bulked-up bodybuilders. In recent years, however, researchers have found that people of both sexes, all ages, and every body type can benefit from regular strength training. This type of exercise strengthens muscles and bones, and it helps control blood sugar and cholesterol levels. It also boosts metabolism even while resting, which can help with weight control. In addition, strength training has been shown to increase self-confidence and decrease stress and depression.

With the introduction of the resistance band these kinds of exercises can now be carried out safely in the home without the use of space-cluttering multi-gyms. In fact you can pack up a band and take it with you wherever you go, thus facilitating important anaerobic exercise any time, any place, anywhere.

Nutrition

When it comes to your overall health and well-being, exercise and diet go hand in hand. The foods you choose will affect your health and fitness; so if you're going to set about making yourself fit through exercise, it's a good idea to look at the things you may be putting into your body that can be harmful, as well as the things that might be missing.

* Do get adequate amounts of B vitamins. These vitamins help maintain the nervous system, which goes into overdrive during times of stress. A deficiency in B vitamins may make it harder to adapt to the increased demands, so it's important to get enough of these nutrients. Good food sources include chicken, legumes, fish, bananas, avocados, and dark green leafy vegetables.

* Do consider taking a multivitamin-mineral supplement. In addition to B vitamins, the demand for many other nutrients is increased when a body is trying to build muscle mass. A moderate-dose multivitamin can provide extra nutritional insurance at such times. Of course, it's also essential to eat regular, balanced meals.

* Do drink plenty of fluids. The first sign of dehydration is fatigue. It's hard to feel relaxed and happy when you're exhausted. New guidelines from the Institute of Medicine recommend that men aim for about 13 8-ounce cups of water and other beverages daily. Women should aim for about nine cups. It's also important that you drink fluids during and after exercise when the body is dehydrated.

* Don't overdo the caffeine. Coffee and other caffeinated beverages can have a dehydrating effect, since they cause increased urination. Three or more cups of coffee per day can also lead to the "caffeine jitters," which

just magnifies anxiety. Coffee too close to bedtime can keep you awake at night. In addition, once a caffeine high wears off, heavy users may experience withdrawal symptoms, including depression and fatigue.

* Don't rely on sugar for a quick pick-me-up. Many people crave sweets when they're under pressure. Eating a sugary snack can deliver a quick burst of energy, but it's soon followed by a crash. Before long, you may find yourself on an emotional rollercoaster of highs and lows.

Is 20 minutes enough?

We probably all know a "gym freak" who needs his or her daily dose of endorphins and will drop anything to make sure they get to the gym at some point in the day. This book is not aimed at that go-for-the-burn kind of mind-set. What it does provide is a program of exercises that once perfected should take around 20 to 25 minutes to complete.

However, whatever you do, don't put a stopwatch on yourself. Twenty minutes is a rough guide, not a time limit. In addition to the 20 minutes of exercise you will need time to warm up and, preferably, to cool down afterwards.

In the early stages it will take far longer than 20 minutes to get through each program because you will need to keep referring to the book to get both the movements *and* the alignments correct. Each section has been written by a teacher in their own particular field and throughout the book they will stress the importance of correct alignment. So it is not just a question of getting the exercise movements learnt and perfected, it is equally as important to be doing them from the correct posture.

Stretching and Toning

Whoever you are, at whatever level of fitness, the chances are you suffer from stiffness and tension from time to time; and there are probably parts of your body that are weaker or less toned than you would like. Modern-day living, sedentary or active, takes its toll on our bodies. Whether you spend hours a day at a desk looking at a computer screen, sitting behind the wheel of your car, or doing manual labor, your body is under strain. But how often do you take time to consider your body? Usually, it is not until we become sick or injured that we realize that it needs some maintenance and care.

The exercises in this section are a blend of many different disciplines, including Yoga-inspired stretches, Pilates-based exercises, classic strength moves, and isolated stretching and toning exercises. The focus is on increasing your body awareness, improving posture, tone, strength, and mobility. The goal is a body that is life-fit. By following this program, you will have the tools to avoid future injury and delay age-related physical decline. Your body will look and feel much more alive.

An ideal fitness regime includes aerobic exercise, muscular strength and endurance work, and flexibility training. These do not have to be present in every workout but should all play a part at some time. Although this section is concerned with stretching and toning the body, it is useful to remember that all these components of exercise are needed.

Aerobic exercise

Taking aerobic exercise does not have to involve a gym and hours on a treadmill. It simply requires you to get moving. Technically, aerobic exercise is a sustained, rhythmical activity that uses all of the major muscle groups of the body and increases your heart and respiratory rates. Apart from the obvious fat-burning potential of aerobic exercise, it is important because it helps reduce the risk of cardiovascular disease associated with a sedentary lifestyle.

More specifically for this section it will warm up your system in preparation for the exercises here, so that you are focused and ready for

toning. You will find your muscles more willing to stretch and you will be less inclined to injure yourself. Test it for yourself and get moving. Walk, run, cycle, swim, or rollerblade—even if it is only for 15 minutes—before following the exercises.

Muscular strength and endurance

Strength and endurance are different qualities. Muscular strength can be measured by the amount of force a muscle produces to execute one single move. Endurance is measured by your ability to repeatedly execute a specific move before your muscles give in. Both of these qualities are vital. Together, they decrease the risk of injury and age-related diseases such as osteoporosis, a weakening of the bones that can affect men and women—but as most people are now aware—affects women more often and more profoundly than men. Without a reasonable amount of strength and endurance, daily activities are much harder for you than they need to be.

Flexibility

Flexibility and stretching are different things. Flexibility refers to the range of movement across a joint, and stretching is the act of lengthening muscle and connective tissue. So the easiest way to think of it is that we stretch to increase our flexibility.

Apart from for those who do little or no exercise, this is probably the most neglected component of fitness. We all have tendencies to muscular imbalances that cannot be rectified by strength training or aerobic exercise alone. We therefore have poor posture, non-specific aches and pains—typically in the lower back, neck, and shoulders—and inhibited breathing patterns, which can dramatically reduce our energy levels.

Inflexible muscles can result in injury even in

fit bodies, when demands on the body are high and as overall flexibility declines with age. Inflexibility seriously impairs the quality of life in sedentary people as mobility is reduced.

The Principles of Toning

Toning exercise is commonly thought of as the "lightweight" cousin of strength-based workouts; however, both strength and endurance can be challenged in a workout that aims to tone the body, as opposed to giving it size or sports-specific training.

Some accepted ideas about what muscles should look like can be unhelpful. It is untrue to say that a bodybuilder has good tone if he or she cannot straighten their arms, just as it is untrue to say that a slim woman has good tone if she has difficulty carrying a heavy briefcase.

The tone of a muscle refers to the tension of that muscle at rest. Good muscle tone indicates adequate strength and flexibility for normal function. So, by definition, a toned muscle is strong and long.

It is not true that strength and size correlate precisely. For those of you who are scared of muscular size, do not worry. The strength exercises here will not bulk you up. It takes a lot of hard work to increase muscle mass. You might see an initial growth in your muscles, but if you are working equally on the stretching aspects, the result will be long, strong, toned muscle, which is a desirable quality in both men and women.

As a general rule, if you can repeat an exercise more than 12 times it will have more of a toning effect than building size. However, bear in mind that if you are starting from a low base, getting some strength first can only be a good thing. So if you try an exercise and can only do eight repetitions well, that's fine! Keep

at it and soon you will be doing 12 without a problem.

Some of the exercises in this this section of the book are isolated toning movements using dumbbells and resistance bands. Others need no such equipment.

A lot of the exercises fall into the category of functional training. This refers to exercises that use a person's own body weight as a "load," or resistance. The major benefit of functional training is that body parts can be strengthened by movements that simulate daily activities, rather than just strengthening muscles in isolation. So the body learns to move cohesively, as one unit.

This method of training is beneficial to everyone, irrespective of age and fitness level. An increased body awareness and improved co-ordination help decrease the chances of injury from normal daily activity and improve performance in sports that require high levels of dynamic, functional movements (anything from tennis to rock-climbing).

Caution

Toning exercises can make you a little stiff and sore if your muscles have not been challenged for a while. It is not until 24 to 48 hours after your workout that you feel the effects on your muscles. This is quite normal. Your muscles have been worked and are growing to meet the new mechanical demands you are placing on them. However, if you feel very sore, you know to ease back a little in subsequent sessions.

The Principles of Stretching

Stretching helps prevent injury, increases co-ordination and range of movement, relaxes both the muscular and nervous system, and makes you feel good!

There is a lot of controversy about whether stretching without warming up will cause injury. The answer to that question is no—if you are calm and focused in your approach to the stretch, paying attention to your breathing, and not trying to force your muscles. Warm muscles stretch more than cold ones, so if you are stretching to increase flexibility rather than simply limbering up your body, warm up thoroughly first, or you will not achieve your goal. Whichever approach you are taking, just make sure that you are stretching within the range that is comfortable at the time.

Simple and developmental stretches

A simple stretch is one where you move into a position that you would describe as having a mild tension, and hold for 10–15 seconds. (This is equivalent to taking two to three deep breaths.) If you are in the right range, the tension should have eased in this time.

A developmental stretch is one where after the first phase of the simple stretch, you stay in the stretch and move a little further into it. You should be staying in the realm of mild tension. Again, after 10–15 seconds the tension will have eased. You can continue this procedure until the muscular tension starts to increase, not decrease. This is the limit of the elastic range of your muscle. Gently come out of the stretch.

The exercises and stretches in this section

aim more to mobilize your joints and gently lengthen your muscles over time, rather than radically or quickly change their length. So be patient, use your breath, and relax into a dialog with your body. Some days it will want to stretch deeply and other days you will feel like

you are made of steel. There is no single reason for this. Cumulative events have profound effects on our bodies. Do not expect yours to stretch as well today as it did yesterday, and you may be pleasantly surprised by the net result of a few weeks' work.

A rule of thumb for stretching is that you should feel light resistance in your muscles, not tingling, shaking, or burning. If your breathing becomes quick or you find yourself holding your breath, you are working too hard—ease off and start again. As your awareness of your body grows, you will know with more certainty exactly how much your body can be pushed.

Muscle Groups

So that you can get an idea of what part of the body you are working as you move through this section of the book, here are the major muscle groups mentioned.

Hip Flexors (Psoas and Iliacus, sometimes known as Iliopsoas) A very strong muscle group at the front of the hip that tips the pelvis forward when not in balance. These muscles lift your leg up in front of you and are very often chronically tight.

Gluteals These are the muscles at the back and side of your hip. They extend your leg out behind you and turn your leg inward and

outward. Toning them will stabilize your hips and give you a great shaped butt. When gluteals are tight, they affect the lower back.

Hamstrings These muscles run down the back of your upper leg. They bend your leg at the knee. Toning the hamstrings protects the knee and shapes the back of the thigh. These muscles are tight if you have difficulty reaching your toes in a forward bend. There are actually three hamstring muscles, the semi-tendinosus and semi-membranosus on the inner thigh, the biceps femoris on the outside.

Quadriceps These are the muscles at the front of the thigh that you can feel working as you go up a flight of steps. Toning them shapes the thigh and protects the knee. These muscles tighten when you are sitting for long periods of time.

Adductors These are the muscles of the inner thigh. Toning these can improve the shape of the thigh. Care needs to be taken in stretching these muscles as they can tear if they are overstretched when very tight.

Abductors These muscles take the leg away from the midline. Good tone here shapes the hips. These too affect the back if they are too tight.

Calves (Gastrocnemius and Soleus)
These are the muscles at the back of the lower leg. Toning these gives good shape to the lower leg. When they are tight, squatting is impossible and the ankles become tight.

Trapezius This is a large, diamond-shaped muscle that runs from your spine to your shoulder blades and up your neck to attach at the base of the head. Working this muscle will both sculpt the back of your shoulders and ease the kind of back and neck pain you get from being desk-bound all day staring at a computer screen.

Pectoralis Major These are two large, flat muscles that run across the surface of your chest. The action of this muscle is both to push away from the body and hug something to your chest. The result of toning the pectorals is different for men and women. For men, exercising these muscles will increase chest size and definition. For women, toning these muscles provides support for the bust.

Latissimus Dorsi These are the big "wing" muscles that attach from the top of the arm and spread out wide all the way from the mid-spine to lower back. When these are weak, the shoulders rise up and performing climbing or chin-up movements is difficult. Toning these tapers the back and makes the waist look smaller.

Erector Spinae These muscles run up the back on either side of the spine. They need to have good tone to support correct posture and enable your spine to move freely.

Rhomboids These are small muscles in the center of your upper back, running between your spine and shoulder blades. Working the rhomboids will help to hold your shoulders back and maintain good posture.

Deltoids These muscles lie across the edge of your shoulders. They consist of three parts: the front/anterior deltoid, the side/lateral deltoid, and the rear/posterior deltoid. These muscles

give your arms their large range of movement. Toning these will help to give a more defined shape to the line across your shoulders.

Rotator Cuff These are four small but very important muscles that act within the shoulder to help hold your arm in place. Strengthening them helps to pull in your underarm and protect your shoulder from extreme ranges of movement.

Biceps These are the famous muscles at the front of your upper arm that body builders like to flex. You use these when you bend your arm or pick things up. Toning these will give shape and definition to your upper arm.

Triceps These are the opposing muscles to the biceps, sitting at the back of the upper arm. You use them to push away from you. Toning your triceps will avoid sagging in the back of your arm.

Forearm Flexors and Extensors These muscles run from your hand to your elbow on both sides of your forearm. Toning these gives your lower arm good shape and helps to avoid conditions like Carpal Tunnel Syndrome (when tendons or ligaments in the wrist become enlarged, often through repetitive movements at work, notably typing).

Technique

Breathing cues are given throughout this section of the book as most of us forget to breathe the moment we begin to concentrate. This habit is never helpful, and particularly so when exercising. Your muscles need a good flow of oxygen-rich blood to perform well and the actions involved in breathing properly can actively support stretching and toning.

I have recommended a number of breaths for the duration of most stretches. Use the breathing to focus on what you are doing and what your muscles and joints feel like. Usually, with each exhalation you can deepen a stretch. But let your body lead.

Where advised to breathe deeply, do not take that as a command to fill your lungs to bursting point. Just breathe slowly until your lungs are full, and then empty them just as slowly and easily. It takes discipline not to rush at first, but you will be rewarded with a much greater sense of calm as you practice it.

If you are breathing well, your ribcage will expand out to the side as you breathe in and draw together as you breathe out. There is no need for your abdomen to push out hard. Let it relax and focus on the sideways movement of your ribs.

Many of us lift our shoulders to get a deep breath in. Keep your shoulders down and again, think of the ribs going outward to draw the breath in. Breathe softly. You should never feel like you have to gasp for air. If your breathing is labored, take a break and begin again. Please pay attention to the Hints & Tips given with each exercise. I have noted the main "cheats" that we all try to get away with. Often they are the same tips even when the exercises are very different, but we need reminding of them time and time again because they are habitual patterns of behavior. This isn't just for your safety; it is to get the most work out of every exercise you do. Half-heartedly moving your arms and legs around will not benefit you much and when you don't see results from all your efforts, you will probably give up!

This is also why it is important to pay attention to how much energy you have when you come to work out. If you really don't have any, do a stretch routine rather than bullying your body into some toning exercises you will do badly. Then, when you do have the energy, you can really put effort into some of the more challenging workouts.

Shifting into neutral

I have used the term "neutral" to describe the ideal position of the spine, the neck, and the pelvis, in standing, sitting, and in lying positions. There are natural curves in the spine that should be maintained for safety and correct posture. (For an in-depth look at how to achieve neutral spine, turn to page 260 for further instruction.)

The cervical spine (neck) curves forward, the thoracic spine (upper back) curves backward, and the lumbar spine (lower back) curves forward again. These curves are slight. You do not want to exaggerate them any more than you want to reduce them.

Maintaining these curves while exercising will ensure correct posture and should put the emphasis of the toning work or stretch on the right part of the body.

Safety and Equipment

Please take responsibility for your body. These exercises are designed for an uninjured, healthy body. They do not presume to correct or rehabilitate injuries.

If you have never taken exercise before, or suffer from any chronic condition which contra-indicates exercise, if you are pregnant or recently postnatal, injured, or recovering from injury, make sure that your health practitioner clears you for exercise before you commence any fitness regime.

All care has been taken in the description of these exercises and the selection of exercises to suit beginners up to intermediate levels, however each body is different. Some people will find some exercises unsuitable. Because of this fact, no responsibility can be taken for injury sustained while exercising.

Use your common sense—stop immediately if any exercise causes pain or discomfort. The chances are that if a movement or position is irritating your body by the third repetition, it will not get any better if you continue. Check with a health practitioner whether that particular exercise is appropriate for you and that there is no underlying condition that needs attention.

Equipment

You do not require any equipment for most of the exercises, but there are some that will be enhanced by the use of a few simple tools. On occasion you will need a comfortable mat, a resistance band, a set of dumbbells, or a towel or cushion.

The mat simply has to provide enough cushioning to ease the pressure on your joints, especially your spine and knees for the floorwork. The simplest foam rubber one will do. If you intend to work on carpet, you may not need one at all.

Resistance bands come in different strengths. If you are a beginner, you may want to buy two. A light to medium one is recommended for the upper body strength exercises and a heavy one for the stretches. If you are strong and at an intermediate level, a heavy (but not extra heavy) one will probably do for all the exercises. Find an extra long band of around two yards. You will need that length for the standing exercises.

The weight of the dumbbells will differ depending on your starting level. As this is a toning workout, go for a weight that you can pick up easily. You only need mild resistance for your muscles to wake up and start working. If you are a complete beginner, 2–3 lb. (1–1.5 kg) is enough. If you are intermediate, 4–5 lb. (2–2.5 kg) will be fine. If you do not want to buy weights, two cans of food or plastic bottles will do!

Clothing

Keep it simple. Wear something that is comfortable and which allows full range of movement at every joint. Make sure your leggings or track pants will not trip you up in the more dynamic exercises!

Our exercise models wear sneakers, but it is not necessary for you to wear them at home, especially for the considerable number of floorwork exercises. Just make sure that you are not going to slip during the standing work if you are wearing socks.

Warm Up / Cool Down

Warming up and cooling down are important components of exercise. They prepare the body for what is to come and enable the body to settle again after the work. This section is about a low-impact form of exercise and has been written so that the exercises gently increase in intensity through the sequences. Therefore, do not start in the middle of a workout—there are variations in the workout options. The first few exercises are, in part, your warm-up for each section. If you are constructing your own workout from the exercises given here, just make sure that the first few movements you do are from the first few exercises in any given section or workout.

Ideally, you will have done a gentle aerobic warm-up before you commence a workout, but even marching on the spot and giving your arms and legs a good shake is better than nothing at all. If you come to do a routine and you are very inflexible or feel cold, try doing the core stretches section before you attempt anything else. It will comprehensively limber up the spine and should start the blood circulating in your limbs enough to ease into the other stretches.

In terms of cooling down, you shouldn't have any problems with these workouts. Finish each workout lying on your back with your arms by your sides and your legs either

outstretched or with your knees bent, and your feet flat on the floor.

Close your eyes and breathe 10 times. Observe your body. You are waiting for your heart rate to settle and your breathing to relax into a full and easy pattern. This should take just a couple of minutes and leave you feeling refreshed and ready to continue your day.

Core Exercises

For the purposes of this section, the core refers to the entire trunk, from neck to hip. The most frequent question asked about the abdominals is how to make them flatter. The most frequent complaint made by people who exercise is that they cannot understand why their abdominals are not flat because they do hundreds of crunches. This is a perfect example of quality of movement being more important than quantity. Abdominals will not necessarily flatten by doing hundreds of crunches because the main muscle responsible for flexing the torso (a crunch) is the Rectus Abdominus. This is the six-pack muscle that runs vertically down the stomach. It is the muscles underneath this layer that are responsible for drawing the abdominal wall backward toward the spine. These muscles are the Transverse Abdominus and the Internal and External Obliques. They support the lumbar spine in all ranges of movement, create a flatter abdominal region and a slimmer waist, and are often referred to as the corset muscles.

The pelvic floor muscles also play a role in core stability. These can be weakened by a sedentary lifestyle, illness, and childbirth. They are equally important for men and women. The muscles of the pelvic floor run internally from the pubic bone back to the tailbone and are vital for good postural support. The simplest way to find these muscles is to imagine that you are trying to stop yourself from urinating. Although it is difficult at first because this is an unfamiliar movement, keep trying to locate these muscles. You are aiming to feel a "lift" of the pelvic floor up into your body. Where you are instructed to draw your abdominals in to protect your spine, include pulling up the pelvic floor. Focus on the drawing up of the pelvic floor and drawing in of the abdominals, without changing the shape of your spine.

Recent research has shown that it is the relative strength of the abdominals, sides of the trunk, and lower back muscles that results in the best support for the lower spine. There are strengthening exercises for all these areas in the core toning section. However, developing strong abdominals, sides, and back will not relieve aches and pains automatically. Tight hip flexors, quadriceps, glutes, and hamstrings, or inflexibility in the spine itself, can exacerbate lower back complaints. So make sure you give enough time and attention to the core and lower body stretches as well.

The classic postural problem in the upper body is slumping. This is caused by the muscles that run down either side of the spine becoming long and weak, allowing the chest to collapse. The head then has to tilt backward just to look straight ahead. This shortening in the muscles of the back of the neck increases tension, restricts full range of movement, and can cause or exacerbate headaches and eyestrain. Doing strengthening and stretching exercises for this area will bring back some balance.

As a bonus, when your upper back starts to lift, you will notice that your waist is more defined and as the pressure is relieved on your diaphragm, your breathing will become more relaxed.

Core Toning

Abdominal Activation

Aim: To activate postural abdominal muscles, flatten the middle, and release lumbar spine.
Muscle Focus: Transverse and Oblique Abdominals and Pelvic Floor Muscles.

Method
- Lie on your back with your knees bent and feet flat on the floor.
- Breathe softly into the sides of your ribs.
- Breathe out; draw your pelvic floor up and your lower abdominals in.
- Repeat 10 times.

Hints & Tips
- Do not jam your lower back into the floor. Focus on maximizing the abdominal work— drawing your abdominals toward your spine.
- Think of bringing your lowest ribs together as you exhale.

Pelvic Tilts

Aim: To activate postural abdominal muscles, flatten the middle, and release the lumbar spine.
Muscle Focus: Transverse and Oblique Abdominals, and Pelvic Floor Muscles.

Method

- Lie on your back with your knees bent and your feet flat on the floor, hip width apart.
- Breathe softly into the sides of your ribs.
- Breathe out, engage your pelvic floor, draw in your abdominals, and roll your spine up off the floor until your weight rests on your shoulders.
- Breathe in and hold the position at the top.
- Breathe out and roll down vertebra by vertebra.
- Repeat 6 times.

Hints & Tips

- Press evenly into the floor with both feet to stabilize your body.
- Articulate your spine by moving slowly and in harmony with your breath.
- Make sure that your chest remains heavy and that your floating ribs stay connected to your abdominals throughout the exercise. That is, don't let them stick out.

Note: If you have very poor range of movement in your lower lumbar spine or particularly weak transverse abdominals and glutes, do this exercise with a glute emphasis to help get the correct range of movement and support for your lower back. Squeeze your glutes as you contract your pelvic floor and deep abdominals, to help your pelvis move so that your lower back comes to the floor as you roll up.

Abdominal Curl

Aim: To strengthen entire abdominal region.
Muscle Focus: Transverse, Oblique, and Rectus Abdominals.

Method

- Lie on your back with your knees bent and your feet flat on the floor, hip-width apart.
- Interlace your hands behind your head so that you can see your elbows in your peripheral vision.
- Inhale softly into the sides of your ribs.
- Exhale and curl your head, shoulders, and upper back off the floor.
- Inhale and curl your spine back down.
- Repeat 10 times.

Hints & Tips

- Keep your hips and lower back relaxed throughout—don't jam your lower back into the floor as you curl forward.
- Keep your shoulders drawn down away from your ears throughout the exercise.
- Look toward your knees rather than at the ceiling as you curl your upper back, but do not pull your chin onto your chest.
- Do not let your abdominals bulge away from your spine.

Oblique Curl

Aim: To strengthen the abdominal region, targeting the waist.
Muscle Focus: Transverse, Oblique, and Rectus Abdominals.

Method

- Lie on your back with your knees bent and your feet flat on the floor, hip-width apart.
- Interlace your hands behind your head so that you can see your elbows in your peripheral vision.
- Inhale softly into the sides of your ribs.
- Exhale, curl your upper body off the floor and simultaneously twist toward your right hip.
- Inhale and curl your spine back down.
- Curl to the other side, then repeat 5 more times each side.

Hints & Tips

- Do not pull yourself into the twist with your elbows, keep them fixed in position and think of drawing your opposite ribs to hips.
- Do not let your abdominals bulge away from your spine.
- Do not pull on your head and neck—make your abdominals do the work.

Single Leg Extension

Aim: To tone and strengthen entire core and improve co-ordination.
Muscle Focus: Transverse, Rectus, and Oblique Abdominals, and Latissimus Dorsi.

Method

- Lie on your back with your legs in the air with 90 degrees at your hips and knees. Interlace your hands behind your head.
- Curl you upper body forward and hold this position throughout.
- Exhale while extending one leg out in front of you and inhale to return to the start position.
- Repeat this 12–20 times, alternating legs.

Hints & Tips

- Your pelvis must stay relaxed in neutral.
- Take your leg only as low as you can control your pelvis and still fully maintain your abdominal control.

Side Double Leg Lift

Aim: To strengthen the core muscles, toning the waist and legs.
Muscle Focus: Transverse and Oblique Abdominals, and Quadratus Lumborum.

Method

- Lie on your side, with your legs just in front of your trunk in a slight "banana" shape.
- Lay your head on your bottom arm and use your top arm for support in front of you. (Use a thin pillow or towel under your head if your neck is uncomfortable.)
- Breathe in to prepare, and as you breathe out, draw your abdominals in and lift both straight legs an inch off the floor.
- Breathe in and control your legs back down to the floor. Repeat 6–10 times.

Hints & Tips

- Do not lift high. Keep thinking of lengthening your legs away from you. If you cannot get your legs off the floor at all, that's fine. Do not give up on the exercise. Just practicing the controlled effort to lift your legs will strengthen the correct muscles.
- Keep your hips stacked one on top of the other—do not let your pelvis roll forward or back.
- Keep your top shoulder drawn down so that your side does the work rather than your supporting arm.

Starfish

Aim: To encourage good posture, and strengthen and tone the back and buttocks to support the spine.

Muscle Focus: Erector Spinae, Latissimus Dorsi, Gluteals, and Deltoid.

Method

- Lie on your front with your hands just wider than your shoulders and your feet wider than your hips.
- Take a breath in and as you breathe out, reach your right hand and left foot as far away from each other as possible.
- Breathe in and relax back to your start position.
- Change sides and repeat on alternate sides 8 times.

Hints & Tips

- Do not lift your hands and feet high off the ground. The exercise is about lengthening. You should feel the work and stretch diagonally across your back.
- Keep your shoulder down even as you reach your hand forward so that you do not increase tension in your neck.

Cobra

Aim: To strengthen the upper back, encouraging good posture.
Muscle Focus: Erector Spinae, Trapezius, and Rhomboid.

Method

- Lie on your front with your legs outstretched behind you, your forearms on the floor either side of your upper body with your palms lined up with the outside of your shoulders.
- Inhale gently into the sides of your ribs, keeping the tops of your shoulders soft.
- Exhale and draw your abdominals in while you lift your head and upper back off the floor.
- Hold here and breathe in.
- Breathe out and lower your upper body.
- Repeat 6 times.

Hints & tips

- Do not let your lower back arch. Keep your abdominals in and isolate the extension to your upper back.
- Press down into your forearms and keep your shoulder blades pulled down.
- Think of lengthening your head away from your shoulders, but do not jut your chin forward.

Front Support

Aim: To strengthen abdominals and improve shoulder and lumbar stability.

Muscle Focus: Transverse Abdominus, Pectorals, and Serratus Anterior (under arm from ribs to shoulder blade).

Method

- Kneel on all fours with your hands underneath your shoulders and your knees underneath your hips.
- Tuck your toes under and as you exhale, lift your knees an inch off the floor and hold for the count of 8.
- Release down and repeat 3–5 more times.

Hints & tips

- Keep breathing continually as you hold the position.
- Keep your abdominals drawn in throughout—do not let your lower back arch or your upper body sag between your arms.

Core Stretching

Knee Hugs

Aim: To lengthen and release lower back and hips.
Muscle Focus: Lumbar Extensors and Gluteals.

Method

- Lie on your back with your knees drawn up toward your chest.
- As you inhale, float your knees away from your chest until your arms are straight.
- Exhale and draw your knees closer to your chest—think of your knees following the breath out of your body.
- Repeat 10 times.

Hints and Tips

- Imagine the air reaching all the way down to your tailbone and lower abdomen as you breathe in. Feel the weight of your tailbone resting on the floor. (If you can.)
- Try not to let your shoulders tense to squeeze your knees in. Use the strength of your arms and be patient. You will increase your flexibility more by working with your breathing than by forcing movement.

Single Knee Hug

Purpose: To release the muscles across the hips and lower back.
Muscle Focus: Iliopsoas, Gluteals, and Lumbar Extensors.

Method

- Lie on your back with one knee hugged into your chest and the other extended along the floor away from you.
- Hold for 3 deep breaths and change sides.
- Repeat the stretch on both sides.

Hints & Tips

- Keep drawing your knee into your chest as you reach your straight leg away so that you feel a stretch across the front of the straight leg.
- If you feel constricted when you hug your knee into your chest, take that knee slightly out to the side to clear your hip.

Lumbar Twist

Aim: To increase mobility throughout the spine and stretch hips.
Muscle Focus: Gluteals, Iliotibial Band, and Spine Extensors.

Method

- Lie on your back with your knees bent, feet flat on the floor wider than your hips, and arms out to the sides.
- Roll your knees to the left. (Your left knee should reach the floor, your right knee may or may not—it's not important to begin with.)
- Hold for 5 deep breaths and change sides.

Hints & Tips

- Let your legs be as heavy and passive as possible.
- You should be feeling a stretch from your top knee through to your hip and lower back. This stretch may extend up to shoulder height.

Thoracic Rotation

Aim: To release upper back and ribs, improve breathing, and reduce shoulder tension.
Muscle Focus: Spine rotators and Pectorals.

Method

- Lie comfortably on your side with your head on a pillow, knees bent, and hands outstretched, palm on palm.
- Inhale to lift the top arm vertically in the air above your shoulders.
- Exhale and open the top arm behind you, bringing the upper body into rotation.
- Inhale, returning your arm to the vertical position, then exhale to palm on palm position; repeat 5 times on each side.

Hints & Tips

- Keep your hips stacked one on top of the other throughout the sequence.
- Do not let your working arm drop behind your shoulder as you open out into the twist. Try to rotate from the bottom shoulder so that your whole spine twists.
- Correct breathing is the key.

Neck Stretch 1

Aim: To relieve tension in the neck and upper back.
Muscle Focus: Neck Extensors and Trapezius.

Method

- Lie on your back with your knees bent and feet flat on the floor, hip-width apart.
- Place your hands on the back of your head with your fingers pointing down your spine and your elbows over your face. Keep your head heavy.
- As you exhale, gently lift your head, bringing your chin toward your chest. Stop when you can feel a gentle stretch.
- Take a full breath in and out, release down, and repeat another 2 times.

Hints & Tips

- Do not pull on your neck. Let the weight of your head fall backward into your hands and very slowly increase the stretch.
- Keep your shoulders down, otherwise you lose the anchor for the stretch.

Cat Stretch

Aim: To mobilize and "connect" the spine and abdominals.
Muscle Focus: Latissimus Dorsi, Erector Spinae, Pectorals, and Abdominals.

Method

- Start on all fours with your hands under your shoulders, knees under your hips, and a neutral spine.
- Breathe in to the sides of your ribs.
- As you breathe out, draw your stomach up toward your spine, bring your ribs and hips close together, drop your tailbone, and curve your spine toward the ceiling.
- Hold here and breathe in to ease any restrictions you feel across your back.
- Exhale and release your spine into an arch, starting from your tailbone, moving through your middle back to your shoulders.
- Breathe in, lifting your breastbone and broadening your chest.
- Breathe out and repeat, curving and arching your spine 5 more times.

Hints & Tips

- Aim to feel the work evenly throughout your spine.
- Do not let your abdominals hang when you are arching your back, keep them drawn in for lumbar support.
- Push into your hands to keep your shoulders down as you lift your chest in the arch.
- If you have a vulnerable lower back, leave out the back arch. Go from a flat back to curving your spine to the ceiling and back to the flat back position.

Cobra Stretch

Aim: To release lower back and stretch abdominals.
Muscle Focus: Abdominals, Quadratus Lumborum (lower back), and Erector Spinae.

Method

- Lie on your front with your elbows under your shoulders.
- Gently press down into your forearms to support the arch of your back. Do not squeeze your lower back.
- Hold for 3 deep breaths and release down flat on your front with your head turned to one side.
- Repeat 1 or 2 more times.

Hints & Tips

- Concentrate on broadening your chest so that the stretch comes right up into your upper back and not just into one or two joints of the lower spine.
- You may feel mild tension in your mid- to lower back. If it is any more than mild, move your elbows forward so that the arch in your lower back is less.
- If this doesn't relieve the pressure, relax down and curl on your side or sit on your heels, relax your torso over your thighs, letting your head hang forward to the floor with your arms relaxed by your side.

Spine and Hip Release

Aim: To relax spine and release hips.

Muscle Focus: Erector Spinae, Gluteals, Semi-tendinosus/Semi-membranosus (back inner thigh), and Adductors.

Method

- Sit on the floor with the soles of your feet together, your knees dropped to the sides making the shape of a stretched diamond.
- Move your upper body forward and let go of the weight of your head, shoulders, and spine.
- Breathe deeply 5–8 times.

Hints & Tips

- Do not pull yourself down into this stretch. Allow gravity to do the work while you concentrate on breathing as smoothly, deeply, and fully as you can.

Lower Body Toning

The muscles in the lower body are the largest and as such tend to be the strongest and the best developed. The reason for this is simple. They have to support the rest of your entire body. Because of this, the lower body can be slow to show the effects of toning exercise. That is unless you are starting from a very low base. If that is the case, the effect of toning these large, slack muscles is very noticeable indeed.

Many women are still convinced that spot reducing is possible—especially when it comes to hips and thighs. Unfortunately, it is not. But that doesn't mean that you should give up on toning, just understand what it can do for you. It can improve the overall appearance of your hips and thighs by redefining the shape of the muscle. And if you are increasing lean muscle mass in your body, you will burn more energy and improve your chances of losing the overlying fat.

For most people, the lower body is where most muscular tightness resides. Hamstrings, gluteals, quads, and hip flexors all have a profound effect on the lower back and when they are not in balance, standing and sitting for long periods of time becomes uncomfortable.

These stretches are not as "portable" as the upper body ones, but even so, try to do even a little stretching where you can throughout your day. In the street you can drop your heel off the sidewalk for a calf stretch. If you feel yourself stiffening up at work, get up and move around at the very least.

Do not neglect the feet and lower leg work. The feet are often overlooked in workouts. Without good strength in the foot, your arches will start to collapse, which will have a knock-on effect on the alignment of your legs and could trouble your knees, hips, and back. And if you lack good mobility in your ankles as you age, you are more prone to fall on an uneven surface.

Simple Glute Squeeze

Aim: To isolate, tone, and strengthen the buttocks.
Muscle Focus: Gluteals and Transverse Abdominus.

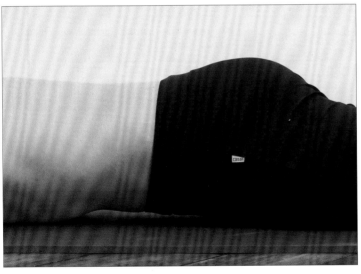

Method

- Lie face down with your hands supporting your forehead as a pillow, elbows wide and resting on the floor.
- Inhale to prepare and as you exhale, draw your abdominals in and squeeze your glutes together.
- Repeat this 10 times.

Hints & Tips

- Use a pillow under your midsection if you have a tendency to arch your back.
- Think of the lower section of your butt where it meets your legs and do not squeeze so hard that your legs roll in and out.
- Make sure both of your glutes are squeezing evenly.

Hamstring Curls

Aim: To isolate, tone, and strengthen the back of the thigh.
Muscle Focus: Abdominals, Gluteals, and Hamstrings.

Method

- Lie face down with your hands supporting your forehead as a pillow, elbows wide and resting on the floor.
- Draw your abdominals in and keep a light squeeze on your glutes.
- As you exhale, slowly bend one knee to 90 degrees.
- Inhale and lower the leg.
- Start with 10 repetitions on each leg and when you can remain absolutely stable through your pelvis, you can move on to doing alternating hamstring curls, which will challenge your stability.

Hints & Tips

- Imagine that your lower leg weighs a ton to increase the resistance in your hamstring.
- Do not lift your tailbone, otherwise you will be working your lower back. If you get halfway and the tail begins to lift, then reassert your abdominal hold, pelvic floorwork, and your glute squeeze. If this does not pull your tail down again, lower your leg down and start again.

Hamstring and Glute Lift

Aim: To tone and strengthen the buttock and back of thigh in unison.
Muscle Focus: Hamstring, Gluteals, and Transverse Abdominus.

Method

- Lie face down with your hands supporting your forehead as a pillow, elbows wide and resting on the floor.
- Extend one leg out behind you and bend the other to 90 degrees at the knee.
- Inhale and flex your foot so that your heel is reaching up to the ceiling.
- Exhaling, squeeze your glute and lift your knee half an inch off the floor.
- Inhale and lower the knee back down again.
- Repeat this lift 10 times and change legs.

Hints & Tips

- Keep your pubic bone pressing into the floor to maintain length in your lower back and increase the work in the glutes.

Side Leg Lift

Aim: To tone the buttocks and outer thigh.
Muscle Focus: Abductors.

Method

- Lie on your side, with your bottom leg bent for stability and your top leg straight and angled a few inches forward of your trunk.
- Exhale to lift your foot just above hip height, reaching your heel away from your hip.
- Inhale, lower, repeat 10 times, and change legs.

Hints & Tips

- "Stack" your hips so that the top hip is directly above the bottom hip. (It usually wants to sink in toward your waist and sometimes roll either forward or back.) Rest your top hand on your hip so that you have to stabilize your pelvis with your abdominals and not your arm.
- You must think of extending your leg as far away from you as possible without moving your hips—otherwise this exercise will feel very easy!

Wall Sit

Aim: To tone and strengthen the buttocks and thighs.
Muscle Focus: Glutes and Quadriceps.

Method

- Stand with your back against the wall so that your head, shoulders, and butt are against the wall.
- Exhale and lift the bottom leg.
- Take your feet 18 to 20 inches away from the wall, hip-width apart. If you like, fold your arms and hold them out in front of you like a Cossack.
- Slowly bend your knees and slide your torso down the wall.
- Stop when your thighs are parallel to the floor and your knees are directly above your ankles.

- Hold this position for the count of 8 before slowly returning to your start position.
- Repeat this exercise 5 times.

Hints & Tips

- (Skiers will know all about this exercise.) Make sure your knees are following the line of your toes and do not extend past them in the squat.
- Try varying the depth of your squat (the deepest will remain 90 degrees) for each repetition of the exercise.
- If you experience knee pain, stop.

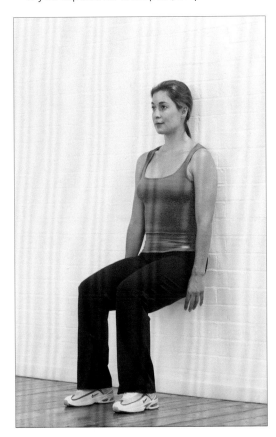

Static Lunges

Aim: To tone the entire leg, hip, and buttock area.
Muscle Focus: Glutes, Iliopsoas, Quadriceps, Hamstring, Adductors, and Abductors.

Hints and tips

- Your back should not arch. Keep your abs engaged and make the lunge shallower if you do not feel in control.

Method

- Stand with your feet together, hands on hips, your spine in neutral, and your eyes focused on a still point in front of you.
- Step forward with one leg, bending your knees until you are in a lunge position, with your front thigh parallel to the ground and your knee directly above your ankle. (Both knees will be bent to a 90-degree angle; your back heel will be lifted off the ground.)
- Exhale, squeeze your glutes, and straighten your front leg. Inhale and bend it back to the lunge position.
- Repeat this 15 times and change sides.

Calf Raise

Aim: To strengthen ankle joints and tone the calves.
Muscle Focus: Gastrocnemius and Soleus.

Method

- Stand with the balls of your feet on a step and your heels extended off the edge. Place a hand on a wall or handrail to maintain your balance.
- Slowly lower your heels below the level of the step and hold for a stretch.
- As you exhale, lift your heels as high as possible without letting your ankles fall out to the sides.
- Hold for a moment at the top of range and feel your calves squeezing.
- Inhale and slowly return to the start position; repeat 10 times.

Hints & Tips

- Keep your kneecaps pulled up so that your legs are straight and all muscles engaged.
- Make sure that your body rises straight up and down and does not sway forward and backward.

  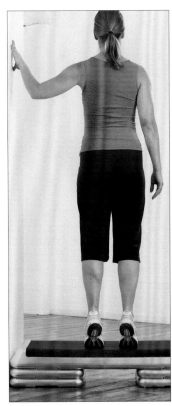

Lower Body Stretches

Japanese Sitting

Aim: To stretch the front of the ankle.
Muscle Focus: Dorsi Flexors of the foot; and the ankle joint itself.

Method

- Kneel on the floor with your toes pointing out behind you and your heels pointing directly to the ceiling.
- Find a plumb line through your body and rest the weight of your torso on your heels.

- Hold here for 3–5 soft breaths. Release the stretch and then repeat. See if you can work up to sitting comfortably like this for a minute or longer!

Hints & Tips

- Keep your feet vertical so that your sitting bones are over the center of your heels.
- If your ankles are uncomfortable, kneel on a folded towel with your feet off the edge and gradually reduce the height of the towel over time.
- If your knees are painful, stop.

Foot Stretch

Aim: To stretch the sole of the foot and the toes.

Focus: Plantar Fascia (connective tissue, not muscle) and Plantar Flexors of the foot.

Method

- Kneel as in Japanese Sitting, opposite, but with your toes tucked under so that they are pointing forward.
- Hold for 3–5 soft breaths, release your toes, and repeat. See if you can build up to 30 seconds sitting in this position.

Hints & Tips

- Make sure that your heels are pointing directly up (as in Japanese sitting) and not rolling in or out.
- Keep your upper body relaxed and vertically above your heels to maximize the stretch.

Adductor Stretch

Aim: To stretch groin and inner thighs and release lower back.
Muscle Focus: Short Adductors.

Method

- From Japanese Sitting position, separate your knees as far as possible, keeping your toes touching.
- Lean forward onto your hands or elbows and let your bodyweight effect the stretch in your inner thighs.

Hints & Tips

- Allow your butt to lift slightly forward of your heels so that you can "hang" in the stretch.

Wall Assisted Glute Stretch

Aim: To stretch the hip area with lower back support, avoiding upper body strain.
Muscle Focus: Gluteals and Adductors.

Method

- Lie on your back with both feet on the wall with your knees at 90 degrees. Cross your right ankle over your left knee, with your right knee staying wide.
- Gently push your right knee toward the wall to increase the stretch.
- Hold for 3–5 deep breaths, increasing pressure on the knee with each exhalation if the muscles allow, and repeat on the other side.

Hints & Tips

- Your hips must stay down on the floor. If this isn't possible, move your hips away from the wall.
- If your tailbone is still anchored and you can take more stretch, move your hips closer to the wall or slide the foot on the wall lower so that your left knee bends in more and increases the stretch.

Lying Quad Stretch

Aim: To stretch the front of the thigh using the floor as resistance.
Muscle Focus: Quadriceps.

Method

- Lie on your stomach with your legs outstretched behind you.
- Bend one knee to bring your heel toward your buttocks. Grasp the ankle and draw your foot into your buttock.
- Keep your inner thighs touching and tuck your pelvis under by pressing your pubic bone down into the floor as you pull your foot in.
- Hold for 3–4 deep breaths and repeat on the other side.

Hints & Tips

- Do not arch your back.
- Watch you do not over-compress your knee. If you have any pain, stop.

Standing Calf Stretch

Aim: To stretch the posterior lower leg.
Muscle Focus: Gastrocnemius, Soleus, and Achilles Tendon.

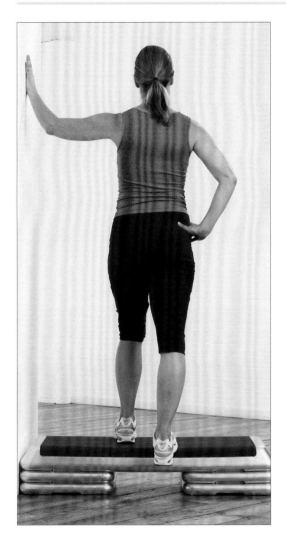

Methods

- Stand with the ball of your right foot on the edge of a step, with your heel extended off the edge. Let your bodyweight fall into your right heel to feel a stretch in your calf.
- Keep your right kneecap pulled up tightly as you press your heel down to stretch into the upper part of your calf.

- Hold here for 3–5 deep breaths. Gently bend your right leg, keeping your weight in the heel. You will feel the stretch move down lower in your calf. Hold again for 3–5 breaths; change legs.

Hints & Tips

- Use your left leg for balance only—try not to let it take too much weight.

Upper Body

The muscles of the upper body are more familiar to the non-specialist than those of the lower body. The image of the well-built male form is based on good tone in the pectorals, biceps, triceps, latissimus dorsi, and deltoids.

Strangely enough, this area is often neglected. Many people cannot do even one press-up—modified or otherwise. Women especially tend to have poor upper body tone and, often through fear of developing large muscles, do nothing at all. Men who do not exercise tend to have strong biceps from tasks involved in day-to-day living, but have weak shoulders, chest, and back.

Fortunately though, when it has been neglected, this area responds very quickly to toning exercises and the appearance of the upper body can change dramatically.

Many of the exercises in this section rely on the maintenance of good posture to tone the isolated muscle groups. The more you use your abdominals to support your spine and focus on which muscles you are targeting, the more effective the result will be.

As is the case with the core and lower body, muscular imbalances respond best to a combination of stretching and toning exercises. Stretching the upper body increases breathing capacity by releasing tension in the ribs. It feels wonderful to relieve pressure and tension in the upper back and neck, an area in which many people store tension.

Doing some of the simple stretches here in the middle of the day is a fabulous way not only of releasing tension, but of keeping it at bay. The simple chest, back, and shoulder releases can be performed anywhere, even in your chair at work. The forearm stretches too can be done at any time, and should be by anyone who spends a lot of time at a keyboard.

Upper Body Toning

Shoulder Shrugs

Aim: To release neck and shoulder tension.
Muscle Focus: Upper Trapezius and Levator Scapula (back of neck to shoulder blade).

Method

- Sitting or standing, let your arms hang down by your sides.
- Inhale and shrug your shoulders as high as possible toward your ears.
- Exhale and drop your shoulders; keep tall through the crown of your head.
- Repeat 10 times.

Hints & Tips

- Your chin should not jut forward as you inhale, this will shorten the back of your neck.
- Do not let your chest sink as you drop your shoulders, you won't get a good shoulder stretch, you will just shorten your neck.
- Keep your spine tall and in neutral, with your abdominals drawn in.

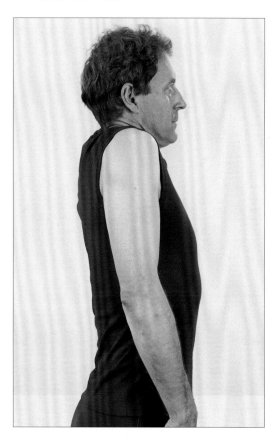

Openings

Aim: To balance rotator cuff to support the shoulders, upper back, and neck.
Muscle Focus: External Rotators.

Method

- Sitting or standing with your spine in a neutral position, imagine that you are holding a tray out in front of you (palms facing upward), with your elbows just in front of your hipbones. Hold the resistance band with a small amount of slack in it.
- Inhale into the sides of your ribs without letting your shoulders rise.

- Exhale and take your hands out to the sides without letting your elbows leave your sides. Your upper arms will remain vertical. This should quickly make you feel your shoulder blades. Imagine them pressing into your back rather than squeezing together.
- Hold for a second at the end of range to maximize the work.
- Repeat 12–15 times.
- As you inhale, return your hands to the front.

Hints & Tips

- Your back should remain neutral as your palms move outward. You need to remain straight to feel the pressure of the shoulder blades pressing into the back.
- Do not let your chin jut forward.

Lateral Raise

Aim: To shape and tone the shoulders.
Muscle Focus: Middle Deltoid.

Method

- Stand in a relaxed, neutral position, with your hands by your sides holding small weights.
- As you breathe out, lift your arms to the sides, keeping your elbows soft and your shoulders down.
- Inhaling, control your arms back down by your sides.
- Repeat 12–15 times.

Hints & Tips

- Keep your shoulders down, abdominals drawn in, and a neutral spine throughout.

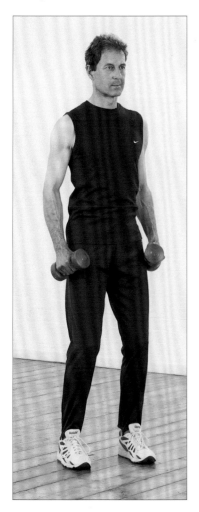

Bicep Curl

Aim: To shape and tone the upper arm.
Muscle Focus: Biceps.

Method

- In a sitting or standing position with your back in neutral, relax your arms in line with your body. Grip the weights with your palms facing upward.
- Exhale and curl them up toward your shoulders.
- Inhale and release them back down again.
- Repeat 12–15 times.

Hints & Tips

- Keep your torso still and back straight. Do not use your shoulder. Let your arms do the work

Tricep Kickback

Aim: To strengthen and tone the back of the upper arm.
Muscle Focus: Triceps.

Method

- Hold a dumbbell in your right hand and stand next to a chair or bench.
- Lean forward at the hips until your upper body is at a 45-degree angle to the floor. Place your free hand on top of the bench or chair for support.
- Bend your right elbow so that your upper arm is parallel to the floor, your forearm is perpendicular to it, and your palm faces in.
- Keep your elbow close to your waist. Pull your abdominals in and relax your knees.
- Keeping your upper arm still, straighten your arm behind you.
- Slowly bend your arm to lower the weight.
- Repeat 12–15 times and change sides.

Hints & Tips

- Keep both shoulders drawn down, away from your ears.
- Keep your spine long and do not let your head hang or your chin jut forward.

Flyes

Aim: To strengthen and tone upper chest.
Muscle Focus: Pectorals and Anterior Deltoid.

Method

- Lie on your back and hold your weights above your chest as if you are hugging a large beach ball.
- As you inhale, open your arms out to the side.
- As you exhale, return to the starting position and repeat 12–15 times.

Hints & Tips

- Keep your elbows slightly soft throughout—you should make a large circle with your arms when they are together and then the arms should not change shape. The feeling is that you are lifting your elbows out to the sides.
- Keep your shoulders down and the weights in line with your chest, not your face.

One-arm Dumbbell Row

Aim: To tone upper back, shoulder, and upper arm, and improve posture.
Muscle Focus: Latissimus Dorsi, Rear Deltoid, Trapezius, and Biceps.

Method

- Stand near a bench or chair, holding a dumbbell in your left hand with your palm facing in.
- Draw your abdominals in and pivot forward from your hips and rest your right hand on the support so that your back is neutral and just short of 90 degrees.
- Allow your left arm to hang down to the floor.
- As you exhale, pull your left arm up until your elbow is pointing to the ceiling and your hand is by your waist.
- Inhale and lower the weight slowly back down.
- Repeat 12–15 times and change sides.

Hints & Tips

- Do not let your shoulder lift toward your ear and keep your abdominals in to support your lower back.

Modified Press Up

Aim: To increase chest and upper arm strength and improve upper body posture.
Muscle Focus: Pectorals, Anterior Deltoid, and Triceps.

Method

- Start on all fours, with vertical arms, hands wider than shoulders, and your knees just back from your hips.
- Keep your abdominals drawn in to stop your lower back from arching.
- Inhale and bend your arms to lower your body toward the floor. Stop when your upper arms are parallel to the floor.
- Exhale and straighten your arms.
- Repeat 8–10 times. Rest and try another set.

Hints & Tips

- Keep drawing your shoulder blades down your back to your waist and pull your abdominals and pelvic floor in for support.
- If you lose good form, reduce the depth of your press-up, or stop.
- Do not let your spine collapse between your shoulder blades. Keep your shoulders down and both upper back and chest broad.

Upper Body Stretching

Side Stretch

Aim: To stretch the sides, shoulders, forearms, and wrists.
Muscle Focus: Quadratus Lumborum, Latissimus Dorsi, and Wrist Flexors.

Method

- Stand with your spine in neutral, your feet just wider than hip-width apart, and knees soft.
- Interlace your fingers and lift your hands above your head with your palms facing upward.
- Inhale and broaden your ribs as much as possible, without shrugging your shoulders.
- Keep your abdominals drawn in, and as you exhale, bend to the right.
- Inhaling, return to center and exhaling, reach to the left.
- Inhaling, return to center and repeat 3 times to each side.

Hints & Tips

- Draw your abdominals in, keep your shoulders down away from your ears, and do not arch your lower back or let your hips twist.

Upper Back Stretch

Aim: To release tension in upper back.
Muscle Focus: Lats, Rhomboids, and Trapezius.

Method

- Stand with your spine in neutral, your feet just wider than hip-width apart and knees soft. Interlace your fingers and reach your hands forward with your palms facing away from you.
- Reach your hands as far forward as you can while pulling your upper back in the opposite direction. Allow your head to incline forward toward your arms without dropping it completely.
- Hold and take 4 deep breaths, increasing the intensity of the stretch with each breath.

Hints & Tips

- Keep your abdominals drawn in and do not push your hips forward.

Chest Stretch

Aim: To release tension in upper shoulders and stretch chest.
Muscle Focus: Pectorals, Anterior Deltoid, and Trapezius.

Method

- Stand with your spine in neutral, your feet just wider than hip-width apart, and knees soft. Interlace your fingers behind you and reach your hands away with your palms facing inward to your back.
- Stretch your hands as far away from you as possible, keeping your spine erect.
- Hold for 4 deep breaths, bringing the breath as high into your collar bones as possible to intensify the stretch, reaching farther away with each exhalation.

Hints & Tips

- Do not let your chin jut forward or arch your lower back as you stretch.

Shoulder Stretch

Aim: To stretch the shoulders.
Muscle Focus: Deltoid, Rhomboid, and Trapezius.

Method

- Stand with your spine in neutral, your feet just wider than hip-width, and knees soft.
- Take your right arm across in front of your chest, with your wrist resting on your left shoulder.
- Keep your shoulders down and push your right elbow toward your left shoulder. (Your wrist may slide over your shoulder.)
- Hold for 3 deep breaths, increasing the stretch with each breath if possible. Repeat on the other side.

Hints & Tips

- Do not let your stretching shoulder lift in an effort to increase the range. Keep your abdominals drawn in and your spine neutral.

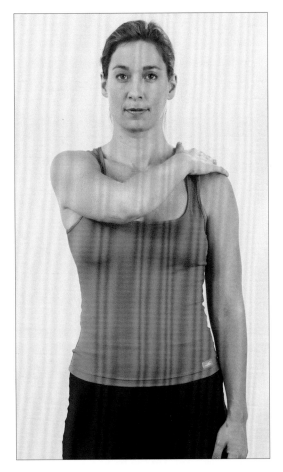 

Tricep Stretch

Aim: To stretch the upper arm and increase range of movement in the shoulder joint.
Muscle Focus: Tricep and Lats.

Method

- Stand with your spine in neutral, your feet just wider than hip-width, and knees soft.
- Reach your right hand into the air and bend your elbow so that your hand is reaching down your spine. Use your left hand to gently press down on your right elbow to increase the stretch.
- Hold for 3 deep breaths and repeat on the other side.

Hints & Tips

- Do not let your head be pushed forward by your arm or try to increase your range of movement by arching your back.
- Keep your abdominals drawn in for support.

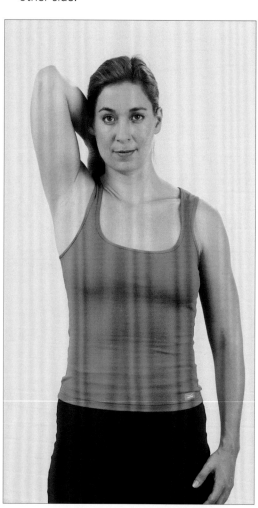 

Back Hand Link

Aim: To increase shoulder mobility and stretch the back of the arm.
Muscle Focus: Trapezius, Rhomboid, Pectorals, Tricep, and Rotator Cuff.

Method

- Stand in neutral with your left arm lifted above your head.
- Bend your elbow so that your left hand is reaching down your spine.
- Reach your right hand behind your back and link with the fingers of your left hand.
- Hold for 3–5 breaths and change sides.

Hints & Tips

- If you can't link fingers, drop a towel or band down from your top hand for your bottom hand to grasp.
- Be careful if you have hypermobile shoulders; don't overstretch.
- Do not let your top upper arm push your head forward; press the back of your head into your arm instead.

Neck Stretch 2

Aim: To release tension in the side of the neck into the shoulder.

Muscle Focus: Trapezius, Sternocleidomastoid (rotates head), Scalenes (from neck to ribcage under collar bone).

Method

- Stand with your spine in neutral, your feet just wider than hip-width apart and knees soft.
- Take your right hand behind your back and hold your right wrist with your left hand.
- Draw down on your right wrist and gently lean your head to the left.
- Hold for 3 deep breaths, release gently, and change sides.

Hints & Tips

- If you are aggressive when stretching your neck, the muscles will not respond well.
- Focus on keeping your shoulders down and level—do not lean to the side, keep the movement limited to the head.

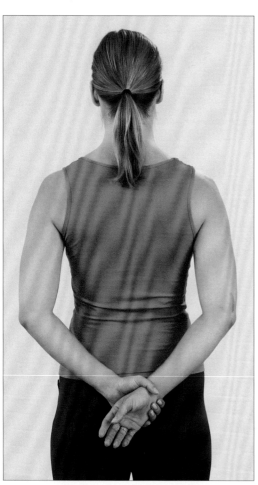
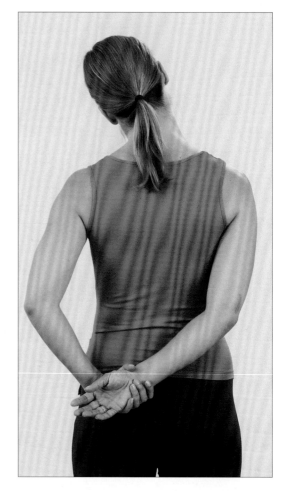

20-Minute Workouts

Now that you are familiar with all the exercises—and your body's capabilities—it is time to incorporate both toning and stretching in individual workouts.

If you intend to work out every day, then vary your choice initially among the first three sections that follow: core, upper body, and lower body. For further variation, return to the earlier sections and do a complete tone workout as given there, followed by its equivalent stretch workout.

If you think you have progressed beyond some of the exercises and workouts, do not give up on them. Simply changing what you do by returning to them—even if it is less intense— can keep boredom at bay and ensure that you do not reach a plateau in your toning and stretching from which you do not progress. You can do two sets of each exercise, or do circuits (that is, repeat the exercise sequence) to increase the intensity.

These workouts can all be repeated on consecutive days without a problem, but use common sense and maintain a balance, so that each area of the body experiences an equal amount of toning and stretching work over time. Take one day a week off so that you come back to your workouts with enthusiasm; if you are worried about losing momentum, then do a gentle stretch routine on that day.

These exercises are yours to experiment with. So long as you warm up, cool down, and begin with some basic exercises, you can make every workout unique!

Core Workout

When in doubt, start here. Even when you have progressed beyond these basic exercises, you can return to this workout as an extended warm-up, or on days when you feel fragile.

These three workouts give you more variation than you have when you are just following the sections. Try them once you are familiar with all the exercises. They are organized to allow you to move as smoothly as possible from one exercise to the next.

Exercise Order

1 Knee Hugs
2 Single Knee Hugs
3 Abdominal Activation
4 Pelvic Tilts
5 Abdominal Curl
6 Oblique Curl
7 Lumbar Twist
8 Single Leg Stretch
9 Side Double Leg Lift
10 Thoracic Rotation
11 Starfish
12 Cobra
13 Neck Stretch 1
14 Front Support
15 Cat Stretch
16 Spine and Hip Release

1 Knee Hugs (See page 38)

2 Single Knee Hugs (See page 39)

3 Abdominal Activation (See page 29)

4 Pelvic Tilts (See page 30)

5 Abdominal Curl (See page 31)

6 Oblique Curl (See page 32)

7 Lumbar Twist (See page 40)

8 Single Leg Stretch
(See page 33)

9 Side Double Leg Lift
(See page 34)

10 Thoracic Rotation
(See page 41)

11 Starfish (See page 35)

12 Cobra (See page 36)

13 Neck Stretch 1 (See page 42)

14 Front Support (See page 37)

15 Cat Stretch (See page 43)

16 Spine and Hip Release
(See page 45)

Lower Body Workout

Splitting the body in two (or three) can be a cunning way to force you back into your sneakers on two consecutive days. While your upper body rests, your lower body works.

Exercise Order

1 Simple Glute Squeeze
2 Hamstring Curl
3 Hamstring and Glute Lift
4 Wall Assisted Glute Stretch
5 Side Leg Lift
6 Lying Quad Stretch
7 Japanese Sitting
8 Foot Stretch
9 Adductor Stretch
10 Static Lunges
11 Wall Sit
12 Calf Raise
13 Standing Calf Stretch

1 Simple Glute Squeeze
(See page 47)

2 Hamstring Curl (See page 48)

3 Hamstring and Glute Lift
(See page 49)

4 Wall Assisted Glute Stretch (See page 57)

5 Side Leg Lift (See page 50)

6 Lying Quad Stretch (See page 58)

7 Japanese Sitting
(See page 54)

8 Foot Stretch
(See page 55)

9 Adductor Stretch (See page 56)   10 Static Lunges (See page 52)   11 Wall Sit (See page 51)

12 Calf Raise (See page 53)   13 Standing Calf Stretch
(See page 59)

Upper Body Workout

This workout will add significant muscle mass only if you begin from a relatively low level of upper body strength.

Exercise Order

1 Side Stretch
2 Chest Stretch
3 Back Stretch
4 Shoulder Shrugs
5 Openings

6 Lateral Raise
7 Shoulder Stretch
8 Bicep Curl
9 Modified Press Up
10 Flyes
11 One Arm Row

12 Back Hand Link
13 Tricep Kickback
14 Tricep Stretch
15 Neck Stretch 2

1 Side Stretch (See page 69)

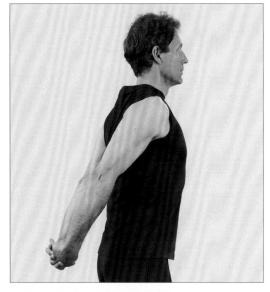

2 Chest Stretch (See page 70)

3 Back Stretch (See page 70)

4 Shoulder Shrugs (See page 61)

5 Openings (See page 62)

6 Lateral Raise (See page 63)

7 Shoulder Stretch (See page 71)   8 Biceps Curl (See page 64)   9 Modified Press Up (See page 68)

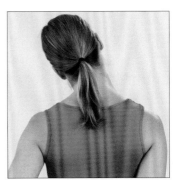

10 Flyes (See page 66)   11 One Arm Row (See page 67)   12 Back Hand Link (See page 73)

13 Tricep Kickback (See page 65)   14 Tricep Stretch
(See page 72)   15 Neck Stretch 2 (See page 74)

Swiss Ball

The term "Swiss Ball" was given to this fantastically versatile piece of equipment by physiotherapists in the United States during the late 1980s when it began to be used for physical therapy and rehabilitation from injury. It was named the "Swiss Ball" as it was first used in Switzerland, though the ball was actually manufactured by an Italian plastics company in 1963. The Swiss Ball is now widely used around the world, in everything from light aerobics classes to professional athletic training institutions, as more and more people learn the benefits of using this simple yet highly effective training aid.

What makes Swiss Balls so good?

We all need to be balanced and stable. Even when sat at a desk all day, stability is required to hold a correct posture. A lack of balance and stability around your joints can lead to injury and referred complaints such as back and neck pain. Effective muscle proprioception (communication with the brain resulting in muscle action) is vital in maintaining balance and stability, especially in sport. The nature and instability of a ball when a body rests against it, makes it the perfect training tool. It helps to improve your center of balance and at the same time strengthen your "core."

All muscles work together in a synergistic chain; by following the exercises and progressions in this section you will learn to create improved balance, stability, and even strength and muscle tone, maximizing the efficiency of this chain. Your muscle control and coordination will be greatly improved, as the instability of the ball requires you to concentrate on your balance as well as the movement that you are performing. Even more important, a Swiss Ball will add fun and variety to your fitness training routine.

Additional benefits of using a Swiss Ball

Low cost
Swiss Balls provide training without the use of expensive equipment, or the need to join a gym. For the price of less than a month's gym membership, you can set yourself up with all that you need for a complete Swiss Ball workout.

Light weight
Unlike other training equipment that would be required to complete some of the exercises shown here, the Swiss Ball is light in weight, making it easier and safer to move around.

Storage and portability
Because the Swiss Ball is lightweight and compact when deflated, it does not require much storage space, unlike bulky frames and benches. This also means that you can take it with you anywhere you go, which is especially beneficial for those who travel regularly, as it enables you to maintain the consistency of your exercise program.

Time efficiency
You can plan your time more efficiently by using a Swiss Ball, as you won't need to work around gym schedules or allow for additional traveling time. You can pick it up whenever you want and wherever you are.

What results can you expect from using a Swiss Ball?
- Enhanced balance, stability, and control of deep muscle tissues
- Improved posture and support around joints
- Greater muscle strength, power, and endurance
- Greater flexibility and range of movement in joints
- Improved metabolism, body weight control, and energy
- Greater enjoyment of everyday activities and sports
- Prevention of muscle and joint atrophy (loss of muscle mass) caused by aging
- Reduced risk of injury

The terminology of the anatomy and muscle groups being worked in each section has been kept to a level where it is easily understandable for a beginner, yet is still informative to those who have good basic knowledge of other training methods. It is outside the remit of this book to go into great anatomical detail, but the guide to muscle areas on pages 86 and 87 is an excellent start to understanding the muscle areas you will be working on.

Safety Precautions

Before commencing any exercise with a Swiss Ball, please ensure you have checked the following:

1. Condition of ball

Examine the Swiss Ball before each use, checking for stress marks and punctures. Purchase an anti-burst ball, designed to take up to 300kg in weight. Always take note of the manufacturers' recommendations with regard to its resistance to weight.

2. Ball size and inflation

To check that you have the right size ball for your body size and that it is inflated correctly, sit on top and in the center of the Swiss Ball. Your hips should be level or slightly higher than your knees, with them ideally flexed to a 90-degree angle, and your feet flat on the floor. Follow the manufacturers' instructions for optimal inflation.

3. Ball storage

Swiss Balls should be stored at room temperature. Do not store the ball in cold temperatures as this can have a negative effect on its expansion properties.

4. Exercise area suitability

Give yourself plenty of free space to perform the exercises. Choose an area of flooring that is non-slip with nothing in close proximity that you could fall onto.

Correct and safe usage

- Make sure that you understand how to do each exercise properly by carefully reading through and following the full instructions before starting your workout. Improper use can cause serious injury.
- Wear appropriate clothing, ensuring that it is not too baggy or slippery. Use footwear that has a sole with good grip.
- When using weights, be cautious. Remember that the ball will be unstable, making the weights harder to manage.
- Allow sufficient rest periods (48 hours) between workouts for recovery and to prevent over-training.
- If you are new to Swiss Ball training it is advisable to build up the exercise intensity and frequency gradually.
- It is advisable to have someone with you to assist your balance at first when progressing to the more advanced stability exercises.

Health

- If you are not used to exercise or have a medical condition, please check with your physician/doctor before commencing any form of exercise.

Equipment

For the exercises in this section you will require the following equipment:

1. Swiss Ball

There are many types and sizes of Swiss Ball available. Follow the individual manufacturer's guidelines to choose the correct size for you. Also ensure that you purchase a hand pump. Do not use an electrically operated pump.

2. Free weights

Dumbbells are available in various guises. Some are fixed weight and others are adjustable. Choose a variety from a few kilos upward.

3. Ankle weights

Ankle weights are an ideal way to add resistance against the movement of a limb, and come in a variety of weights. Choose a medium weight for the exercises in this section.

4. Medicine ball

Medicine balls are easy and comfortable to hold, and are available in various resistance levels.

5. Exercise mat

If you are exercising on a shiny surface or a hard wood floor, it would be advisable to use a mat for grip and comfort.

How to choose the correct size of Swiss Ball

The following sizes should be used as a general guide:

HEIGHT	BALL SIZE REQUIRED
Up to 5' 6"	55 cm (22 in.)
5' 7" – 6' 0"	65 cm (26 in.)
6' 1" – 6' 9"	75 cm (30 in.)

Please note that each manufacturer will provide their own size guidelines; so be sure to follow their individual recommendations.

Muscles

To provide you with a better understanding of the location of areas that are being worked please refer to the following diagrams. Main muscle group names are listed for each exercise.

Major anterior muscle groups

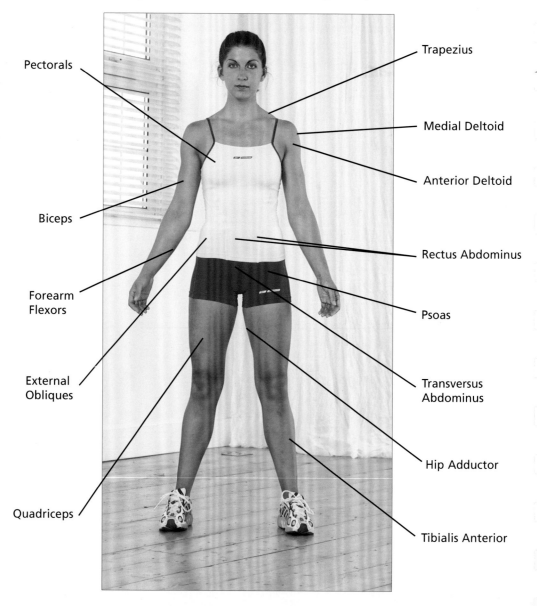

Pectorals

Biceps

Forearm Flexors

External Obliques

Quadriceps

Trapezius

Medial Deltoid

Anterior Deltoid

Rectus Abdominus

Psoas

Transversus Abdominus

Hip Adductor

Tibialis Anterior

Major posterior muscle groups

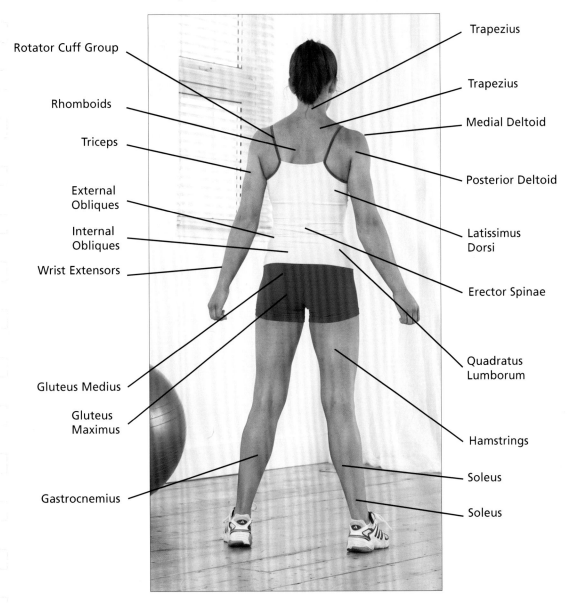

Rotator Cuff Group

Rhomboids

Triceps

External
Obliques

Internal
Obliques

Wrist Extensors

Gluteus Medius

Gluteus
Maximus

Gastrocnemius

Trapezius

Trapezius

Medial Deltoid

Posterior Deltoid

Latissimus
Dorsi

Erector Spinae

Quadratus
Lumborum

Hamstrings

Soleus

Soleus

Activating and Holding the Correct Posture

To perform the exercises within this section correctly and safely, it is important that you learn how to position your body in neutral alignment. Finding this alignment will increase the effectiveness of the exercise by activating the abdominal and pelvic stabilizing muscles used to form a supportive girdle around the lower back.

Neutral alignment is when all major joints (or selected joints, depending on the exercise) are in line with one another. For example, your body and legs would be neutrally aligned when you can draw a straight line from your shoulder to your ankles passing through your hips and knees.

To help you hold a neutral position and compensate for the instability of the ball, you require support from the core muscle groups. You will see references to the "core" throughout this section and the rest of the book. The core muscles are stabilizers that have very deep attachments to their access of movement. For example, the Transversus Abdominus has a stabilizing role in preventing your pelvis from tilting while in a bridge position with legs straight. The main aim of activating your core when doing exercises using the Swiss Ball is to effectively recruit the midsection musculature, learning to control the position of the lower back during the various dynamic movements used in this section.

Your stabilizing muscles will be stressed to a variety of intensities with each exercise. You can control the instability to a degree by altering the inflation of the ball. If the ball is fully inflated and more solid it will require greater stability than if it were softer, forming a wider contact area with the floor.

Here are some examples of the neutral alignment and correct postures that you will need to master:

Seated on the Ball

1 Place yourself directly in the center of the Swiss Ball.
2 Sit on the ball with your feet flat on the floor.
3 Knees should be bent to 90 degrees.
4 Activate and tighten your abdominal muscles to support and straighten your midsection.
5 Keep your eyes fixed straight ahead so that your neck is straight.
6 Hold your torso vertical and neutrally aligned from shoulders to hips.

Lying on the Floor

1 Lie on your back on the floor with your knees bent and feet flat on the floor.
2 Pull your navel in, imagining that you are trying to get it to the floor as you tighten your lower abdominal muscles.
3 Place your finger tips either side of your lower abdominals so that you can feel them flatten and tighten as you pull your abdominals in.
4 Keep your back flat on the floor from your shoulders to your pelvis, making sure that there is no arch in the small of your back.
5 Continue to breathe normally as you hold your abdominal muscles tight.

Reverse Bridge Position

1 Lie on your back on top of the ball with your knees bent at 90 degrees.
2 The ball should be positioned so that it sits directly between your shoulder blades.
3 Place your feet shoulder width apart.
4 Activate and tighten your abdominal muscles to maintain a neutral alignment, forming a straight line from your shoulders to your knees.
5 Do not let your pelvis drop and move out of alignment.
6 Place your hands on your hips and fingers on the lower abdominals to feel that they are engaged and to maintain symmetry and balance in your upper body.

Grip Positions

Throughout the exercise descriptions in this section, references will be made to the different grip positions required when using weights. They are as follows:

Over hand grip

Under hand grip

Palm inward grip

Gaining Balance and Familiarity

Lying on the Ball

The first stage in familiarizing yourself with the Swiss Ball is to practice lying on it.

1 Start by lying on top of the ball with fingers and toes touching the floor for stability.
2 Shift your body weight from your toes to your fingers, rolling the ball back and forth.
3 Now try shifting your weight from side to side, touching your toes and fingers on one side, then rolling over to toes and fingers on the other side.
4 Finally, try finding your center of balance on the ball by lifting fingers and toes off the floor.

Sitting on the Ball

The second stage in finding your center of balance is to practice sitting on the Swiss Ball.

1 Sit on the center of the ball.
2 Lift your feet off the floor and raise your arms out in front of you. Start with one leg at a time and progress to both legs. You'll be amazed how quickly you are able to tune your balance and become stable on the ball.

Warm Up/Cool Down with the Swiss Ball

Performing a warm-up prior to strenuous exercise of any kind is crucial. A warm-up with light aerobic and flexibility exercises is important because it:

- Prepares the muscles and joints for the activity ahead by increasing blood flow and muscle temperature.
- Reduces the risk of injury to muscles, tendons, and ligaments by making them more pliable, allowing you to move through a full range of motion more safely and effectively.
- Encourages circulation to the muscles, heart, and lungs by raising the flow of blood. This increased blood volume helps supply muscles with additional oxygen and nutrients required for exercise.
- Allows you to get into the right frame of mind through increased central nervous system function, helping you enhance factors such as muscle control and coordination, which are essential when using a Swiss Ball.

An exercise warm-up should last at least 15 minutes and should focus on all areas of the body. This should start with light but brisk aerobic style movements that work large muscle group areas together. Once this has been achieved your muscles will be more pliable and ready for the flexibility exercise phase of your warm-up.

These exercises can also be used at the end of your workout as a cool down phase. When performing any strenuous exercise your muscles tend to shorten with some of the fibers staying more contracted than normal. Performing flexibility exercises after your workout will help to correct and further improve muscle length, which will also aid recovery.

Jogging on the Spot

Areas Worked: A great warm up starting point using the large muscle groups in your legs.

1 Lift alternate legs, pushing off your toes and flexing your knees.
2 Swing your arms back and forth in an opposite order to your legs.

Technique

- Bend your elbows to 90 degrees and lift your hands high as you swing your arms.
- Keep your eyes fixed straight ahead so that your neck is in a neutral position.
- Activate and tighten your abdominal muscles to help maintain a neutral alignment.

Hints & Tips

- Progressively increase the speed of your steps and the height of your knees.
- Control your breathing with your steps. For example, breathe in for 5 steps and out for 5 steps.

Seated Bounce on Ball

Areas Worked: All the main muscle groups in your legs and core.

1 Sit on the ball with your feet flat on the floor. Push through your heels and extend your hips and knees slightly as if you are about to stand up.
2 Relax your legs before you lose contact with the Swiss Ball, sinking back into it. Repeat this movement for 2 to 3 minutes, or as long as desired.

Technique

- Place yourself directly in the center of the Swiss Ball.
- Start with your knees bent to 90 degrees.
- Sit straight with your abdominal muscles activated and tightened.
- Keep your eyes fixed straight ahead so that your neck and back are neutrally aligned.

- Relax your arms and rest your hands on your thighs. Avoid using them to assist the lift.

Hints & Tips

- Progressively increase the speed and height of the bounce to enhance the warm up intensity.

Seated Leg Rotations

Areas Worked: Warm up and mobility for the muscles in front of, and surrounding, the hip.

1 Sit on the ball with your feet flat on the floor. Extend one leg at the hip and knee so that it is straight.
2 Rotate your extended leg at the hip moving it in so that your foot passes the central line of your body, moves down toward the floor, and then up and out to the side. Repeat this movement for 8 to 10 repetitions.

Technique

• Place yourself directly in the center of the Swiss Ball.
• The leg on the side that you are not working should be bent to 90 degrees at the knee, and your foot flat on the floor.
• Your extended leg should stay straight for the whole movement.
• Keep your eyes fixed straight ahead and avoid leaning your shoulders forward when lifting the leg.
• Relax your arms and rest your hands on your hips.

Hints & Tips

• Sit straight with abdominal muscles activated and tightened.
• Progressively increase the size of the circles.

Ball and Raise Reach

Areas Worked: A good final warm up exercise that includes a full body stretch.

1 Stand holding the Swiss Ball in front of you.
2 Swing the ball out to the right and up, placing your weight on your right foot. Lower the ball back to the center with your weight on both feet.
3 Swing the ball out to the left and up, now placing your weight on your left foot. Continue to swing to each side for 10–15 repetitions.

Technique

- Fully extend your arm and reach as far as possible to achieve a full stretch.
- Your legs should be straight with each reach.
- Keep your eyes fixed on the ball throughout the movement.

Hints & Tips

- Manage your breathing so that you breathe out each time you stretch out and up, and breathe in when the ball returns to the center.

Midsection Stretches

Spinal Flexion and Extension

Areas Worked: The length of your vertebrae, from neck to pelvis
Name of Main Muscle Group: Erector Spinae

1 Position yourself on your hands and knees so that your arms and thighs are vertical. Tuck your chin in and tilt your pelvis back so that you are flexing your back and creating an arc.

2 Lift your head and tilt your pelvis forward so that you are extending your back and creating a dip. Hold the top of each movement for 3 seconds then repeat for 6 repetitions.

Technique
- Keep your hands and knees fixed in position.
- Lift the center of your back as high as possible when flexing as if it is being lifted by a crane.
- When extending your back do so through as large a range as possible but ensuring that it is pain free.

Hints & Tips
- Relax your abdominal muscles when extending your back.
- Focus on your breathing. Breathe out when flexing and breathe in when extending.

Ball Reach and Back Flex

Areas Worked: The length of your vertebrae, from neck to pelvis and between shoulder blades
Name of Main Muscle Groups: Erector Spinae and Rhomboids

1 Kneel down with the Swiss Ball at arms length in front of you. Extend your arms out and place your hands on the top of the ball.
2 Drop your head between your shoulders and slowly sit back onto your heels. Flex your back, arching it outwards as much as possible so that you feel a stretch along the length of your back. Hold this position for 15–20 seconds, and then relax.

Technique

- Keep your arms stretched out as if pulling back against the ball.
- Flex the center of your back as much as possible when arching it, as if it was being pulled back by someone behind you.

Hints & Tips

- Contract your abdominal muscles when flexing your back to aid the range of the stretch.

Spinal Lateral Flexion

Area Worked: Muscles at the side of your spine and torso
Name of Main Muscle Groups: External Obliques, Quadratus Lumborum, and Latissimus Dorsi

1 Lie sideways onto the Swiss ball. Extend your outside arm above your head, and lower your hand toward the floor. Alternatively, wrap your inside arm around the ball to help your balance.
2 Arch your body over the ball so that you can feel a stretch all the way down your side. Hold this position for 15–20 seconds, and then repeat on your other side.

Technique
- Position yourself so that your side is in the middle of the top of the ball.
- Extend your outside leg, and move your inside leg back a little to aid stability.

Hints & Tips
- Inflating the Swiss Ball to its maximum will create a bigger stretch down your side.

Seated Pelvic Rotations

Areas Worked: Stretch and mobility for the muscles around the lower back and pelvis.
Name of Main Muscle Groups: External Obliques, Internal Obliques

1 Sit on the ball with your feet flat on the floor.
2 Rotate your pelvis, forming large circles to the side, front, side, and back. Repeat this movement for 10 repetitions clockwise, and then counter clockwise.

Technique

- Place yourself directly in the center of the ball.
- Your knees should be bent to 90 degrees.
- Activate and tighten your abdominal muscles.
- Keep your eyes fixed straight ahead of you so that your neck and back are neutrally aligned.

- Relax your arms and rest your hands on your thighs.
- Keep control throughout the pelvic rotation.

Hints & Tips

- Progressively increase the size of the rotations and circles that you are forming.
- Keeping your feet firmly planted on the floor will help you to control the range of movement.

Lumbar Rotations

Areas Worked: Stretching and mobility for the soft tissue surrounding the lumbar vertebrae used in rotation of the lower back.
Name of Main Muscle Groups: External Obliques, Erector Spinae

1 Lie on the floor, on your back, with your lower legs resting on top of the Swiss Ball and arms out to the side.
2 Slowly rotate your lower back, rolling the ball and legs over to one side, and pause.

3 Tighten your abdominal muscles and bring your legs back to the starting position.
4 Repeat on the other side, and continue this for 8 to 10 repetitions.

Technique

- Your thighs should be in a vertical position.
- Keep your back flat and in the neutral position.
- Position your arms out to the side to aid stability.
- Move slowly and always through a pain free range.

Hints & Tips

- Relax your abdominal muscle when rolling your legs to the side.
- Focus on your breathing. Breathe out when rotating out to the side and breathe in when returning to the center.

Lower Body Stretches

Lying Hamstring Stretch

Areas Worked: Back of upper legs
Name of Main Muscle Group: Hamstrings

1 Lie on the floor, on your back, with your bottom about a foot away from a wall. Place the Swiss Ball against the wall and hold it there by pushing your feet against it, with your knees bent.
2 Extend your legs so that your heels roll over the ball until your legs become straight.
3 Hold, and then slowly bend your knees rolling your heels back over the ball, and to the starting position.
4 Continue this movement for 8 to 10 repetitions.

Technique

• Maintain your back in a neutral position, not allowing your lower back and pelvis to lift off the floor.
• Move slowly and avoid locking out your knees.
• Position your arms out to the side to aid stability.

Hints & Tips

• Relax your neck and shoulders by keeping your head on the floor.
• Move closer to the wall to increase the stretch. Move further away if the stretch is too intense.
• Breathe out when extending your legs, and breathe in when returning to the starting position.

Standing Hamstring Stretch

Areas Worked: Back of upper legs
Name of Main Muscle Group: Hamstrings

1 Stand on your left leg facing the Swiss Ball. Extend your right leg and place your foot on top of the ball.
2 Gently lean your shoulders forward until you feel a stretch in the back of the right leg. Hold the stretch for 15–20 seconds and then relax, and repeat with your left leg.

Technique

- Stand with your shoulders and hips square on to the Swiss Ball.
- Keep your back neutral and look straight ahead as you shift your weight by leaning your shoulders forward.
- Place your hands on the thigh of the leg that you are stretching but do not push down.

Hints & Tips

- If you are quite inflexible, start with the foot of the leg that you are standing on rotated out at 45 degrees to make it easier.

Standing Quadriceps Stretch

Areas Worked: Front of upper legs
Name of Main Muscle Group: Quadriceps

1 Stand on your left leg facing away from the Swiss Ball.
2 Bend your right leg behind you and place your foot on top of the ball.
3 Slowly bend your left leg until you feel a stretch in the front of the right leg.
4 Hold the stretch for 15–20 seconds and then relax, and repeat with your left leg.

Hints & Tips

- Activate and tighten your abdominal muscles to help keep yourself balanced and stable.

Technique

- Keep your back neutral and look straight ahead as you bend the leg that you are standing on.
- The upper part of the leg that you are stretching should be vertical.
- Position yourself so that your standing leg does not bend past 90 degrees.
- Place your hands on your hips.

Hip Flexor Stretch

Areas Worked: Front of hip/thigh
Name of Main Muscle Groups: Psoas and Rectus Femoris

1 Stand over the Swiss Ball, so that your left leg is forward and bent, and your right leg extended back.
2 Bend your left leg, leaning your weight and right thigh into the ball.
3 Hold the stretch for 15–20 seconds and then relax, and repeat with your left leg.

Technique

- Keep your back neutral and look straight ahead.
- Position your body over the center of the ball with your shoulders and hips facing forward.
- Your front foot should be flat on the floor, but only place the toe of the back foot down.

Hints & Tips

- Lower yourself onto the ball to increase the stretch.
- Place one hand on the ball to steady it.

Gluteal Stretch

Areas Worked: Muscles in the back of the hip and bottom
Name of Main Muscle Groups: Gluteus Medius and Gluteus Maximus

1 Lie on the floor, on your back, with the lower part of your right leg resting on top of the Swiss Ball.
2 Rotate your left hip and place the outside of your left ankle over your right knee, which acts as an anchor.
3 Put gentle pressure against the inside of your left knee until you feel a stretch in your left buttock.
4 Hold for 15–20 seconds and repeat on the other side.

Technique
- Keep your back flat and in the neutral position.
- The thigh of the leg that is on the ball should be vertical.
- Move slowly and always through a pain free range.

Hints & Tips
- Gradually increase the range of the stretch throughout the 15-20 seconds as the muscles lengthen.
- Bringing the knee of the leg that is resting on the ball closer into your body will also increase the stretch.

Outer Thigh Stretch

Areas Worked: Outer thigh and waist
Name of Main Muscle Groups: Gluteus Medius and Quadratus Lumborum

1 Lie on the floor, on your right side.
2 Lift your right leg and rest it on top of the ball.
3 Gently lift your shoulders away from the floor so that you are flexing at the waist.
4 Hold for 15–20 seconds and then repeat on the other side.

Technique

- Rest your other leg on the floor behind the ball.
- Your shoulders and hips should remain in a vertical position throughout the stretch.
- Lift your shoulders slowly as the muscle relaxes and lengthens.
- Keep your hip in contact with the floor during the stretch.

Hints & Tips

- Position your hands on the floor to aid stability and hold the stretch.
- Progressively increase the range of the stretch by lifting your shoulders and side away from the floor.

Standing Inner Thigh Stretch

Area Worked: Inner thigh
Name of Main Muscle Group: Adductors

1 Stand with the Swiss Ball to your right hand side. Place the inside of your right ankle on the ball, with the leg straight.
2 Slowly bend your left leg, lowering your body, until you feel a stretch in the inner thigh of the right leg.
3 Hold the stretch for 15–20 seconds and then relax, and repeat with your left leg.

Technique

- Keep your back neutral and look straight ahead as you bend the leg that you are standing on.
- Face your shoulders and hips forward.
- The leg that you are stretching should be completely straight.
- Place your hands on your hips.

Hints & Tips

- Gradually increase the stretch as your inner thigh relaxes.
- Activate and tighten your abdominal muscles to help keep yourself balanced and stable.

Upper Body Stretches

Standing Chest Stretch

Areas Worked: Chest and front of shoulders
Name of Main Muscle Groups: Pectoral and Anterior Deltoid

1 Stand up, holding the Swiss Ball behind you with your hands either side.
2 Slowly lift the ball until you can feel the stretch across your chest and front of shoulders.
3 Hold the stretch for 15–20 seconds and then repeat once more.

Technique

- Stand with your feet hip width apart, and knees slightly bent.
- Maintain the neutral position in your back, stopping yourself from leaning forward.
- Keep your head up and eyes fixed straight ahead.
- Your arms should be straight, with the palms of your hands against the ball.

Hints & Tips

- Tighten your abdominals to assist the upright posture.

Kneeling Chest Stretch

Areas Stretched: Chest and front of shoulder
Name of Main Muscle Groups: Pectoral and Anterior Deltoid

1 Kneel down with the Swiss Ball beside you to your left. Extend your left arm and place your hand on the top of the ball.
2 Slowly lower your left shoulder until you feel the stretch. Hold for 15–20 seconds, and then repeat on the other side using your right arm.

Technique

- Keep your arm stretched out on the ball so that your hand is in line with your shoulder.
- Your other arm and legs should all be positioned vertically.
- Face the floor to keep your neck and back neutrally aligned.
- Your hips and shoulders should be parallel to the floor.

Hints & Tips

- Keep your hips and shoulders parallel to the floor.
- Gradually increase the stretch by lowering your shoulder on the side that you are stretching.

Back of Shoulder Stretch

Areas Worked: Back of shoulder and between the shoulder blades
Name of Main Muscle Groups: Posterior Deltoid and Rhomboids

1 Kneel down on the floor with the Swiss Ball in front of you. Place your right arm across your body toward your left shoulder so that it is resting on top of the ball.
2 Lower your shoulders down toward the ball until you can feel a stretch in the back of the right shoulder.
3 Hold this position for 15–20 seconds, and then repeat with your left arm.

Technique

- Rest your forearm and elbow on the ball.
- Keep your shoulders straight and parallel to the floor as you lower them down.

Hints & Tips

- Place your other hand on your thigh to control your weight against the ball.
- Contract your abdominal muscles to hold your back in a neutral position.

Single Arm Lat Stretch

Areas Worked: Side of upper back
Name of Main Muscle Group: Latissimus Dorsi

1 Kneel down with the Swiss Ball in front of you.
2 Extend your left arm and place your hand on top of the ball.
3 Slowly sit back onto your heels, and drop your shoulders toward the floor until you feel the stretch.
4 Hold this position for 15–20 seconds, and then repeat with your right arm.

Technique
- Keep your arm stretched out as if pulling back against the ball.
- Face the floor, keeping your neck and back neutrally aligned.
- Your hips and shoulders should be parallel to the floor.

Hints & Tips
- Progressively increase the stretch by lowering your shoulders toward the floor.
- Place your other hand on the floor to help control the height of your shoulders.

Combination Stretch

Areas Worked: Side of upper back and lower back
Name of Main Muscle Groups: Latissimus Dorsi, External Obliques and Quadratus Lumborum

1 Kneel down with the Swiss Ball in front of you. Extend your arms and place your hands on top of the ball. Slowly sit back onto your heels, and drop your shoulders toward the floor until you feel the stretch.
2 Hold this position for 10 seconds, and then roll the ball to your left, holding for 10–15 seconds.
3 Finally, roll the ball to your right and hold for 10–15 seconds.

Technique

- Keep your arms stretched out as if pulling back against the ball.
- Position your head between your shoulders, facing the floor, to keep your neck and back neutrally aligned.
- Your hips and shoulders should be parallel to the floor.
- Roll the ball to each side by walking your hands over the surface of the ball.

Hints & Tips

- Keep your hips and knees facing straight ahead throughout to obtain the best stretch.
- Progressively increase the stretch by lowering your shoulders toward the floor.

Shoulder Arcs

Areas Worked: Mobility of the shoulder
Name of Main Muscle Groups: Anterior/Posterior Deltoid and other deep muscle tissues

1 Kneel down with the Swiss Ball in front of you. Extend your left arm and place your hand on top of the ball.
2 Slowly roll the ball around, forming an arc at arm's length toward your feet. Hold for a few seconds, and then roll the ball in an arc back to the starting position.
3 Repeat this movement 2 to 3 times, and then do it on the other side using your right arm.

Technique

- Keep your arm stretched out on the ball throughout the movement.
- Your other arm and legs should all be positioned vertically.
- Face the floor to keep your neck and back neutrally aligned.
- Roll the ball to each side by walking your hand over the surface of the ball.

Hints & Tips

- Keep your hips and shoulders parallel to the floor.
- Keeping a light touch with your fingers will help you to roll the ball more smoothly.

Upper Back Rotations

Areas Worked: Upper back (vertebrae) mobility
Name of Main Muscle Groups: Latissimus Dorsi, Erector Spinae

1 Lie on the floor, on your back, with your legs straight. Hold the Swiss Ball up in front of you with your arms straight.
2 Slowly lower the ball to your left until your left hand touches the floor and hold for 3–4 seconds.
3 Return back to the starting position, and repeat on the right hand side. Continue this for 8 repetitions.

Technique

- Hold your back and neck in a neutral position.
- The position of your hands should be directly above your shoulders in the starting position.
- Keep both arms straight as you rotate to each side.
- Make sure that your pelvis stays in contact with the floor throughout the rotations.
- Move slowly and always through a pain-free range.

Hints & Tips

- Keep your eyes looking straight up to maintain a neutral neck position.
- Aim to get the arm on the side you are rotating flat on the floor for a full range movement.
- Focus on your breathing. Breathe out when rotating out to the side and breathe in when returning to the center.

20-Minute Workouts

Make sure that you have warmed up and stretched correctly, using the exercises in the Warm Up / Cool Down section, before starting any of the 20-minute Swiss Ball exercise routines listed below.

Having warmed up, start the first exercise, completing the first set of designated repetitions (progressively increasing the exercise intensity and range of movement). Rest for 30 seconds and then complete your second set.

When all of your sets for each exercise are complete, rest for 40–60 seconds, and then move on to the next exercise. Continue in this way until you have completed all the exercises in this workout. It is advisable to perform a cool down and stretch after the workout is complete.

Always check with your doctor before starting any exercise routine.

Total Body Stability Routine

Press Ups, Kneeling on the Floor

Sets: 2
Repetitions: 12–15
Areas Worked: Chest, front of shoulders, back of upper arms, and core

1 Kneel on the floor, leaning forward with your arms extended and your hands resting on top of the ball.
2 Bend your arms, bringing your chest toward the ball until your elbows reach

an angle of 90 degrees. Pause, and then extend your arms, pushing your chest away from the ball and returning to the start position.

Technique
- Activate and tighten your abdominal muscles to help maintain a neutral back position.
- Pivot on your knees as you lower your upper body toward the ball.
- Stop at the bottom of the movement, when you feel a stretch across your chest and shoulders.

Mid Row, Leg Extended

Sets: 2
Repetitions: 12–15
Areas Worked: Upper back, between the shoulder blades, back of shoulders, front of upper arms, and core

1 Lie face down on the Swiss Ball, with your right leg elevated off the floor, and the toes of your left leg on the floor.
2 Start with your upper arms out to the side and extended down toward the floor, holding the weights with an over-hand grip.
3 Lift your elbows up past shoulder level, bending your arms.
4 Pause, and then extend your arms, returning the weights back toward the floor.
5 Repeat, elevating your left leg.

Technique

- Hold your leg extended and foot off the floor for the duration of the exercise.
- Focus on control and keeping balanced as you lift the weights.
- Position your elbows out to the side at a 90-degree angle as you flex your arms.
- Stop at the bottom of the movement, making sure that the weights don't touch the floor.
- Ensure that your forearms are vertically positioned throughout the exercise.
- Keep your torso still during the movement.
- Make sure that your shoulders do not lift away from the ball as you raise your elbows.

Forward Hand Walk

Sets: 2
Repetitions: 8–10
Areas Worked: Shoulders and core

1 Lie face down on the Swiss Ball with your arms extended, hands on the floor, and legs extended at the hip.
2 Walk your hands forward, rolling the ball underneath you until it reaches your feet.
3 Pause and walk your hands back, rolling the ball back underneath you until you reach the start position.

Technique

- Lie on the ball with your hips resting on the center.
- Position your hands on the floor so that they are directly below your shoulders.
- Activate and tighten your core muscles to maintain a neutral position with a straight line running from your shoulders to your ankles.
- Make sure that your back doesn't arch and your hips don't rotate during the exercise.
- Face the floor throughout the movement to keep your neck neutrally aligned.
- Lift, reach, and place your hands one at a time.
- Avoid locking your elbows when your arms are straight.

Seated Bicep Curls, Leg Extended

Sets: 2
Repetitions: 12–15
Areas Worked: Front of upper arm and core

1 Sit on the ball with your feet flat on the floor.
2 Take hold of a weight in both hands with an under-hand grip, positioning them down by your side.
3 Extend one leg off the floor.
4 Flex your arms at the elbows, lifting the weights toward your shoulders.
5 Pause, and then extend your arms, lowering the weights back down to the start position.
6 Repeat, using your other leg.

Technique

- Position yourself on the center of the Swiss Ball.
- Bend one knee to 90 degrees with your foot on the floor.
- Hold your extended leg off the floor for the duration of the exercise.
- Activate and tighten your abdominal muscles, holding your back straight.
- Keep your eyes fixed straight ahead so that your neck and back are neutrally aligned.
- Hold the weights straight as you flex and extend your arms.
- Ensure that your upper arms stay vertical throughout the movement.

Reverse Bridge Single Leg Extension

Sets: 2
Repetitions: 12–15
Areas Worked: Front of upper leg and core

1 Attach an ankle weight around each ankle.
2 Lie on your back on top of the ball in the reverse bridge position, with your knees bent at 90 degrees and your right foot elevated off the floor slightly.
3 Extend your right knee, lifting your foot until your leg is straight.

4 Pause, and then flex your knee, lowering your foot back down toward the floor.
5 Repeat the exercise using your left leg.

Technique

- The ball should be positioned so that it sits directly between your shoulder blades.
- Activate and tighten your abdominal muscles to help maintain a neutral alignment.
- Stabilize your weight with the foot that is on the floor.
- Keep your upper leg static and horizontal as you extend and flex your knee.
- Stop at the bottom of the movement when your knee reaches a 90-degree angle.

Bridge

Sets: 2
Repetitions: 10–12
Areas Worked: Butt, back of upper legs, and core

1 Position yourself lying on your back on the floor, heels resting on top of the ball.
2 Extend your hips, lifting your bottom off the floor.
3 Hold at the top of the movement for 3 seconds, and then flex your hips, dropping your bottom back down toward the floor.

Technique

- Start with your feet on the ball and your butt just off the floor, so that you are not resting your full weight down on the floor.
- Lift your pelvis up by extending your hips so that only the back of your shoulders are in contact with the floor.
- Activate and tighten your core muscles to maintain the neutral position, with a straight line from shoulders to hips.
- Make sure that your back doesn't arch during the exercise.

Sitting on the Ball

Sets: 2
Time: As long as you can, or up to 1 minute
Area Worked: Core

1 Sit on the ball with feet flat on the floor.
2 Extend your arms and legs forward.
3 Balance for 10 second intervals.

Technique

- Place yourself directly in the center of the Swiss Ball.
- Activate and tighten your abdominal muscles.
- Keep your eyes fixed straight ahead so that your neck and back are neutrally aligned.
- Extend your arms and legs straight so that they are not in contact with the floor.

Total Body Strength and Tone Routine

Chest Press

Sets: 2
Repetitions: 12–15
Areas Worked: Chest, front of shoulder, back of upper arm. It also activates the muscles of the core for stability of the mid section.

1 Lie on your back on top of the ball in the reverse bridge position, with your knees bent at 90 degrees.
2 Take hold of a dumbbell in each hand with an overhand grip.
3 Bend elbows to 90 degrees and position them out level with your shoulders.
4 Extend both arms up, pushing the weights away, until they are straight.
5 Pause and then slowly bend arms, allowing them to return to the start position.

Technique

- The ball should be positioned so that it sits directly between your shoulder blades.
- Place feet shoulder width apart.
- Activate and tighten your abdominal muscles to help maintain a neutral alignment.
- Be careful not to let your pelvis drop and move out of alignment. You should form a straight line from shoulders through to knees.
- Ensure that forearms maintain a vertical position throughout the movement.
- Stop at the bottom of the movement when you feel a stretch across your chest and shoulders.

Mid Row

Sets: 2
Repetitions: 12–15
Areas Worked: Upper back, between shoulder blades, back of shoulders, and front of upper arms

1 Position yourself lying prone on the Swiss Ball, with legs stretched out and toes on the floor.
2 Start with your upper arms out to the side and extended down toward the floor, taking hold of the weights with an overhand grip.

3 Lift elbows up past shoulder level, bending your arms.
4 Pause, and then extend your arms, returning the weights back toward the floor.

Technique
- Your elbows should move out to the side at a 90-degree angle as you flex your arms.
- Stop at the bottom of the movement, making sure that the weights don't touch the floor.
- Ensure that your forearms are vertically positioned throughout the exercise.
- Keep your torso still during the movement.
- Make sure that your shoulders do not lift away from the ball as you raise your elbows.

Seated Shoulder Press

Sets: 2
Repetitions: 12–15
Areas Worked: Front of shoulders and back of upper arms

1 Sit on the ball with feet flat on the floor.
2 Take hold of a weight in both hands with an overhand grip, positioning them just above shoulder level.
3 Extend your arms, pushing the weights above your head.
4 Pause, and then flex your arms, lowering the weights back down to the starting position.

Technique

- Place yourself directly in the center of the Swiss Ball.
- Knees should be bent to 90 degrees.
- Activate and tighten abdominal muscles.
- Keep your eyes fixed straight ahead so that your neck and back are neutrally aligned.
- Start with your elbows pointed out to the side, keeping forearms vertical.
- Extend your arms straight up so that they are vertical when fully extended.

Seated Bicep Curls

Sets: 2
Repetitions: 12–15
Area Worked: Front of upper arm

1 Sit on the ball with feet flat on the floor.
2 Take hold of a weight in both hands with an underhand grip, positioning them down by your side.
3 Flex your arms at the elbows, lifting the weights toward your shoulders.
4 Pause, and then extend your arms, lowering the weights back down to the starting position.

Technique

- Position yourself on the center of the Swiss Ball.
- Bend your knees to 90 degrees.
- Activate and tighten abdominal muscles, holding your back straight.
- Keep your eyes fixed straight ahead, so that your neck and back are neutrally aligned.
- Hold the weights straight as you flex and extend your arms.
- Ensure that your upper arms stay vertical throughout the movement.

Squat Against Wall

Sets: 2
Repetitions: 12–15
Areas Worked: Front of upper legs and buttocks

1 Place the Swiss Ball against the wall and lean your lower back into it.
2 Stand with feet shoulder width apart.
3 Flex your hips and your knees, lowering your buttocks down toward the floor, and rolling the ball up your back.
4 Pause and then extend your hips and knees, lifting yourself straight and back to the start position.

Technique

• Start with your legs straight, feet placed ahead of the ball and parallel to each other, back neutrally aligned, as you rest against the ball.
• Activate and tighten your abdominal muscles, tilting pelvis forward slightly to help maintain a neutral alignment as you flex your hips and knees.
• Look straight ahead and keep your shoulders back as you lower yourself down.
• Stop at the bottom of the movement, just before your knees reach a 90-degree angle.
• Keep your back in contact with the ball throughout the exercise.

Prone Hamstring Curls

Sets: 2
Repetitions: 12–15
Area Worked: Back of upper legs

1 Secure an ankle weight around each ankle.
2 Lie prone on the Swiss Ball with arms extended, hands on the floor, and legs extended straight.

3 Flex your knees, lifting your feet up. Pause, and then extend your legs, lowering your feet back down to the start position.

Technique

- Lie on the ball with your hips resting on the center.
- Position your hands on the floor so that they are directly below your shoulders.
- Hold a neutral position with a straight line running from your shoulders to your knees.
- Make sure that your back doesn't arch and your hips don't flex during the exercise.
- Keep your knees and feet together as you flex your knees.
- Flex your knees from straight legs to a 90-degree angle.

Abdominal Crunch Basic

Sets: 2
Repetitions: 15–20
Area Worked: Abdomen

1 Position yourself lying on your back on the floor, with legs flexed and heels resting on top of the ball.

2 Roll your shoulders forward, lifting them off the floor.

3 Hold at the top of the movement for 3 seconds, and then relax back down toward the floor.

Technique

- Start with your legs flexed to 90 degrees and feet on the ball.
- Extend arms, positioning your hands on the outside of each knee.
- Activate and tighten your abdominal muscles to roll and lift your shoulders forward as you reach your hands toward your ankles.
- Make sure that only your shoulders lift away from the floor, and not your back.

Back Extension with Toes on Floor

Sets: 2
Repetitions: 12–15
Areas Worked: Lower back and sides of midsection

1 Lie prone on the Swiss Ball, so that your navel is on the center of the ball, with legs extended.
2 Extend your back, lifting your chest away from the ball, and rotate your torso to the right.
3 Pause, and then lower your chest and shoulders back down to the ball and starting position.
4 Repeat, extending your back and rotating your torso to the left.

Technique
- Keep your legs extended straight behind you, with toes on the floor.
- Hold arms out at a 90-degree angle to your body with your elbows bent.
- As you extend your back, slowly rotate your torso so that you are looking out to the side.
- Keep your hips square on the ball as you rotate.

Midsection Stability, Strength and Tone Routine

Abdominal Curl on Ball

Sets: 2
Repetitions: 12–15
Area Worked: Abdomen

1 Lie on the Swiss Ball, with your knees bent at 90 degrees.
2 Extend your arms, with your hands on top of your thighs.
3 Raise your shoulders away from the ball.
4 Hold for 3 seconds and then slowly lower your shoulders back to the start position.

Technique

- Position yourself so that your mid back and upper pelvis are resting against the ball.
- Place your feet shoulder width apart.
- Drop your pelvis down slightly so that it is pressing into the ball as you raise your shoulders.
- Activate and tighten your abdominal muscles, to flex your midsection and lift your shoulders forward, as you reach your hands toward your knees.
- Stop at the bottom of the movement, just before your shoulders touch down on the ball.

Abdominal Curl Rotation

Sets: 2
Repetitions: 12–15
Areas Worked: Abdomen and sides of midsection

1 Lie on the Swiss Ball, with your knees bent at 90 degrees.
2 Extend your right arm, with your hand on top of your left thigh.
3 Reach your right arm along your thigh and raise and rotate your upper body and shoulders toward the left and away from the ball.
4 Hold for 3 seconds and then slowly lower yourself down, straightening your shoulders back to the start position.
5 Repeat, using your left arm and rotating toward the right.

Technique

- Position yourself so that your mid back and upper pelvis are resting against the ball.
- Place your feet shoulder width apart.
- Drop your pelvis down slightly so that it is pressing into the ball as you raise your shoulders.
- Activate and tighten your abdominal muscles to flex and rotate your midsection and lift your shoulder forward as you reach your hand toward your knee.
- Stop at the bottom of the movement just before your shoulders touch down on the ball.

Reverse Curl

Sets: 2
Repetitions: 12–15
Area Worked: Lower abdomen

1 Position yourself lying on your back on the floor with your knees bent and feet raised.
2 Place the ball between your legs.
3 Flex your abdomen, tilting and lifting your pelvis off the floor.
4 Hold for 3 seconds and then lower your pelvis back down.

Technique

- Lie with your back flat on the floor.
- Position the ball between your legs, flexed to a 90-degree angle, so that the ball is in contact with your knees and lower legs.
- Make sure that your back doesn't arch or lift during the exercise.

Lying Lateral Flexion

Sets: 2
Repetitions: 12–15
Area Worked: Sides of midsection

1 Lie on your left hand side against the Swiss Ball, legs extended and feet on the floor.
2 Laterally flex your midsection, lifting your pelvis away from the floor.
3 Pause, and slowly lower your pelvis, returning back to the start position

Technique

- Position yourself against the ball so that it is in contact with the side of your rib cage.
- Your legs should be straight, with your feet staggered.
- Bend both arms, resting one over the ball and the other on the side.
- Start with your midsection flexed toward the floor.
- Lift your pelvis away from the floor as you flex, until your body and legs form a straight line.
- Activate and tighten your abdominal muscles to help maintain a neutral position.

Reverse Bridge Torso Rotation

Sets: 2
Repetitions: 12–15
Areas Worked: Sides of midsection and core

1 Lie on your back on top of the ball in the reverse bridge position, with your knees bent at 90 degrees.
2 Take hold of the medicine ball with both hands, and position your arms straight up.
3 Rotate your upper body to the right, rolling onto your shoulder on top of the ball.
4 Pause, and then slowly roll back with the Swiss Ball in the center of your shoulders.
5 Repeat the exercise, rotating your torso and rolling on your shoulder the other way.

Technique

• Start with the ball positioned so that it sits directly between your shoulder blades.
• Place your feet shoulder width apart.
• Activate and tighten your abdominal muscles to help maintain a neutral alignment.
• Form a straight line from shoulders through to your knees.
• Hold onto the medicine ball with your arms up, so that they are vertical, and level with your shoulders.
• Keep your arms straight throughout the movement, arcing the ball over as you roll onto your shoulder.
• Rotate your torso, rolling onto the side of your shoulder, so that it is placed in the middle of the ball.

Alternate Arm and Leg Back Extensions

Sets: 2
Repetitions: 12–15
Area Worked: Length of back

1 Lie face down on the Swiss Ball with your arms and legs extended.
2 Extend your back, lifting your left arm and right leg off the floor.
3 Hold for 3 seconds, and then lower your arm and leg back to the floor.
5 Repeat the exercise with your right arm and left leg.

Technique

- Place the opposite hand and toe on the floor to those that are elevated.
- Keep your arms and legs straight when lifting and when static.
- Position your head so that you are facing the floor.

Resistance Band

Theory Behind Resistance Band Training

The term resistance training refers to using an increased force against a body movement for the purpose of developing greater muscle tone, strength, endurance, and power. Resistance training can also provide other benefits such as improved weight control through increased metabolism, as well as injury prevention. In recent years resistance training has become an integral part of a balanced fitness routine. Traditionally, to include this type of training into your lifestyle would mean joining a gym or investing in large and heavy exercise equipment. Not everybody has the luxury of a gym membership or the space to install home equipment, but there is a way to get all the benefits of resistance training without either of these things.

The solution is the resistance band. Made from pliable materials such as rubber and latex, resistance bands are compact, light, and safe. These bands were first used in physical rehabilitation to aid recovery from injury and illness. Now they are widely used in aerobic studies and homes around the world.

Benefits of Using Resistance Bands

Low cost

Resistance bands provide training without the use of expensive equipment or the need to join a gym. For the price of one month's gym membership, or less, you can set yourself up with everything you need for a complete resistance workout.

Lightweight

Unlike other resistance training equipment that provides resistance through weight, the bands are light, making them easier and safer to move around.

Storage and portability

Because the bands are lightweight and compact they do not require any storage space, unlike bulky free weights and benches. This also means that you can take them anywhere, which is especially beneficial when traveling, enabling you to maintain exercise consistency.

Constant resistance during exercise movement

Resistance training equipment normally provides gravity-generated resistance, which means it can be lost during some parts of the exercise. Bands provide constant resistance throughout the exercise, and therefore more benefit.

Time efficiency

You can plan your time more efficiently by using resistance bands, as you won't need to work around gym schedules or allow for additional traveling time. You can pick them up whenever you want and wherever you are.

Safe

The band only provides resistance when you want it. The resistance is progressive and controlled by you, making it safer and easier on the joints. This also makes it suitable for people of all ages. The band eliminates the mishaps

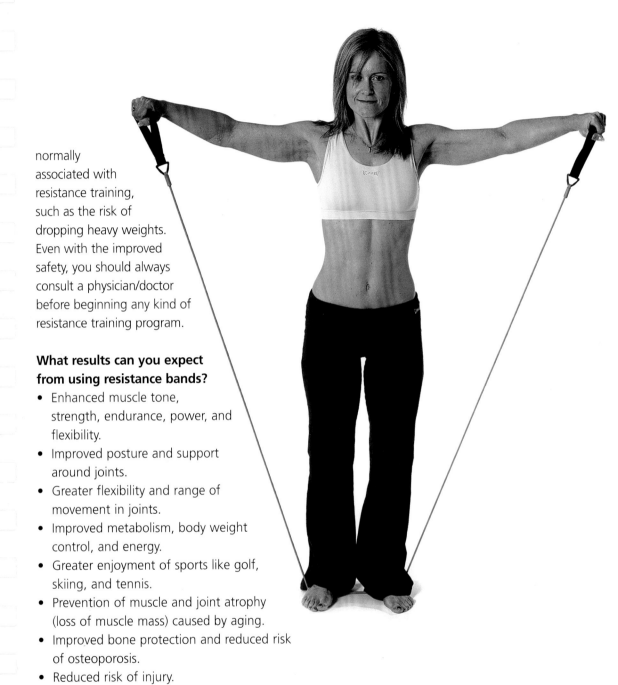

normally associated with resistance training, such as the risk of dropping heavy weights. Even with the improved safety, you should always consult a physician/doctor before beginning any kind of resistance training program.

What results can you expect from using resistance bands?

- Enhanced muscle tone, strength, endurance, power, and flexibility.
- Improved posture and support around joints.
- Greater flexibility and range of movement in joints.
- Improved metabolism, body weight control, and energy.
- Greater enjoyment of sports like golf, skiing, and tennis.
- Prevention of muscle and joint atrophy (loss of muscle mass) caused by aging.
- Improved bone protection and reduced risk of osteoporosis.
- Reduced risk of injury.

The terminology of the anatomy and muscle groups being worked in each section has been kept to a level where it is easily understandable for a beginner, yet is still informative to those who have a good basic knowledge of other training methods. It is outside the remit of this book to go into too much anatomical detail.

For a full exposition of the body's muscle groups please turn to page 86 in the Swiss Ball section, or alternatively, you can consult the text guide on page 20 in the section on Stretching and Toning.

Safety Precautions

Before commencing any exercise with resistance bands, please check the following:

Ensure all equipment is in good working order:

- Examine the resistance band before each use, checking for small tears or punctures. Damage to the band can cause it to snap under tension. If you do find damage, discard it and replace it with a new one.

Band storage:

- Resistance bands should be stored at room temperature and in a dark place. Do not store the bands in sunlight, as long exposure may cause damage to the bands' elastic properties.

Exercise area:

- Give yourself plenty of free space to perform the exercises. Choose an area that is nonslip.

Correct and safe usage:

- Make sure that you understand how to do each exercise properly by carefully reading through and following the full instructions before starting your workout. Improper use may cause serious injury.
- When positioning the band around or attaching it to an anchor point, ensure that it is at the specified level for the exercise and is secure. Do not attach the band to any loose objects. If using a door, ensure that others around know this, and don't try to use the door.

- Do not use the resistance band in a way that may cause it to flick toward the head and cause facial injury.
- Select a band with a suitable level of intensity starting with the lowest. Only increase the level of resistance when you can comfortably complete the specified number of repetitions.
- Be careful not to place the band around any part of the body or limbs that could result in cutting off circulation.
- Work each muscle through a full range being careful not to hyperextend or lock the joint.
- Allow sufficient rest periods (48 hours) between resistance workouts for recovery and to prevent overtraining.
- If you are new to resistance training, build up the exercise intensity gradually.

Health:

- Some bands contain latex, which can cause an allergic reaction. There are latex-free bands available to prevent an adverse reaction.
- If you are new to exercise or have a medical condition, check with your doctor before commencing any form of exercise.

Warm Up / Cool Down:

- It is important to warm up before undertaking any exercise routine. Please follow the warm-up procedures in either the Stretch and Tone section or the Swiss Ball section, or, follow the routine on page 182.

Equipment

For the exercises in this section you will require the following equipment:

Resistance bands: There are many types of band available. Traditionally the resistance band is without fixed handles. They are generally made of latex and come as a flat sheet (#2) in various thicknesses and colors, which denote the intensity of each band. A knot can be tied in each end to attach a handle or to make a loop to hold onto. The other type is generally referred to as a resistance tube (#1). These are mainly latex-free and come with handles already attached. Whichever you choose, be sure to get quality bands to limit the chance of them breaking. To avoid confusion, "bands" and "tubes" have been used in the same context within this section, and are called "bands".

Ankle strap: An ankle strap (#3) is required so that the band can be attached to it, and then comfortably placed around your leg for lower body exercises.

Door anchor: Some exercises require the band to be anchored to create a suitable resistance angle. The simple yet effective door anchor loop (#4) can be closed in the door to provide a solid anchor point. If there isn't a suitable doorway, the band can be placed around a pole or similar fixed object capable of holding that level of resistance.

Chair or Swiss ball: Some exercises require a chair or similar object to sit or hold onto for balance.

How to choose the correct strength of band

Different manufacturers make bands of varied resistance levels in different colors. Be sure to follow their specific instructions. The most common bands are:

- Light resistance (yellow) is recommended for use by seniors, and to improve the smaller muscle groups of the upper body.
- Medium resistance (green) is for average strength, and to work small to medium muscle groups such as the back and hips.
- Heavy resistance (red) is recommended for the average man or active woman and can be used to develop muscle groups such as the arms, shoulders, chest, and legs.
- Extra heavy resistance (black) is recommended for use by advanced men and women to develop large and strong muscle groups.

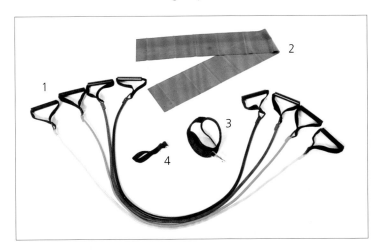

Correct Exercise Posture

Correct postural positioning is imperative when exercising to prevent injury and to obtain the maximum benefit from your routine.

Poor posture:
On the left is an example of poor posture. Many people unknowingly form this position with head down and shoulders rounded forward. This posture will only lead to problems in the future.

Correct posture:
On the right is an example of good/correct posture.
- Standing tall, head and neck straight with eyes focused straight ahead.
- Shoulders relaxed and back, with chest out.
- Abdomen pulled in and muscles held tight.
- Pelvis curled under slightly so that buttocks are tucked in to form a neutral position.
- Feet placed hip width apart with weight distributed evenly and toes pointing forward.
- Knees slightly bent.

Grip Positions

Throughout this section, references will be made to the different grip positions required. They are as follows:

Overhand grip

Underhand grip

Palm-inward grip

Exercises

Chest Press

Chest

This is a multiple joint exercise designed to work the major muscle groups in the front of the upper body in a forward pushing movement.

Attach the resistance band to a door anchor, or around a sturdy object of a suitable height (e.g. a pole), ensuring that it is positioned at shoulder height.

Position yourself with the band coming from behind you, your feet in a split stance, and leaning forward slightly with abdominal muscles tight. Hold the handles of the band in each hand with an overhand grip and elbows bent at 90 degrees. Ensure that elbows and wrists are all elevated to shoulder height and are parallel to the floor.

Extend both arms forward until they are straight and then slowly bend arms back to the start position, stopping when you feel a slight stretch across your chest and shoulders. To make the exercise harder, step further forward, or make it easier by moving closer to the attachment.

Muscle groups worked in this exercise:
Chest (pectorals), front of shoulders (anterior deltoid), and back of upper arms (triceps).

Breathing tip: Breathe out as you extend arms forward.

Incline Chest Press

Chest

This is a multiple joint exercise designed to work the major muscle groups in the upper body in a forward and upward pushing movement.

Attach the resistance band to a door anchor, or around a sturdy object, ensuring that it is positioned at waist height.

Position yourself, as in the standard Chest Press exercise, with the band coming from behind you, your feet in a split stance, and lean forward slightly with abdominal muscles tight. Hold the handles of the band in each hand, with elbows crooked at 90 degrees. Ensure that both forearms and wrists are elevated at a 40-degree angle to your shoulders and parallel to the angle of the band.

Extend both arms forward and up to just above head level, maintaining the 40-degree angle and until arms are straight, then slowly bend arms back to the start position, stopping when you feel a slight stretch across your chest and shoulders.

Muscle groups worked in this exercise:
Upper chest (upper pectorals), front/middle of shoulders (anterior deltoid and medial deltoids), and back of upper arms (triceps).

Breathing tip: Breathe out as you extend arms forward.

Decline Chest Press

Chest

This is a multiple joint exercise designed to work the major muscle groups in the front of the upper body in a forward and downward pushing movement.

Attach the resistance band to a door anchor, or around a sturdy object, ensuring that it is positioned just above head height.

Position yourself, as in the standard Chest Press exercise, with the band coming from behind you, your feet in a split stance, and leaning forward slightly with abdominal muscles tight. Hold the handles of the band in each hand with elbows bent at 90 degrees and elbows at shoulder height. Ensure that both forearms and wrists are lowered at a 40-degree angle to your shoulders and parallel to the angle of the band.

Extend both arms forward and down to waist level, maintaining the 40-degree angle and until arms are straight, then slowly bend arms back to the start position, stopping when you feel a slight stretch across your chest and shoulders.

Muscle groups worked in this exercise:
Lower chest (lower pectorals), front of shoulders (anterior deltoid), and back of upper arms (triceps).

Breathing tip: Breathe out as you extend arms forward.

Single Arm Chest Flys

Chest

This exercise is designed to isolate the primary muscles of the chest and front of shoulder, in a shoulder and arm adduction movement. Attach the resistance band to a door anchor, or around a sturdy object, ensuring that it is positioned at shoulder height. You only need the use of one end of the band for this exercise, so ensure that the other end is securely attached to the anchor point.

Position yourself in the correct standing exercise posture, with your feet hip-width apart. The band should be on the side that you are working. From this position take hold of the handle with your arm extended out to the side and at shoulder height. Ensure that your elbow is pointing behind you and rotate your wrist so that the palm of your hand is facing forward. Slowly rotate your body away from the band until you feel resistance against your chest and shoulder.

Working against the resistance, bring your arm across in front of you, to just past mid-chest level, maintaining a slight bend in the elbow throughout the full range of the movement. Then slowly back to the starting position, stopping when you feel a slight stretch across your chest and shoulder. Your shoulders should remain parallel to your hips throughout the exercise to ensure that you don't rotate your upper body.

Muscle groups worked in this exercise:
Chest (pectorals), front of shoulder (anterior deltoid).

Breathing tip: Breathe out as you bring your arm across in front of you.

Latissimus Pull Down

Upper Back

This is a multiple joint exercise designed to work the major muscle groups in the back of your upper body in a wide body pull-up movement.

Attach the resistance band to a door anchor, or around a sturdy object of a suitable height (e.g. a pole or beam) ensuring that it is positioned above head height.

Position yourself kneeling down facing the anchor point with the band coming from above you. Keeping your back straight and abdominal muscles tight to help support this posture, hold the handles of the band in each hand with palms facing forward and arms extended toward the anchor point.

Pull the band down in a straight line by bending arms, keeping a wide arm position, until your elbows pass the line of your back and reach your sides. You should feel a slight stretch across your chest—if not ensure that you are squeezing shoulder blades together at the bottom of the movement. Then extend your arms following the same line, until they are back to the start position. At this point they should be fully extended before beginning your next repetition. Check that your back remains straight and still throughout the exercise and prevent any swaying back and forth.

Muscle groups worked in this exercise:
Back (latissimus dorsi), back of shoulders (posterior deltoid), and front of upper arms (biceps).

Breathing tip: Breathe out as you pull down.

Close Grip Pull Down

Upper Back

This is a multiple joint exercise designed to work the major muscle groups in the back of the upper body in a close arm pull-up movement, with slightly more emphasis on the arms than the Latissimus Pull Down.

Attach the resistance band to a door anchor, or around a sturdy object of a suitable height ensuring that it is positioned above head height.

Position yourself kneeling down facing the anchor point with the band coming from above you. Keeping your back straight and abdominal muscles tight to help support this posture, hold the handles of the band in each hand with palms facing each other and arms extended toward the anchor point. Ensure that your hands are approximately 6-8 inches (15-20cms) apart.

Pull the band down in a straight line by bending both arms, maintaining the close hand position with elbows in tight, until they reach your sides and hands touch your chest. You may feel a slight stretch across your chest. Then extend your arms following the same line, until they are back to the start position. At this point they should be fully extended before beginning your next repetition. Ensure that your back remains straight and still throughout the exercise to prevent any swaying back and forth.

Muscle groups worked in this exercise:
Back (latissimus dorsi), back of shoulders (posterior deltoid), and front of upper arms (biceps).

Breathing tip: Breathe out as you pull down.

Standing Mid Row

Upper Back

This is a multiple joint exercise designed to work the major muscle groups in the upper back in a pulling/rowing movement.

Attach the resistance band to a door anchor, or around a sturdy object of a suitable height ensuring that it is positioned at around shoulder height.

Position yourself with the band in front of you, your feet in a split stance and body upright, with abdominal muscles tight. Hold the handles of the band with palms facing down and arms extended forward until they are straight. Elbows and wrists should be elevated to shoulder height and parallel to the floor.

Slowly bend elbows pulling them back past the line of your shoulders, ensuring that elbows and wrists remain elevated to shoulder height and parallel to the floor. Then slowly straighten your arms back to the start position, stopping when they are fully extended. To make the exercise harder step further back, or make it easier by moving closer.

Muscle groups worked in this exercise:
Upper back (lower trapezius), back of shoulders (posterior deltoid), between shoulders (rhomboids), and front of upper arms (biceps).

Breathing tip: Breathe out as you pull arms backward.

Bent Over Row

Upper Back

This is a multiple joint exercise and an alternative to the Mid Row, designed to work the major muscle groups in the upper back in a pulling/rowing movement.

Place the resistance band under the arches of both feet. Position yourself with feet shoulder-width apart, a slight bend in the knees and bent forward at the waist. The lumbar region of your back should be straight and not arched over. Keep abdominal muscles tight. Hold the handles of the band and extend your arms down toward the floor until they are straight and vertical.

With an overhand grip, bend elbows, pulling them back past the line of your shoulders, retracting shoulder blades and keeping your forearms vertical. Then slowly straighten your arms back to the start position, stopping when they are fully extended. Ensure that your back remains still throughout the exercise and prevent any swaying back and forth. You can move feet wider apart to make the exercise harder, or closer to make it easier.

Muscle groups worked in this exercise:
Upper back (lower trapezius), back of shoulders (posterior deltoid), between shoulders (rhomboids), and front of upper arms (biceps).

Breathing tip: Breathe out as you pull arms up.

Band Pull Over

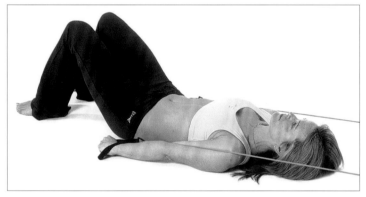

Back

This is a single joint isolation exercise designed to work the muscle groups in the middle/side of the back and assisted by those in the lower chest. These muscles are used in a movement similar to closing a large pull-down window.

Attach the resistance band to a door anchor, or around a sturdy object of a suitable height, ensuring that it is positioned just above floor level.

Position yourself lying flat on your back so that the anchor point is above your head. You can bend your knees to take the pressure off your lower back. Take hold of both handles with an underhand grip and extend them above your head, keeping them shoulder-width apart and near to the floor. When arms are extended, check that your lower back is flat on the floor and abdominal muscles are tight. This will help prevent any unwanted arching.

With tension already in the band, pull the band over and down, creating a large arc until your hands reach the side of your legs. Pause, and then slowly allow your arms to return back up and over following the same line, until they are back to the start position.

Muscle groups worked in this exercise:
Back (latissimus dorsi) and lower chest (lower pectorals).

Breathing tip: Breathe out as you pull down.

Upright Row

Shoulders

This is a multiple joint exercise designed to work the major muscle groups in the upper back and shoulders in an upright, arm lifting movement.

Place the resistance band under the arches of both feet. Position yourself with feet hip-width apart, and in the correct standing exercise posture. Keep abdominal muscles tight. Swap the handles of the band to opposite hands so that it crosses over and hold the handles with a close overhand grip. Extend arms down toward the floor until they are straight, but don't round your shoulders.

With elbows leading, lift the handles of the band until your hands reach your chin, keeping them as close to your body as possible throughout the movement. Elbows should be high and form a "V" with shoulder blades retracted. Then, slowly straighten your arms back to the start position, stopping when they are fully extended. Ensure that your back remains still throughout the exercise to prevent any swaying back and forth. You can keep feet wider apart to make the exercise harder, or closer to make it easier.

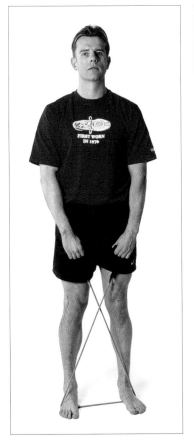 

Muscle groups worked in this exercise: Upper back/neck (upper and lower trapezius), front and middle of shoulder (anterior and medial deltoid), and front of upper arms (biceps).

Breathing tip: Breathe out as you pull arms up.

Shoulder Press

Shoulders

This is a multiple joint exercise designed to work the major muscle groups in the top of the shoulder and the back of the upper arm, in an upward pushing movement.

Place the resistance band on top of a swiss ball or chair and position yourself so that you are seated on top of the band. Sit straight with shoulders back and abdominal muscles tight. Using an overhand grip, hold the handles of the band with your hands to the side of each shoulder at around shoulder height.

Extend both arms above your head until they are straight and then slowly bend your arms taking them back to the start position, with your hands returning level with your shoulders. Make sure that your forearms remain vertical throughout the movement.

Muscle groups worked in this exercise:
Front of shoulders (anterior deltoid), top of shoulders (upper trapezius) and back of upper arms (triceps).

Breathing tip: Breathe out as you extend arms up.

Lateral Raise

Shoulders

This is a single joint exercise designed to isolate the muscles in the middle of the shoulder in a lateral arm elevation movement.

Place the resistance band under the arches of both feet. Position yourself with feet hip-width apart and in the correct standing exercise posture. Keep abdominal muscles tight. Take hold of the handles with an overhand grip, palms facing inward and arms straight by your side.

Slowly elevate your arms up and out to the side, until your hands are just above shoulder height, pause, and then slowly bring your arms back to the starting position, keeping arms extended. Ensure that your back remains still throughout the exercise to prevent any swaying or throwing of weight. To make the exercise harder, move feet further apart, or make it easier by moving them closer together.

Muscle group worked in this exercise:
Middle of shoulder (medial deltoid).

Breathing tip: Breathe out as you bring your arms out to the side.

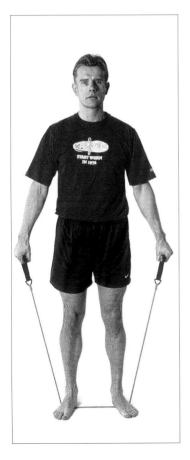

Single Arm Lateral Raise

Shoulders

This is an alternative single joint exercise that allows you to focus on one side at a time. It's designed to isolate the muscle in the middle of the shoulder in a lateral arm elevation movement.

Attach the resistance band to a door anchor, or around a sturdy object, ensuring that it is positioned at floor level. You only need the use of one end of the band for this exercise, so ensure that the other end is securely attached to the anchor point.

Position yourself with feet in a split stance and in the correct standing exercise posture. Keep abdominal muscles tight. The band should be coming from the opposite side to which you are working. From this position bring the band across the front of your body, taking hold of the handle with an overhand grip, palm facing inward, and holding your arm straight by your side. There should be some resistance at this point.

Slowly elevate your arm up and out to the side, until your hand is just above shoulder height, pause, and then slowly bring your arm back to the starting position, keeping it extended. Repeat with the other arm. Ensure that your back remains still throughout the exercise and prevent any swaying or throwing of weight. To make the exercise harder, step further away from the anchor point, or make it easier by moving closer.

Muscle group worked in this exercise:
Middle of shoulder (medial deltoid).

Breathing tip: Breathe out as you bring your arm out to the side.

Shoulder Front Raise

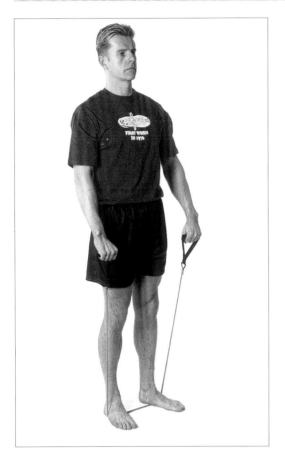

Shoulders

This is a single joint exercise designed to isolate the muscles in the front of the shoulder in a forward arm elevation movement.

Place the resistance band under the arches of both feet. Position yourself with feet hip-width apart and in the correct standing exercise posture. Keep abdominal muscles tight. Take hold of the handles with an overhand grip and arms straight by your side.

Slowly elevate your arms up in front of you, until your hands are just above shoulder height, pause, and then slowly bring arms back to the starting position, keeping arms extended throughout the full range of movement. Ensure that your back remains still throughout the exercise and prevent any swaying or throwing of weight. To make the exercise harder, move feet further apart, or make it easier by moving them closer together.

Muscle group worked in this exercise: Front of shoulder (anterior deltoid).

Breathing tip: Breathe out as you bring your arms up.

Single Arm Front Raise

Shoulders

This is an alternative single joint exercise that allows you to focus on one side at a time. It's designed to isolate the muscle in the front of the shoulder in an arm elevation movement.

Attach the resistance band to a door anchor, or around a sturdy object, such as a pole, ensuring that it is positioned at floor level. You only need the use of one end of the band for this exercise, so ensure that the other end is securely attached to the anchor point.

Position yourself so that the band is coming from behind you, with feet in a split stance, and in the correct standing exercise posture. Keep abdominal muscles tight. Take hold of the handle with an overhand grip and arm straight by your side.

Slowly elevate your arm up in front of you, until your hand is just above shoulder height, pause, and then slowly bring it back to the starting position, keeping your arm extended throughout the full range of movement. Then repeat using the other arm. Ensure that your back remains still throughout the exercise and prevent any swaying or throwing of weight. To make the exercise harder, step further away from the anchor point, or make it easier by moving closer.

Muscle group worked in this exercise: Front of shoulder (anterior deltoid).

Breathing tip: Breathe out as you bring your arm up.

Reverse Flys

Shoulders

This is a single joint exercise designed to isolate the muscles at the back of the shoulder in a shoulder blade adduction/pulling-arms-to-the-rear movement. This is an area commonly neglected in training and everyday activities; it is therefore an important area to include in your program.

Attach the resistance band to a door anchor, or around a sturdy object, ensuring that it is positioned at shoulder height.

Position yourself with the band in front of you and in the correct standing exercise posture, with your feet in a split stance. Take hold of the handles with a palms-inward grip, your arms extended forward at shoulder height, and a very slight bend in the elbows. There should be tension in the band already.

Working against the resistance, bring your arms apart and out to the side, keeping arms at shoulder height. Retract shoulder blades together, pause, and then slowly bring arms back to the starting position, with arms extended. Ensure that your back remains still throughout the exercise and prevent any swaying or throwing of weight. To make the exercise harder, step further back or make it easier by moving closer to the attachment.

Muscle groups worked in this exercise:
Back of shoulder (posterior deltoid) and between shoulder blades (rhomboids).

Breathing tip: Breathe out as you bring your arms out to the side.

Lying Internal Shoulder Rotation

Rotator Cuff

The Rotator Cuff is a group of four muscles located at the front, top, and back of the shoulder joint originating from the shoulder blade. They are responsible for creating outward, inward, and upward circular motion or rotation in the shoulder. The following exercises will help you to create strength in the shoulder joint and prevent shoulder instability. These exercises are especially beneficial to those who play sports that require overarm motions, such as serving in tennis.

Rotator Cuff

This is a single joint isolation exercise designed to work the muscle group that stabilizes the shoulder joint. The muscles worked in this exercise are typically recruited in racket sports and when performing an overarm throwing action.

Attach the resistance band to a door anchor, or around a sturdy object of a suitable height, ensuring that it is positioned at floor level. You will only be using one handle.

Position yourself lying flat on your back so that the anchor point is above your head. You can bend your knees to take the pressure off your lower back. Take hold of the handle with an underhand grip, bending arm at the elbow. Position your upper arm so that it is at 90 degrees to your body with your shoulder and elbow touching the floor. Slowly rotate your shoulder allowing your hand to move down toward the floor at head height and as far as you can comfortably go. There should not be any pain. If pain is present, raise your hand away from the floor slightly. This is the correct starting position.

With tension already in the band, rotate your shoulder by lifting your hand up and over in an arc, pivoting on the elbow. Rotate as far as is comfortable and without the shoulder lifting away from the floor. Pause, and then slowly allow your shoulder to rotate back by lifting your hand back up and over, following the same line, until it is back to the start position. Make sure your upper arm and elbow stay fixed in position. Repeat using your other hand.

Muscle group worked in this exercise: Rotator cuff.

Breathing tip: Breathe out as you move your hand in the direction of your feet.

Lying External Shoulder Rotation

Rotator Cuff

This is another highly beneficial single joint isolation exercise designed to work the muscle group that stabilizes the shoulder joint. The muscles worked in this exercise are typically recruited in racket sports when performing a backhand return shot, setting up for a serve, volley, and overarm throw.

Attach the resistance band to a door anchor, or around a sturdy object of a suitable height ensuring that it is positioned at floor level. You will only be using one handle.

Position yourself lying flat on your back so that the anchor point is by your feet. As before, you can bend your knees to take the pressure off your lower back. Take hold of the handle with an overhand grip, bending your arm at the elbow. Position your upper arm so that it is at 90 degrees to your body with your shoulder and elbow touching the floor. Get into the start position by rotating your shoulder, allowing your hand to move down toward the floor at waist height, and as far as it can comfortably go. There should not be any pain. If pain is present, raise your hand away from the floor slightly.

With tension already in the band, rotate your shoulder by lifting your hand up and over in an arc, pivoting on the elbow and stopping when it reaches the floor at head height.

Pause, and then slowly allow your shoulder to rotate back by lifting your hand back up and over following the same line, until it is back to the start position. Make sure that your upper arm and elbow stay fixed in position and that your shoulder does not lift away from the floor throughout the exercise.

Muscle group worked in this exercise: Rotator cuff.

Breathing tip: Breathe out as you move your hand in the direction of your head.

Standing External Shoulder Rotation

Rotator Cuff

This is an alternative single joint isolation exercise designed to work the muscle group that stabilizes the shoulder joint. The muscles worked in this exercise are typically used in racket sports when performing a backhand return shot, setting up for a serve, or playing golf.

Attach the resistance band to a door anchor, or around a sturdy object of a suitable height ensuring that it is positioned at elbow height. You will only be using one handle.

Position yourself in the correct exercise posture sideways on to the anchor point, with the band on the opposite side to the one that you're working. Take hold of the handle with a palm-in grip, bending the arm 90 degrees at the elbow. Position your upper arm so that it is tight to your body. Get into the start position by rotating your shoulder so that your forearm is across your body.

With tension already in the band, rotate your shoulder by swinging your arm around to the side, pivoting your elbow on your hip, and stopping when it is parallel with the band. Pause, and then slowly allow your shoulder to rotate back by swinging your arm back across your body, following the same line, and until it reaches the start position. Make sure that your upper arm and elbow stay fixed in position and that your shoulders and midsection don't sway during the exercise.

Muscle group worked in this exercise: Rotator cuff.

Breathing tip: Breathe out as you move your arm out to the side.

Bicep Curls

Arms

This is a single joint exercise designed to isolate the muscles in the front of the upper arms in a hand lifting movement, flexing at the elbow.

Place the resistance band under the arches of both feet. Position yourself with feet hip-width apart, and in the correct standing exercise posture. Keep abdominal muscles tight. Take hold of the handles with an under-hand grip, and arms straight by your side.

Slowly elevate your hands in front of you by flexing at the elbow, keeping a strict position with the upper arms locked by your sides. Pause when your hands are at chest height, but not touching your chest, and then slowly straighten arms back down to the starting position, stopping when your hands reach the side of your legs. Ensure that your back and upper arms remain still throughout the exercise to prevent any swaying. To make the exercise harder, move feet further apart, or make it easier by moving them closer together.

Muscle group worked in this exercise: Front of upper arms (biceps).

Breathing tip: Breathe out as you bring your hands up.

Individual Bicep Curls

Arms

This is an alternative to the standard bicep curl, allowing you to concentrate on working each arm individually, though it is more time consuming.

Place the resistance band under the arches of both feet. Position yourself with feet hip-width apart, and in the correct standing exercise posture. Keep abdominal muscles tight. Take hold of the handles with an under-hand grip, and arms straight by your side.

Slowly elevate one arm in front of you by flexing at the elbow, keeping a strict position with the upper arm locked by your sides. Pause when your hand is at shoulder height, but not touching your shoulder, and then slowly straighten arm back to the starting position, stopping when your hand reaches the side of your leg. Ensure that your back and upper arms remain still throughout the exercise to prevent any swaying or throwing of weight. Repeat with the other arm. To make the exercise harder, move feet further apart, or make it easier by moving them closer together.

Muscle group worked in this exercise: Front of upper arms (biceps).

Breathing tip: Breathe out as you bring your hands up.

Bicep Hammer Curls

Arms

This is a similar single joint exercise to the standard Bicep Curl, putting additional emphasis on the forearm in a hand-lifting movement when flexing at the elbow.

Place the resistance band under the arches of both feet. Position yourself with feet hip-width apart, and in the correct standing exercise posture. Keep abdominal muscles tight. Take hold of the handles with a palms-in grip and arms straight by your side.

Slowly elevate your hands in front of you by flexing at the elbow, keeping palms facing in and a strict position with the upper arms locked by your sides. Pause when your hands are at shoulder height, but not touching your shoulders, and then slowly straighten arms back to the starting position, stopping when your hands reach the side of your legs. Ensure that your back and upper arms remain still throughout the exercise to prevent any swaying or throwing of weight. To make the exercise harder, push feet further apart, or make it easier by moving them closer together.

Muscle group worked in this exercise: Front of upper arms (biceps).

Breathing tip: Breathe out as you bring your hands up.

Tricep Extension

Arms

This is a single joint exercise designed to isolate the muscles in the back of the upper arms in a reaching-out movement, when extending at the elbow and pulling down.

Attach the resistance band to a door anchor, or around a sturdy object of a suitable height (e.g. a pole), ensuring that it is as far as possible above head height.

Position yourself so that the band is as vertical as possible, with feet hip-width apart, and in the correct standing exercise posture. Keep abdominal muscles tight. Take hold of the handles with an overhand grip and with elbows locked in by your sides, bend your arms until hands are at shoulder height.

Slowly extend your arms, pushing the handles down until they touch your thighs, pause, and then bend your arms, returning your hands back to the start position. Ensure that you keep your upper arm and elbows fixed by your sides and do not let them spring out. Keep shoulders and back still throughout the exercise to prevent any swaying or throwing of weight.

Muscle group worked in this exercise: Back of upper arms (triceps).

Breathing tip: Breathe out as you straighten arms.

Tricep Overhead Extension

Arms

This triceps exercise is designed to isolate the muscles in the back of the upper arms and work it through a different angle to the previous triceps exercise. Muscle areas are used in a reaching-out movement, extending at the elbow, as if you were going to hit an object with a hammer.

Place the resistance band under one foot, standing on a part of the band that allows a good level of tension. Ensure that the band is coming out from the back of your foot. You only require one handle for this exercise.

Position yourself with feet in a close split stance and the band under your back foot. Keep abdominal muscles tight. With the band behind you, take hold of the handle with the opposite hand to the foot that is on the band, with an inverted palm-in grip. Extend your arm above your head, and then bend the elbow so that your forearm is behind your head. Keep upper arm vertical.

Slowly extend your arm, pushing the handle up in the air until your arm is straight, pause, and then bend your arm returning your hands back to the start position. Ensure that you keep your upper arm vertical and still throughout the exercise. Repeat exercise with the other arm. Make sure that your neck is comfortable during the exercise by looking straight ahead and not craning it forward.

Muscle group worked in this exercise: Back of upper arms (triceps).

Breathing tip: Breathe out as you extend arm up.

Triceps Kickbacks

Arms

This final triceps exercise is an alternative to the over-head triceps extension, and can be more comfortable if you have a limited range of movement in your shoulders. It also works the triceps under less tension.

Attach the resistance band to a door anchor, or around a sturdy object of a suitable height ensuring that it is positioned at floor level. Only one handle is required.

Position yourself with the resistance band in front of you, feet in a split stance, leaning your upper body forward to about 45 degrees. Rest the hand that you're not using on the thigh of your leading leg for support. Take hold of the handle with a palm-in grip; your upper arm should remain close to your side with elbow bent and then elevated to shoulder height.

Starting with your hand below your shoulder, slowly extend your arm, pulling the handle back behind you until your arm is straight, pause, and then bend your arm, returning your hand back to the start position. Ensure that you keep your upper arm horizontal and held in position throughout the exercise. Repeat exercise with the other arm. To make the exercise harder, step further away from the anchor point, or make it easier by moving closer.

Muscle group worked in this exercise: Back of upper arms (triceps).

Breathing tip: Breathe out as you extend arm back.

Squat

Legs & Hips

This is a multiple joint exercise designed to work the major muscle groups of the legs in the front of the thighs and buttocks. These groups are used in a seated-to-standing movement and when skiing.

Place the resistance band under the arches of both feet. Position yourself in the correct standing exercise posture, with feet shoulder-width apart. Take hold of the handles with an overhand grip and bring them up to shoulder level with the palm of your hands facing forward. The band should be behind your arms.

Slowly bend your knees, keeping your heels down, and push your weight back slightly as if you were about to sit down, stopping just before your legs reach a 90-degree angle. Pause, and then extend your legs pushing through your heels until you are back to the starting position. Try to keep your back and lower legs as vertical as possible throughout the exercise. Avoid pushing your knees forward past the toe line as you bend your knees. You can move feet wider apart to make the exercise harder, or closer to make it easier.

Muscle groups worked in this exercise: Front of thigh (quadriceps), buttocks (gluteus maximus).

Breathing tip: Breathe out as you extend legs.

Lying Leg Extension

Legs & Hips

This is a single joint exercise designed to isolate the muscle group in the front of the upper leg in a forward leg kick action.

Using the ankle strap, attach the resistance band around the ankle of the leg that you're starting with.

Position yourself lying on your front, taking hold of both handles with your hands above your head and elbows firmly on the floor. Bend the knee of the leg you're exercising so that your foot is near to your buttocks.

Extend your leg at the knee, keeping the upper part of the leg still, until your leg is straight and your foot touches the floor. Pause, and then slowly bend the knee again, bringing your foot back to the starting position. Repeat using your other leg. Ensure that your hips remain still and keep knees together throughout the exercise.

Muscle group worked in this exercise: Front of thigh (quadriceps).

Breathing tip: Breathe out as you extend leg.

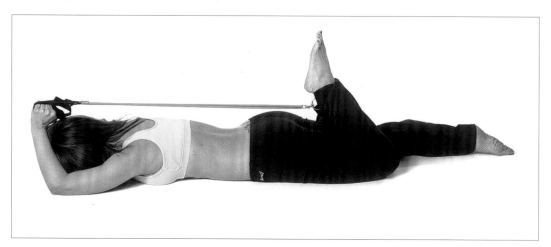

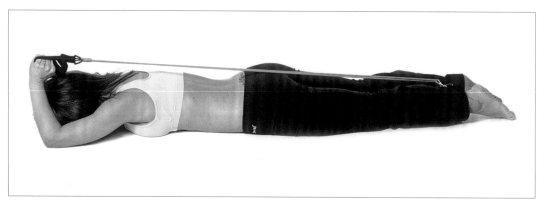

Standing Leg Extension

Legs & Hips

This is an alternative exercise to the Lying Leg Extension, designed to isolate the muscle group in the front of the upper leg.

Attach the resistance band to a door anchor, or around a sturdy object, ensuring that it is positioned at floor level. You only need to use one end of the band for this exercise, so ensure that the other end is secure. Attach the loose end to an ankle strap, and then place around the ankle of the leg that you are starting with.

Position yourself so that the band is coming from behind you and in the correct standing exercise posture. Stand on one leg, flexing the other at the hip so that the thigh is at 45 degrees. Bend the knee of the elevated leg so that your foot drops back. Keep abdominal muscles tight. Place a stable object next to you, to hold onto for support, if necessary.

Extend your leg at the knee, keeping the upper part of the leg still, until your leg is straight. Pause, and then slowly bend the knee again. Bring your foot back to the starting position. After completing your repetitions, swap legs. Ensure that your hips remain still throughout the exercise. To make the exercise harder, step further away from the anchor point, or make it easier by moving closer.

Muscle group worked in this exercise: Front of thigh (quadriceps).

Breathing tip: Breathe out as you extend leg.

Lying Hamstring Curl

Legs & Hips

This is a single joint exercise designed to isolate the muscle group in the back of the upper leg.

Attach the resistance band to a door anchor, or around a sturdy object, ensuring that it is positioned at floor level. You only need to use one end of the band for this exercise, so ensure that the other end is secure. Attach the loose end to an ankle strap and then place around the ankle of the leg that you are starting with.

Position yourself lying on your front, with the band coming from behind your feet and both legs straight.

Bend the knee of the leg you're exercising until your heel is near to your buttocks. Pause, and then slowly extend your leg again. Bring it straight and back to the starting position. Repeat using your other leg. Ensure that your hips remain still and keep your knees together throughout the exercise.

Muscle group worked in this exercise: Back of upper leg (hamstrings).

Breathing tip: Breathe out as you bend the knee.

Standing Hamstring Curl

Legs & Hips

This is an alternative exercise to the Lying Hamstring Curl, designed to isolate the muscle group in the back of the upper leg.

Attach the resistance band to a door anchor, or around a sturdy object, ensuring that it is positioned at floor level. You only need to use one end of the band for this exercise, so ensure that the other end is secure. Attach the loose end to an ankle strap, and then place around the ankle of the leg that you are starting with.

Position yourself so that the band is coming from in front of you and in the correct standing exercise posture, with knees in line. You can place a stable object next to you to hold onto for support.

Whilst supporting all your weight with one leg, flex the other at the knee until the lower leg is at 90 degrees to the upper. Pause, and then extend the leg at the knee until your leg is straight. Repeat using your other leg. Ensure that your hips remain still and keep both knees together throughout the exercise. To make the exercise harder, step further away from the anchor point, or make it easier by moving closer.

Muscle group worked in this exercise: Back of upper leg (hamstrings).

Breathing tip: Breathe out as you bend the knee.

Calf Flex

Legs & Hips

This is an alternative calf exercise, designed for working one leg at a time. It isolates the major muscle group at the back of the lower leg.

Place both resistance band handles over the toes of one foot.

Position yourself in the correct standing exercise posture. Take hold of the middle of the band with an overhand grip and bring them up to chest level. Extend the leg with the band attached, so that it is straight and off the ground.

Keeping the leg straight, push your toes down against the band pivoting at the ankle, as if pushing on a brake pedal. Pause, and then lift your toes back as far as possible and to the start position. Repeat with the other leg. You can move hands wider apart to make the exercise harder, or closer to make it easier.

Muscle groups worked in this exercise:
Back of lower leg (calf).

Breathing tip: Breathe out as you push toes down.

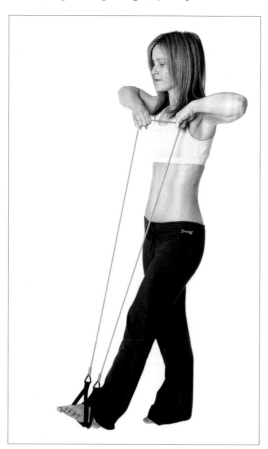

Lying Side Leg Raise

Legs & Hips

This is a single joint isolation exercise designed to work the muscle group that abducts the leg. This muscle has an important role in stabilizing the hip.

Tie the ends of the resistance band together so that it forms a loop, just over two feet (60cms) in diameter.

Position yourself lying on your side in a straight line with shoulders and hips vertical. Place both legs through the middle of the band so that it sits just above the knee. Slightly bend the leg that is on the floor for added support.

Keeping your foot flexed, lift (abduct) the top leg, aiming to get it to a 40- to 45-degree angle to the floor. Pause, and then slowly lower your leg back down until it reaches the start position, but not touching the other leg. Make sure that hips remain fixed during the exercise and that they don't rotate back when lifting your leg. Repeat using your other leg.

Muscle group worked in this exercise:
Outer thigh/hip (gluteus medius).

Breathing tip: Breathe out as you lift leg up.

Standing Outer Thigh

Legs & Hips

This is an alternative single joint exercise to the Lying Side Leg Raise, providing the same benefits but in a standing position.

Attach the resistance band to a door anchor, or around a sturdy object, ensuring that it is positioned at floor level. You only need to use one end of the band for this exercise, so ensure that the other end is secure. Attach the loose end to an ankle strap, and then place around the ankle of the leg that you are starting with.

Position yourself in the correct standing exercise posture so that you are side on to the anchor point with the band attached to the leg that is furthest away. The leg that you are working should be slightly crossed over the front of the one that you are standing on. You can place a stable object next to you to hold onto for support.

Whilst supporting all your weight with one leg, lift (abduct) the other out to the side until it reaches a 40- to 45-degree angle. Pause, and then lower your leg until it crosses the supporting leg. Repeat using the other leg. Ensure that your leg is straight and the upper body remains still throughout the exercise to prevent any flexing of the waist. To make the exercise harder, step further away from the anchor point, or make it easier by moving closer.

Muscle group worked in this exercise:
Outer thigh/hip (gluteus medius).

Breathing tip: Breathe out as you lift leg out to the side.

Inner Thigh

Legs & Hips

This is a single joint isolation exercise designed to work the muscle group that adducts the leg. This muscle also has an important role in stabilizing the hip from the inner thigh.

Attach the resistance band to a door anchor, or around a sturdy object, ensuring that it is positioned at floor level. You only need to use one end of the band for this exercise, so ensure that the other end is secure.

Position yourself in the correct standing exercise posture so that you are side on to the anchor point. Attach the loose end of the band to an ankle strap, place it around the ankle of the leg that is closest to the anchor, and abduct (lift) your leg toward the anchor. You can place a stable object next to you to hold onto for support.

Whilst supporting all your weight with one leg, adduct the other, bringing it across the supporting leg. Pause, and then bring it back across and out to the side, returning to the start position. Repeat using the other leg. Ensure that your leg is straight, and your upper body remains still throughout the exercise to prevent any flexing at the waist. To make the exercise harder, step further away from the anchor point, or make it easier by moving closer.

Muscle group worked in this exercise: Inner thigh/hip (adductors).

Breathing tip: Breathe out as you bring leg in.

Lunge

Legs & Hips

This is a multiple joint exercise designed to work the major muscle groups of the legs in the front of the thighs and buttocks. These groups are worked in a seated-to-standing movement. It is similar to a squat, but enables you to focus on each leg individually.

Position yourself in the correct standing exercise posture, and then take a large step forward with one foot and place the band underneath it. Keep both legs extended, feet parallel, with your leading foot flat and the heel of your back foot raised. Hold the handles of the band with an overhand grip, and bring them up to shoulder level with the palm of your hands facing forward. The band should be behind your arms. Slowly bend your knees, stopping just before the knee of your back leg touches the floor, and both legs are bent to a 90-degree angle. Pause, and then extend your legs pushing through the heel of the leading leg until you are back to the start position. Try to keep your back as vertical as possible throughout the exercise. Ensure that the knee of your leading leg remains in line with your ankle as your knee bends.

Muscle groups worked in this exercise:
Front of thigh (quadriceps), buttocks (gluteus maximus).

Breathing tip: Breathe out as you extend legs.

Hip/Leg Extension

Legs & Hips

This is a multiple joint exercise designed to work the major muscle group of the buttocks. This group is used in movements such as the pushing-down action when pedaling a bicycle. It activates similar areas to the squat, but with more emphasis on the buttocks.

Position yourself on your hands and knees, or elbows if it is more comfortable. Place the resistance band in the arch of one of your feet; take hold of both handles with a palms-in grip and with the band on the inside of your arms. Raise the knee of the side you are working toward your chest and make sure that your back is completely straight.

Slowly extend your hip and leg, pushing your foot directly behind you, stopping when it forms a straight line with your body and with your foot at hip height. Pause, and then flex your hip and bend your knee bringing it back toward your chest and to the start position. Abdominal muscles should be held tight to prevent your back from arching. Keep your foot fixed in position with toes down throughout the exercise to prevent the band from slipping off. Repeat on your other side.

Muscle group worked in this exercise: Buttocks (gluteus maximus).

Breathing tip: Breathe out as you extend hip leg.

Hip Flexion

Legs & Hips

This is a single joint exercise, designed to isolate the muscle group in the front of the hip. This muscle group is typically used when lifting your knee toward your chest; it is therefore an important part of most sporting movements, especially running.

Attach the resistance band to a door anchor, or around a sturdy object, ensuring that it is positioned at floor level. You only need to use one end of the band for this exercise, so ensure that the other end is secure. Attach the loose end to an ankle strap and then place around the ankle of the leg that you are starting with.

Position yourself so that the band is coming from behind you and in the correct standing exercise posture. Stand on one leg, extending the other at the hip and knee so that the thigh is at 30 degrees behind you. Keep your body upright and abdominal muscles tight. Place a stable object next to you so that you can hold onto it for support.

In a forward movement, flex your hip, allow the knee to bend, and lift the knee as high as possible toward your chest without moving your back out of the upright position. Pause, and then slowly lower your knee, extending your hip and leg back to the starting position. Repeat using the other leg. Ensure that your upper body remains still throughout the exercise. To make the exercise harder, step further away from the anchor point, or make it easier by moving closer.

Muscle group worked in this exercise: Hip flexors (iliopsoas).

Breathing tip: Breathe out as you lift knee.

Abdominal Curl

Midsection

To provide a fully-balanced workout, some exercises are needed that don't require a resistance band. This is a basic, yet effective, exercise designed to work the major muscle group of the abdomen. The muscle group is used when flexing your ribcage toward your pelvis, and provides vital support to your midsection.

Position yourself lying flat on your back, with your knees bent and feet on the floor. Straighten your arms and rest your hands on the top of your thighs. Pull your chin in toward your chest very slightly so that your head lifts away from the floor. Breathe out and flatten your stomach as if pulling your belly button toward your lower back then squeeze the muscles so that they are tight. Hold this position throughout the exercise.

Reach your hands up your thighs and touch the top of your knees, curling your shoulders toward your pelvis, but not lifting your lower back. Pause, and then slowly uncurl, sliding your hands back down your thighs until you are back to the start position, but not resting down completely. Focusing on a reference point on the ceiling will help you to fix your head and neck in position for the duration of the exercise.

Muscle group worked in this exercise: Abdomen (rectus abdominis).

Breathing tip: Breathe out as you reach to knees.

Abdominal Reverse Curl

Midsection

This is another abdominal exercise designed to work the major muscle group of the abdomen, with more emphasis on the lower portion. No resistance band is required for this exercise.

Position yourself lying flat on your back. Breathe out and flatten your stomach as if pulling your belly button toward your lower back, then squeeze the muscles so that they are tight. Raise your legs so that your thighs are at 90 degrees to the floor, with feet elevated. Rest your arms on either side of your body to aid stability.

Raise your legs and bring knees back toward your head; your buttocks should lift from the floor very slightly. Pause, and then slowly uncurl, lowering your pelvis until your legs return to the start position. Focus on contracting your abdomen and not the movement of the legs. Keep your neck and shoulders relaxed and on the floor throughout the exercise.

Muscle group worked in this exercise:
Abdomen (rectus abdominis).

Breathing tip: Breathe out as you raise your legs toward you.

Abdominal Curl Twist

Midsection

This exercise works the major muscle groups of the front and side of the abdomen.

Lie on your back; thighs 90-degrees to your body, feet elevated to knee height. Your arms should be bent with fingertips touching either side of your head. Pull your chin in toward your chest so head lifts away from the floor.

Lift your shoulders away from the floor and curl them toward your pelvis, rotating at the waist. Flex your hip on the opposite side bringing your knee toward the opposite elbow. Slowly uncurl and extend the hip until you are back to the start position.

Muscle groups worked in this exercise:
Center of abdomen (rectus abdominis), external obliques.

Breathing tip: Breathe out as you reach elbow to knee.

Dorsal Raises

Midsection

This is a basic yet effective exercise designed to work the major muscle group down the middle of your back, on either side of your spine. The muscle group, which is made up of four muscles, is worked when extending your back, and provides vital support. Position yourself lying flat on your front with neck straight so that you are facing the floor. Legs should be straight and arms extended above your head.

Lift your left arm and right leg, extending it at the hip, and keeping this arm and leg straight. Pause, and then slowly lower your arm and leg back down to the floor until you reach the start position. Then repeat with your right arm and left leg. Only lift as far as is comfortable. Your range of movement in the hip and shoulder should be increased progressively.

Muscle group worked in this exercise:
Length of back (erector spinae).

Breathing tip: Breathe out as you lift opposite arm and leg.

Kneeling Resisted Abdominal Curl

Midsection

This abdominal exercise is a progression from the standard Abdominal Curl. It is designed to work the major muscle group of the abdomen against a controlled resistance with more emphasis on the upper portion.

Attach the resistance band to a door anchor, or around a sturdy object of a suitable height, ensuring that it is positioned at least at head height when standing.

Position yourself kneeling down with the band in front of you. Take hold of the handles with a palms-in grip then place them on either side of your head. Lean forward so that your back is parallel to the floor, and with your buttocks elevated away from your heels.

Breathe out and flatten your stomach as if pulling your belly button toward your lower back, then squeeze the muscles so that they are tight. Hold the contraction throughout the exercise.

Pull down against the resistance by rolling your shoulders toward your pelvis, and elbows to thighs. Pause and then slowly uncurl, raising the shoulders until you are back to the start position. Keep the angle in your hips and legs fixed throughout the exercise so that the target muscles are not being assisted.

Muscle group worked in this exercise: Abdomen (rectus abdominis).

Breathing tip: Breathe out as you roll shoulders toward your pelvis.

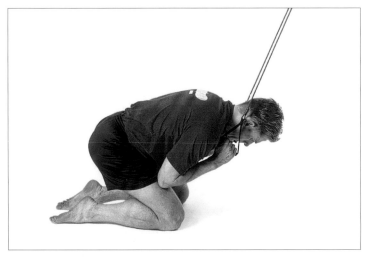

Side Bends

Midsection

This exercise is designed to work the muscles on either side of your midsection. They are worked in a lateral flexion (bending side to side) movement.

Attach the resistance band to a door anchor, or around a sturdy object, ensuring that it is positioned at floor level. You only need to use one end of the band for this exercise, so ensure that the other end is securely attached to the anchor point.

Position yourself with feet shoulder-width apart, and in the correct standing exercise posture. Keep abdominal muscles tight. The band should be coming from the side you are working on. Taking hold of the handle with an overhand grip, hold your arm straight and out to the side at a 45-degree angle to your body. There should be some resistance at this point.

Holding your lower body still and hips level, flex your midsection, leaning away from the anchor point and aiming to touch your free hand on the side of your knee. Pause, and then straighten your midsection back to the upright starting position. Turn around and repeat on your other side. Ensure that you don't sway your hips during the exercise. To make the exercise harder, step further away from the anchor point or make it easier by moving closer.

Muscle group worked in this exercise: Sides of midsection (external obliques).

Breathing tip: Breathe out as you laterally flex away from the anchor point.

20-Minute Workout

The 20-Minute Workout has been designed so that it is suitable for everyone, whether you're new to resistance training and want an effective and achievable starting point, or if you have time constraints and need a time-efficient workout. As you progress, you can vary the workout by including some of the exercises we have outlined in the previous chapter. The initial 20-Minute Workout includes all the major muscle groups and multi-joint exercises to ensure that the whole body has been worked, and because the workout has been formulated with time efficiency in mind, idle periods, such as resting time between sets, have been utilized for flexibility exercises, saving you valuable time and enabling you to get more from your workout.

Exercise Format Example: Having warmed up, start the first exercise, Chest Press. Complete your first set of 12–15 repetitions (using it to progressively increase the exercise intensity and range of movement). Hold the Chest Stretch flexibility exercise for 15 seconds, then complete your final set of 12–15 Chest Press repetitions. Reposition the equipment for the next exercise and start its first set. Continue in this format until you have completed all the exercises in this workout.

Warm Up

A pre-resistance band warm-up should be performed for at least 10 minutes and should focus on all areas of the body. As the 20-Minute Workout was designed to suit people with a small amount of training time, the full workout has been condensed to add flexibility exercises into the program, making it more achievable, beneficial, and safe.

Here are some simple, yet effective, aerobic exercises that you can use in your pre-resistance band workout warm-up program in any environment. The warm-up exercises can also be used at the end of your workout as a cool-down phase.

Jogging on the Spot

Gentle jogging is a great way of warming up, as you are using the large muscle groups in your legs and controlling your body weight. You can do this on the spot, or moving forward as if in an open area. To get the most from this exercise as a warm-up, progressively raise knees higher and use large opposite arm and leg movements, lifting hands to head level.

Star Jumps

Star jumps are good for warming up areas that are not used much in jogging, because you are moving your limbs out to the side and back in, rather than forward and backward, as in jogging. Therefore areas such as the middle and the top of the shoulder and the outer and inner thigh are being prepared.

Start by standing straight with feet together and arms by your side. Jump feet out, landing in a wide stance, and simultaneously lift arms out to the side and above your head, keeping them straight. As soon as your feet touch the floor, jump back to the start position. Continue to repeat this movement.

Shadow Punch / Leg Strides

This warm-up exercise is great as it allows you to progressively work the chest, arms, shoulders, and upper back, as well as legs, hips, and midsection through slight rotation. This also helps you to develop cross-body coordination by using an opposite arm and leg movement.

Start with one arm forward with the palm of your hand facing down and in a fist, and the opposite leg forward. The other arm should be bent and close to your body, with the palm of your hand facing up with a clenched fist, and opposite leg back. Keeping the weight on your toes, jump, swapping your leg position in one large stride. Simultaneously punch your other arm forward and bring the extended one back. Once your toes have made contact with the ground, jump back to the start position and continue to repeat.

Chest Press

Sets: 2
Repetitions: 12–15
Direction of resistance: From behind

Hold the handles of the band in each hand with an overhand grip and elbows bent at 90 degrees. Ensure that elbows and wrists are all elevated to shoulder height and are parallel to the floor.

Extend both arms forward until they are straight, and then slowly bend arms back to the start position, stopping when you feel a slight stretch across your chest and shoulders. To make the exercise harder, step further forward, or make it easier by moving closer to the attachment.

Muscle groups worked in this exercise:
Chest (pectorals), front of shoulders (anterior deltoid), and back of upper arms (triceps).

Breathing tip: Breathe out as you extend arms forward.

Latissimus Pull Down

Sets: 2
Repetitions: 12–15
Direction of resistance: From above/in front

Hold the handles of the band in each hand with palms facing forward and arms extended toward the anchor point.

Pull the band down in a straight line by bending arms, keeping a wide-arm position, until your elbows pass the line of your back and reach your sides. You should feel a slight stretch across your chest—if not, ensure that you are squeezing your shoulder blades together at the bottom of the movement. Then extend your arms following the same line, until they are back to the start position. At this point they should be fully extended before beginning your next repetition.

Muscle groups worked in this exercise:
Back (latissimus dorsi), back of shoulders (posterior deltoid), and front of upper arms (biceps).

Breathing tip: Breathe out as you pull down.

Shoulder Press

Sets: 2
Repetitions: 12–15
Direction of resistance: From underneath

Sit up straight with shoulders back and abdominal muscles tight. Using an overhand grip hold the handles at the side of each shoulder, and at shoulder height.

Extend both arms above your head until they are straight and then slowly bend arms, taking them back to the start position, with your hands returning level with shoulders. Make sure that your forearms remain vertical throughout the movement.

Muscle groups worked in this exercise: Front of shoulders (anterior deltoid), top of shoulders (upper trapezius), and back of upper arms (triceps).

Breathing tip: Breathe out as you extend arms up.

Stretch between sets: Triceps

Stand straight. Raise one arm up above your head, bend it at the elbow and place your hand behind you, touching between your shoulder blades. Lift the other arm above your head and cup your hand just above the elbow of the first arm. Ease the first arm back until you feel the stretch in the back of the upper arm. Hold this stretch for 15 seconds and then repeat with your other arm.

Squat

Sets: 2
Repetitions: 12–15
Direction of resistance: From underneath

Place band under both feet and position them shoulder-width apart. Take hold of the handles with an overhand grip at shoulder level with the palm of your hands facing forward.

Slowly bend your knees, keeping your heels down, as if you were about to sit down, stopping just before you reach a 90-degree angle. Pause, then extend your legs, pushing through your heels until you are back to the starting position. You can keep feet wider apart to make the exercise harder or closer to make it easier.

Muscle groups worked in this exercise: Front of thigh (quadriceps), buttocks (gluteus maximus).

Breathing tip: Breathe out as you extend legs.

Stretch between sets: Quadriceps
Stand on your right leg. Bend the knee of your left leg and take hold of your ankle with your left arm, lifting it up behind you, so that your heel is near to your buttocks. Make sure that your body is completely straight with hips forward, legs close together, and knees in line. Hold the stretch for 15 seconds and repeat with your right leg.

Standing Hamstring Curl

Sets: 2
Repetitions: 12–15
Direction of resistance: From front

Attach one end of the band to an ankle strap and then place around the ankle of the leg that you are starting with. You can place a stable object next to you to hold onto for support.

Flex one leg at the knee until the lower leg is at 90 degrees to the upper. Pause, and then extend the leg at the knee until your leg is straight. Ensure that your hips remain still and keep both knees together throughout the exercise. Repeat using your other leg. To make the exercise harder, step further away from the anchor point, or make it easier by moving closer.

Muscle groups worked in this exercise:
Back of upper leg (hamstrings).

Breathing tip: Breathe out as you bend the knee.

**Stretch between sets:
Lying Hamstrings**
Bend one leg at the knee with your foot on the floor. Place the band over the foot of the other leg and extend it so that it is straight. Keeping your lower back and buttocks flat on the floor, flex the hip of the straight leg, bringing your thigh back as far as possible without bending at the knee. Use the band to aid and progressively increase the stretch. Hold the stretch for 15 seconds and then repeat with the other leg.

Abdominal Curl

Sets: 2
Repetitions: 12–15
Direction of resistance: No band required

Lie flat on your back, with your knees bent and feet on the floor. Breathe out and flatten your stomach, as if pulling your belly button toward your lower back, then squeeze the muscles so that they are tight. Hold this position throughout the exercise.

Reach hands up your thighs and touch the top of your knees, curling your shoulders toward your pelvis. Pause, and then slowly uncurl, sliding your hands back down your thighs until you are back to the start position.

Muscle group worked in this exercise:
Abdomen (rectus abdominis).

Breathing tip: Breathe out as you reach to knees.

Stretch between sets: Lie Flat
Rest between sets of Abdominal Curls by lying completely flat on your back, with legs stretched out straight and arms extended and touching the floor above your head. Hold this position for 20 seconds.

Dorsal Raises

Sets: 2
Repetitions: 12–15
Direction of resistance: No band required

Lie flat on your front with head straight. Legs should be straight and arms extended above your head.

Lift your left arm and right leg, extending it at the hip and keeping both arm and leg straight. Pause, and then slowly lower your arm and leg back down to the floor until you reach the start position. Then repeat with your right arm and left leg.

Muscle group worked in this exercise:
Length of back (erector spinae).

Breathing tip: Breathe out as you lift your opposite arm and leg.

Stretch between sets: Lower Back

Lie on your back; bend your knees, bringing them up toward your chest. Place your arms behind your knees and gently pull them in close to your body. You can increase the area of the stretch by rolling your shoulders forward and tucking your head in. Hold the stretch for at least 15 seconds.

Core Training

Most people have an appreciation for the role that general fitness plays in health and longevity, but find the solution to developing a totally fit and functional body somewhat elusive. Everyone knows that nutrition and activity is an important part of keeping fit and well, but how do you enable your body to function and perform at its optimum level?

The answer to achieving fitness and wellbeing is in developing the core part of your body, and this section will show you how to do that. What was once the hallmark of the elite athlete or prima ballerina is now the benchmark of fitness for every individual. Core strength and stability has meaning for all of us.

The core, in general, is defined as the central or basic part of a whole system—a foundation upon which you build. When speaking about your body, your core is the complex system of muscles, tendons and ligaments that comprise your body's foundation, roughly the area traditionally known as your trunk or torso.

What does this foundation do? It links the powerful movements of your upper and lower extremities, as well as maintaining internal organ function and acting as a life support system. Our core muscles stabilize us as we move or prepare to move our arms and legs. All movement originates at your core, hence it is your primary source of stability. Whether you're running, twisting, lifting weights, or picking up a suitcase, your core keeps your body stable and balanced.

What is core training?

Core training simply means exercising the muscles, tendons, and ligaments that connect your spine and pelvis area around the center of your body. It encompasses several aspects, most important of which are strengthening

and stretching. Some muscles become weak from underuse and poor posture, while others become overworked and tight.

This imbalance in the body happens gradually as we succumb to everyday postural habits and challenges. It's not easy to maintain a healthy posture when computer screens and reading material cause us to bend our necks down, and sitting in one position for a long time leads to a slouching spine.

How do I benefit from core training?

You may imagine that the need for core training is most relevant for athletics, where precise coordination is needed for throwing, kicking, or running. But what about everyday life? The absence of core strength can lead to the common problem of backache, or injuries resulting from lifting simple items. This guide aims to help you gain the necessary core strength to avoid these injuries and aches and pains.

For all individuals, core training offers a higher level of general fitness. We will feel better and will notice that all of our daily activities seem easier. We won't tend to pull a muscle quite so quickly, perhaps a load won't seem so heavy, or we will generally function better throughout the week. An increase in muscle density will provide increased calorie burning capacity, which should also trim excess fat.

For athletes, core training gives more power to a swing or more distance in a throw, and they are not as prone to injury. Children will have healthier bodies, be able to move more dynamically, and will learn other athletic activities more quickly.

Those who are rehabilitating from a back injury will also benefit from core training, which will help to rebuild strength and protect against future recurrences. Pregnant women can tone their bodies not only for the physical ordeal of constantly lifting and moving extra weight during pregnancy, but also the challenge of giving birth and the many physical tasks they face afterward.

Seniors can build life and vitality into their best years. They can enhance stability and balance, which guards against potentially harmful falls. They can also guard against incontinence.

By following your own instincts and expending consistent effort, you will feel better, look better, function better, and protect yourself against everyday injuries, aches, and sprains.

Let's find our core

The area between your upper chest and the bottom of your torso defines your power center, the source of coordination and stability for your arm and leg movements. The most dynamic part of your core is the area from the bottom of your ribcage down to your lower pelvic region.

Your lumbar vertebrae provide the bone structure for this area, allowing for a highly flexible yet highly powerful transmission of power between your upper and lower body. The muscles, tendons, and ligaments of this core region provide stability and balance for your body in motion or at rest.

Let's take a tour of the muscle groups involved and get acquainted with what makes up the core. Your abdominals are composed of three muscle groups:

- **Rectus abdominus:** The set of long, vertical muscle tissue along the front of the abdomen that people associate with the "sixpack" or washboard stomach, which originates at the pubic bone.
- **Internal and external obliques:** Muscles that are located at the waist (side), and cross in the abdominal section to provide

stability. Externals lie on the side and front of the abdomen, around your waist, while internals lie underneath, running in the opposite direction.

- **Transverse abdominals:** These run horizontally and are the deepest of the muscles for stability, wrapping around your trunk and spine for protection and stability.

Your abdominal muscles or abs work together for each exercise, but you can target each of the individual groups separately. Your very own "six pack" of rectus abdominus may even make an appearance once you reduce body fat, but that is just scratching the surface.

Your real foundation lies deep inside and

includes the iliopsoas, intra-spinal, and pubococcygeal muscles that act as stabilizers and as a mechanism for transferring power:

- **Iliopsoas:** The key to core power in a balanced and smoothly functioning body is the iliopsoas. This is a muscle group comprising the iliascus and psoas muscles.
- The **iliascus** muscle "fans" the pelvic anterior surface and connects with the psoas through a common tendon at the lesser trocanter. This means that it connects with your leg.
- The **psoas** muscle is a large hip flexor that plays a key role in creating the tensile strength that stabilizes the spine. There are two psoas muscles, one attaching on each side of the lumbar spine, starting at vertebrae T12 and directly linking the ribcage and trunk with the legs by running through the pelvis. The psoas helps transfer weight from the trunk to the legs and is counterbalanced by the obturators, a small group of muscles that attach within the pelvis. The psoas also enjoys a reciprocal relationship with the erector spinae and rector abdominis, working with your gluteal muscles for locomotion.

Your spine is superficially defined by your erector spinae, a set of three distinct muscles, and at a deeper level by the intra-vertebral muscles:

- **Erector spinae:** These provide longitudinal spine stability.

There are a group of superficial muscles of the arms, shoulders and upper back that surround the scapula (shoulder blades):

- **Levator scapulae:** Hold the scapula against the trunk.

- **Serratus:** Holds the scapula against the thoracic wall (chest area/upper part of the body).
- **Trapezius:** Muscles that draw back the shoulders and pull the head backward or to one side.
- **Rhomboids:** Hold the scapula against the thoracic wall.
- **Latissimus dorsi:** A broad, flat muscle on each side of the mid back area that allows shoulder adduction and extension.

The most often overlooked yet crucial link in the chain of core support is your perineum. This sheet of muscular fibers, known as the pelvic floor, is made of both interconnected voluntary and involuntary muscles. The most important muscular group within the perineum is Levator Ani, because it essentially sustains your various organs (the bladder, the vagina, the intestines, the uterus).

Alignment and posture

The most important principle of a core training regimen is the alignment of all the parts of your body. Alignment is the key word at a time when many of us perform sedentary tasks that allow us to slump or slouch while reaching our heads closer for information on computer screens and the pages of books. Core development requires that you strive to adhere to a strong functional alignment that counters the slouching habits of your normal daily life.

Part of the benefit of this guide is the repeated postural cues given as part of the exercises. Use that repetition to reinforce the movements, for functional alignment is a conscious act. Many refer to good posture as a "neutral" position; but just remember that alignment is an ongoing behavior that requires attention and deliberation.

Here are some guidelines for achieving alignment:

- Roll your hips under (this elongates the lower spine and allows the psoas to relax), as if you have a weight hanging from your tailbone pulling you down.
- Stretch up from the top of your head (this elongates the upper spine). Your chin is slightly tucked back.
- Press down in your underarms to further stretch the ribcage and spine. You will notice that this helps to "seat" the shoulders rather than allow them to be contracted upward by your levator scapulae and trapezius muscles.
- Gently pull your navel back away from your pants or shirt and toward your spine.

necessary, especially for exercises involving the Swiss Ball. Functionally, you don't want loose or sliding clothing to disrupt or get in the way of your exercise.

We already know that alignment is a key aspect to the proper performance of each exercise. Therefore, each of us should try to check our body position and posture in a mirror during the exercise. If you don't have a mirror, maybe you can arrange to have a personal trainer or friend keep an eye on you.

Consult your physician

Consult your physician first to be sure you are medically prepared to try these exercises. Please check all the guidance you receive here against your own good common sense and prepare yourself with a medical checkup before initiating a program.

The content of this book is provided for informational purposes only, and is not intended to be a substitute for professional medical advice, diagnosis, or treatment. Never disregard medical advice or delay in seeking it because of something you have read in this book.

Seek professional advice

Everyone's body is slightly different, and it helps to have a professional's opinion about the exact way in which you train your body and perform the exercises. Ask the opinion of someone you trust who understands physical training.

Keep a personal workout journal

Always record your workouts. Put a date and time on them. Record what you observe to know which workouts left you feeling great, and which ones left you feeling terrible.

As you embark upon your training regimen, create a workout journal or log that helps you

Breathing

In general, breathe out when you contract muscles and breathe in as you release, then relax and return to your original position. You actively work your abdominal muscles on your inhalation and exhalation, along with expanding and contracting your ribcage. Your ribcage is lifted through the effort of your underarm press, and you keep it centered over your pelvis by rolling your pelvis under and pressing back in your lower spine.

What to wear

When exercising your core area, you might benefit from wearing relatively tight-fitting clothing. This offers several advantages, both in function and form. For men and women, some degree of functional support and retention are

- **Incline bench:** Check the stability of the base and the padding on the anchor.
- **Weight machine:** This should include the standard stacked weights and a cable system—specifically the apparatus necessary for lat pulldowns, rows, etc.
- **Roman chair:** For anchoring lower body and suspending the upper—you may substitute a padded table and partner to provide anchor.
- **Suspensory rack:** A freestanding rack with forearm pads for leg lifts—you may substitute parallel bars of any device that suspends the upper body and leaves the legs hanging free.
- **Medicine balls:** Normally supplied in a range of weights from 1–10lbs.
- **Staff:** A stretching pole—this should be as long as your arm-span.
- **Swiss Ball:** The correct size allows you to sit with knees bent at a 90 degree angle.
- **Bosu (1/2 Swiss Ball):** A half ball mounted on plastic bottom or Reebok Core Board.
- **Step platform:** Needs to have an adjustable height, ensure that it will not slide out from underneath you.
- **Handled resistance band:** Typically color-coded degrees of resistance.
- **Nautilus:** Use this or any specialty machine or home device for crunches, flys, etc.
- **Exercise mat:** Keep it clean—you'll be spending some time on it.

track performance. This log can be as simple as a pencil and notebook diary or as comprehensive as a computer-based program that allows you to record sets, repetitions, aches and pains, and frequency of workouts. These can certainly come in handy when you wish to see which exercises have been effective for you and which have possibly caused discomfort, and the benefit is that you may track trends over time.

Equipment

- **Handweights/small dumbbells:** These should be easy to grip.
- **Ankle weights:** You can wear these weights around your ankles by using the Velcro closure.

Core training programs

Time management

Continue your cardiovascular routine, while you are exploring a new core training program. If you do not already have some method of increasing your heart rate at variable pace over time, find one. Core training should not detract from other vital fitness activities. Time is usually a constraint, so perhaps you could take a break from normal gym activities in order to exercise your core.

Designing a training program

The best training program for you is one you design for yourself with guidance. You must answer the basic questions of which exercises to perform and how frequently they should be performed.

Your program will emphasize stretching and range of motion initially; a "Core of Core" approach. Get the basics down and don't shock your body until it has a foundation of flexibility established. Then you can move on to a more comprehensive approach that entails trying all the exercises in the guide step by step.

Daily practice

It is good to test yourself a little bit each day. However, the greatest threat to fitness and flexibility is injury. It is better to make gradual progress over a longer time period; everyone needs to exercise and move their body daily in some way.

Sets and repetitions

Many people wonder how many repetitions or sets they should do. Repeat the exercises with relative comfort in mind. Do not overstretch yourself. Aim for three sets of 8–12 repetitions. Start with only one if that is all you feel confident about doing. Do one repetition of a new exercise and get the feel of it. Then try two and aim to eventually try three. Coach yourself with just the right amount of patience and you will progress without suffering any injury.

Specialist groups

The following is a list of specialty groups that warrant special consideration in this guide:

- Pregnant women
- Seniors
- Those with back injuries and pain
- Younger athletes
- Elite athletes
- Healthy individuals

Remember that every individual is different; some progress rapidly and some progress slowly. Some injure themselves easier; some are more resilient. Common sense is your best guide for which exercises you undertake.

For seniors and pregnant women, the Bosu Ball or balance board may not represent an acceptable risk, so these two may choose to develop balance skills while sitting on the Swiss Ball. Young and elite athletes start with good balance skills which may be readily enhanced by the Bosu or balance board. It is a matter of adapting functional need to acceptable risk levels. Some will be able to handle any and all of the exercises regardless of condition, others will not. Try challenging ones gently and slowly at first. All back injuries are different, all pregnancies are different. You can test yourself and ask a personal trainer to join you as you make your own personal program.

Core influences

Training your core muscles will help correct postural imbalances, prevent injuries and develop efficient, functional movement patterns. Additionally, it will also activate your sensory awareness. This mind/body aspect of core training becomes clearer when looking at how martial arts have influenced it.

In general, the martial arts call upon the individual to harness the strength of the entire body. Noted for its graceful beauty and subtle power, T'ai Chi Chuan is a martial art with Daoist influences, stressing postural alignment. Its practice requires attention that is both inwardly focused and rooted in the environment.

Likewise, core influences can be found in the study of movement disciplines such as Pilates and yoga. Some types of yoga emphasize a long spine and are adequate for everyone. Pilates also increases core strength, endurance and lung capacity. These movement and alignment disciplines emphasize the functional necessity of core strength.

All athletic endeavors require core awareness. For instance, swimming calls for fundamental emphasis on core strength. Swimmers traditionally have strong, flexible core muscles because they must generate power from both arms and legs without the restriction of the ground. Stamina and power for long distance endeavors, such as extreme butterfly swimming in harsh open water, comes directly from the core.

Warm Up / Cool Down

Always warm up first. Your body's connective tissue feels more elastic when your core temperature is elevated slightly. Follow the warm-up on page 182, and add these stretches, too.

Warm Up Twists

Area of concentration: Erector spinalis, abdominals

Start position: Stand with your feet slightly wider than shoulder width apart, eyes focused forward, arms relaxed at your side.

Tuck your chin under and lift your head toward the ceiling from its crown (the very top of the head). Imagine you are being stretched upward by a rope attached to the crown of your skull. Allow your knees to flex and roll your hips under as you imagine the southern tip of your spine being pulled down by an attached weight. Open your hips so that your knees are vertically in line with your feet. Press forward at the fold of the hip joint, which is located at the front of the pelvis where your leg meets your trunk.

Pressing down in the armpits also seats the shoulders in a natural position so that levator muscles are not tugging them upward toward your head and tightening vertebrae along the way.

Exercise: Begin the twists by slowly rotating your waist around your spine, which should feel like a straight column, back and forth. Imagine your whole body rotating around a central vertical axis. Your arms should dangle loosely by your sides. Concentrate on the feeling of balance in your feet. Allow your arms to follow your waist as it twists slightly faster, however, never lead the movement with your arms. The arms should follow the core. Repeat for a slow count of 30, approximately 1 minute or until you feel loose.

End position: Slow your rotation and return to a standing posture. Your feet should be slightly wider than shoulder width apart, hips tucked under, knees flexed, and chin pressing back. Your spine should be long, your head up, and your tailbone down. Your arms should be relaxed at your side. Breathe through your nose in a relaxed manner.

Be aware: The twisting movement comes from turning the waist back and forth around the axis of the spine. Do not force the twist with surface muscles. Feel it originate from your core area.

Double Arm Stretch

Area of concentration: Erector spinae

After you have twisted and moved your way to a loose and warm core body temperature, you can start to activate the muscles, ligaments, and tendons that you will be toning and strengthening. Begin with a double arm stretch up, which opens the chest and upper spinal area as well as the arms and allows your spine to elongate.

Start position: Start with your feet together, eyes focused forward, hands clasped in front of your face, and imagine your spine as a straight cylindrical column. You could vary this by unclasping your hands.

Exercise: Reach for the ceiling, remembering to keep your shoulders "seated" by pressing down in the armpits. Reach and release 8–12 times, breathing out on the way up and in as you bring your arms down.

End position: Return your arms to your side, hips tucked under, knees flexed, and chin pressing back. Your spine should be long, your head up, and your tailbone down. Your arms should be relaxed at your side. Breathe in a relaxed manner through your nose, feeling a distinct contraction and release of your abdomen muscles coupled with the expansion and contraction of your rib cage.

Be aware: Remember to press down at the heels and feel your weight on the ground while you simultaneously reach upward. This provides a good stretch for the spine.

Straight Leg Stretch Down

Area of Concentration: Glutes, psoas, erector spinae

In this exercise, while stretching your back, you will also have the opportunity to identify your hip joint and stretch the leg tendons and muscles that support you. The straight leg stretch mimics a seated position stretch of the same nature, yet it offers the added benefit of being a weight bearing position. This warmup includes the suggestion that you lock your knees in order to create straight legs. This helps to better stretch the hamstrings and related tissues. If you find locking your knees uncomfortable, try to make your legs as straight as possible and work slowly into the position as you gain flexibility.

Start position: Your feet are slightly narrower than shoulder width, eyes focused forward, arms raised.

Exercise: Bending at your hip fold, where your legs join your core, keep your spine straight, and bend as far toward a 90-degree angle as is comfortable. Reach straight down with your fingers touching back to back in repeated reach and releases. You could also bend down with your fingers outstretched, as shown here. Try 8–12 repetitions.

End position: Your feet should be slightly narrower than shoulder width, eyes focused forward, arms at the side.

Be aware: You must keep stretching your spine straight and do not allow your neck to sag as you reach and stretch your arms and back. Bending comes from the hip joint only, just as if you were seated flat on the ground.

Side Reach Oblique Stretch

Area of concentration: Obliques, psoas, lower spine, glutes

Now you are ready to start more dynamic leg movements in association with core stretching. This weight shifting from leg to leg serves to enhance your balance and further elevates your body temperature. You will learn to feel grounded and adjust your posture and alignment in order to maintain balance. You will also learn to stretch dynamically rather than statically, a more realistic test for your body and mind.

Start position: Stand with your feet slightly wider than shoulder width apart and your eyes focused forward. Keep your knees bent, hips rolled under to elongate the spine as you flex at the hip fold, bend the right knee and place weight over the right leg.

Exercise: Pressing the right heel into the ground extend your left arm over your head. The left leg extends straight while the right leg bends. Feel the stretch along the left side of your body.

Retract the right arm and stand straight. Stretch the left arm up and stretch the other side of your body. Do 8–12 repetitions on each side.

End position: Your feet are slightly wider than shoulder width, eyes focused forward, arms at the side.

Be aware: Breathe out with every contraction, moving from the initial position to the stretch extension. Then relax the abdomen and inhale with every return to the initial position.

Double Lumbar Roll

Area of concentration: Abdomen, obliques, lower lumbar spine

This is a fun stretching exercise that can work as a warm-up or as an exercise. The use of a mat makes it a bit more comfortable. Those with back pain may want to try a single leg version first.

Start position: Lie on the exercise mat, keeping your spine long. Retract both legs to a 90-degree knee bend (or right angle, like a corner). Keep your feet flat, and your hands extended to your side for stabilization.

End position: Both legs rest on the mat.

Be aware: This movement is less effective if you swing your legs rather than move them slowly. Make sure you feel only a stretch and no sharp pain. Breathe easily and without holding through the repetitions.

Exercise: Roll both knees over to the right very slowly, allowing the rest of your back to lift off the mat only to accommodate the pull of the legs. You should feel a stretch in your lower spine as the erector spinae release and elongate. As you keep your shoulder blades on the mat, roll both legs to the left side slowly and feel the stretch. Try this 8–12 times.

Cross Body Oblique / Glutes Stretch

Area of Concentration: Psoas, glutes, lower spine

Seated stretching exercises allow you the opportunity to effectively isolate the hamstring/gluteal and erector spinae muscles without weighted pressure. Many basic hamstring stretches can be performed in a seated or standing position.

There are many variations of the basic seated "hurdler" stretch which may be substituted according to personal preference and background. This particular cross body stretch provides ancillary iliopsoas muscle benefits as well.

Start position: Sit on the exercise mat. Keep your spine long, and retract your right leg to a 90-degree knee bend. Keep your left leg out straight with your toes pointed up.

Exercise: Place your right foot flat on the mat to the left side of your left knee. Place your left arm to the right side of your right knee. Gently twist toward the right, pressing gently against your leg with your arm. Breathe out as you twist and hold.

Swap over your legs and repeat for the other side.

End position: Seated, both legs flat on mat.

Be aware: The stretch must be gradual and relaxed; do not force this stretch by levering your arm against your leg.

Frontal Lean and Retraction

Area of concentration: Abdominals, erector spinae

The frontal lean and retraction exercise allows you to dynamically explore your range of motion and slowly stretch yourself. You will see variations of this movement in dance classes, yoga studios, and pilates regimens. As long as you are careful with your knees, this should not present a problem for most individuals. Pregnant women may wish to be careful when stretching back and sitting on their legs. Go only as far as is comfortable.

Start position: From the prone position, face down on the floor or mat, keeping your spine long and extended. Press yourself up on to your hands and knees to form a "tabletop" position, still facing downward. Your arms and legs resemble the four legs of a table, while your back forms the tabletop.

Exercise: Slowly shift your weight forward over your arms. Allow your muscles to extend for this movement.

Next, slowly shift your weight all the way back to your legs, bending your knees to receive your body until you are as far back as comfortable. Your buttocks will move toward your heels as you stretch back.

Those with tender knees may want to be careful in choosing their range of motion for this movement. Go only as far as comfortable, feel the stretch, then return to center. Repeat 8–12 times.

End position: Resume the "tabletop" kneeling position. Your weight should be equally distributed between your hands and knees.

Breathe comfortably in this position and do not hold your breath.

Be aware: Remember to keep your spine long. Those of us with tender knees may wish to skip the mat version of this exercise and perhaps substitute a Swiss Ball stretch. The aim for a person in this situation is to avoid placing a "sheer load" on the knee joint, which stresses the anterior cruciate ligament. Continue breathing in a relaxed fashion throughout the exercise, assuring that you do not hold your breath.

Core Exercises

Kegels

Area of concentration: Pubococcygeal

The pubococcygeal muscle, also popularly referred to as the PC muscle or the Kegel muscle, sustains the pelvic floor. The PC muscles stretch from the pubic bone in the front to the coccyx (tail) bone in the back.

The PC muscles support the pelvic organs like a hammock. Their identification and training are essential to good health and development of core strength. The maintenance of these muscles is vital to sexual health as well as control of excretory functions. In fact, this is the muscle that contracts in the moment of male ejaculation or female orgasm.

But why are they called Kegels? In 1948, gynecologist Dr. Arnold Kegel identified the pelvic floor. He realized that the simple exercise of contracting and relaxing the PC muscle resulted in muscle toning. Done properly, Kegel exercises strengthen weak PC muscles and strengthen the foundation in our quest for a stronger core.

Start position: The first step in performing a kegel is to identify what it is you are actually working on. The simplest and most direct way is to do a simple test: interrupt the flow of urine. The muscles used to do this in women or men are the PC muscles. Be careful not to tense the stomach, buttocks, or thigh muscles as they can take over from the PCs. Lie down on your back in a comfortable position with your entire spine elongated and as much of it touching the ground as possible. Make sure all your muscles feel relaxed and you are looking straight up at the ceiling. Place your feet shoulder-width apart and bend your knees to a 90-degree angle, with your hands down by your side.

Exercise: Contract your PC muscle and hold that contraction for three seconds. Remember to continue to breathe normally and maintain relaxation in all the surrounding muscles. This may not be so easy in the beginning. Relax the PC muscle.

End position: At the end of the repetition of contraction and relaxation, stay calm and relaxed on your back, noticing that you haven't used your buttocks muscles or your abdomen muscles. Try up to eight repetitions.

Be aware: For most people it takes more that two weeks to notice results, but be sure to maintain the integrity of the exercise by not over-forcing and causing the larger surrounding muscle groups to interfere. You want to work the PC only with this exercise. We'll get to the other ones next.

Double Legged Roll Back

Area of concentration: Lower spine

The Roll Back is a fun exercise that can work as a warm-up or exercise. Use of a mat makes contact on the spine easier. Be sure that you don't use momentum to complete this exercise.

Start position: Lie on the exercise mat, keeping your spine long. Retract your legs to a 90-degree knee bend (or right angle, like a corner). Keep your feet flat and your hands relaxed over the upper chest or shoulder joints.

Exercise: Keeping your shoulder blades on the mat, tuck your knees toward your chest, and roll your hips up and toward the ceiling. You will feel yourself roll back. Hold the upright position of your legs for a second, then slowly lower them back to the mat.

End position: Both legs rest on the mat.

Be aware: This movement is less effective if you swing your legs rather than move them slowly. You may also tuck tightly during your roll.

Abdominal Crunch

Area of concentration: Abdominals

Doing a crunch correctly requires a measure of patience. Experience suggests that it is extremely challenging to isolate the abdomen muscles if you are tempted to grab the head and strain your body to lift. For this reason, crossing your arms across your chest removes the temptation for the crunch to turn into a neck-pulling exercise.

Start position: Lie on the floor or a mat, facing the ceiling, with your spine comfortably relaxed and touching the surface along its entire length. With your feet flat on the ground and shoulder width apart, flex your knees to a right-angle position. Roll your hips under to elongate your lower spine. Relax your arms and hands on your chest, with palms facing downward. Breathe comfortably.

Exercise: Contract your abdomen muscles until you lift your shoulder blades off the ground. Keep your lower back flat and do not lift it off the mat. Concentrate to thrust your chest toward the ceiling while your chin stays tucked in. Hold at the top of the movement for two seconds and squeeze your muscles. Lower yourself slowly back to the mat. Repeat this eight times.

End position: Lie flat keeping your spine long and abdominal muscles relaxed.

Be aware: In the enthusiasm and strain of the exercise, it is often tempting to lift the chin toward the ceiling as part of the overall exertion. Resist this urge and only lift your shoulder blades as high as you can by using your abdominal muscles. Breathe as regularly as possible throughout the exercise. Each contraction of the abdomen muscles should correspond with an exhalation, while each relaxation should correspond with an inhalation.

Oblique Crunch or Side Crunch

Area of concentration: Obliques

The side crunch is a very stable way to work your obliques, while protecting your spinal position. As always, care is necessary to assure that you don't pull up with your neck, as curiosity induces you to sneak a peek at your feet. Looking isn't necessary. Feeling the obliques do some toning work is necessary.

Start position: Lie on the floor or a mat, facing the ceiling. Your spine should be comfortably relaxed and touching the surface of the floor along its entire length. With your feet flat on the ground and shoulder width apart, flex your knees to a 90-degree angle position (or right angle, like a corner). Roll your hips under, creating a tucking feeling as you elongate your lower spine. Keep your arms and hands comfortably relaxed, palms down beside you. Breathe in and out comfortably and don't hold your breath.

Exercise: Contract your right side muscles to draw your upper body down toward your feet as you remain lying on your back. Feel the sensation of reaching with your right hand toward your right foot in the muscles at the side of your body. Allow the exercise to be driven not by your arm muscles, but from your side. Maintain a long spine throughout the

motion. Now release and return to the start position, then repeat the process to your left side. Hold at the end of each crunch for a second, squeeze your oblique muscles, then actively release that squeeze and allow them to freely elongate as you crunch over to the other side.

End position: Lie flat with an elongated spine with your abdominal muscles relaxed.

Be aware: In the enthusiasm and strain of the exercise, it is often tempting to lift the chin toward the ceiling as part of the overall exertion. Resist this urge and keep your chin tucked in. Breathe as regularly as possible throughout the exercise.

Bridge

Area of concentration: Transverse abdominis, lower spine

This exercise strengthens the supporting muscles and tendons of the pelvic region.

Start position: Lie on the floor or a mat, facing the ceiling, with your spine comfortably relaxed and touching the surface along its entire length. With your feet flat on the ground and shoulder width apart, flex your knees to a right-angle position. Roll your hips under to elongate your lower spine. Relax your arms and hands at your side, releasing any tension in your abdominals, and breathe comfortably.

Exercise: Keep your gaze fixed on the ceiling, gently contract your gluteals, and feel your heels press into the ground as your hip joint moves toward the ceiling. Imagine your pelvic crease—the two lines where your abdomen joins your legs—reaching for the ceiling, as you allow your hip joints to relax and open. Once you have reached a comfortable end to your range of motion, begin to slowly lower yourself back to the floor, gradually releasing your muscles.

End position: Lie flat on the ground or mat, eyes to ceiling and arms at your side.

Be aware: Keep your scapulae (essentially your shoulders) and spine flat during the exercise. Resist the urge to look at your feet during the movement. Continue to breathe naturally, without holding your breath during any portion of the exercise.

Bridge with Extension

Area of Concentration: Transverse abdominis, psoas

Building upon the base provided by the bridge, you can add more stability and balance skills to your exercise.

Start position: Lie on the floor or a mat, facing the ceiling, with your spine comfortably relaxed and touching the floor along its entire length. With your feet flat on the ground and shoulder width apart, flex your knees to a right angle position. Roll your hips under to elongate your lower spine. Relax your arms and hands at your side as you release any tension in your abdominals and breathe comfortably.

Exercise: Keeping your gaze fixed on the ceiling, gently contract your gluteals, feeling your heels press into the ground as your hip joint moves towards the ceiling. Allow your hip joints to relax and open.

Once you have reached a comfortable end to your range of motion, begin to slowly transfer weight to your left foot on the ground, and extend your right leg straight. Lower the right leg to the ground, then shift your weight to the right foot and extend the left. Upon completing the desired repetitions of this exercise, lower yourself back to the surface, feeling your muscles relax. Try eight repetitions.

End position: Resume the flat on the ground or mat position, eyes to ceiling and arms at side, ready for another repetition if desired.

Be aware: Keep your scapulae (essentially your shoulders) and spine flat during the exercise. Resist the urge to look at your feet during the movement. Do the exercise deliberately and slowly, developing stability and control.

Elevated Leg Rotation

Area of concentration: Rectus abdominus, psoas

Many exercises that strengthen core stability also heighten your awareness of the deeper muscles that govern your spinal alignment and posture. This exercise recruits both the rectus abdominus surface muscles and the deep psoas muscles. The iliopsoas musculature largely governs our stability, from simple walking around to high stress weight and direction change in elite athletics, or extra weight bearing during pregnancy. In this case we are learning to release and relax the psoas.

Start Position: Lie on the floor or a mat facing the ceiling, with your spine comfortably relaxed and touching the surface along its entire length. With your legs flat on the ground and toes up, roll your hips under to elongate your lower spine. Relax your arms and hands with your palms down beside you.

Exercise: Pulling in your front abdominal muscles (rectus abdominus), while your back stays flat, lift your left leg toward the ceiling and attempt to keep it as straight as possible while pointing your toe toward the ceiling. Rotate your left leg once in a clockwise direction, making a circle as big as your foot. Rotate once in the opposite direction.

Slowly lower your left leg to the ground, returning to your ready position. Repeat this process with the right leg, working up to eight repetitions for each leg.

End position: Lie flat and elongate your spine. Relax your abdominal muscles.

Be aware: It is better to only lift your leg as far as you can go without bending it, just gradually pointing the toe higher and higher as you gain awareness of your psoas muscle and learn to release it.

Cross-Legged Oblique Crunch

Area of Concentration: Obliques

The Cross-Legged Oblique Crunch offers you the opportunity to add some subtle refinement to your core. By crossing your legs, you lengthen the pelvic region.

You will see many different hand positions associated with the Crunch, which are all fine and can add or subtract from the degree of difficulty. However, experience suggests that it is extremely challenging to isolate the obliques if you are tempted to grab the head and strain your body to lift. For this reason, you should cross your arms over your chest to remove the temptation to turn the Oblique Crunch into a neck-pulling exercise.

Start position: Lie on the floor or a mat, facing the ceiling, with your spine comfortably relaxed and touching the floor along its entire length. With your feet flat on the ground and shoulder-width apart, flex your knees to a right angle position. Roll your hips under to elongate your lower spine. Cross your left leg over your right one. Relax your arms and hands over your chest, with your palms facing downward, right below your neck. Breathe in and out comfortably.

Exercise: Contract your abdomen muscles until you lift your shoulder blades off the ground. Your lower back should stay flat and not lift off the mat. Twist, using your oblique muscle until your right shoulder is aimed toward your left kneecap. There is no need to actually try to touch the kneecap.

Hold at the top of the movement for a second and squeeze your muscles. Lower yourself slowly back to the mat. Repeat this motion eight times, then reverse your leg cross and do the exercise for the left side.

End position: Lie flat with an elongated spine and with your abdominal muscles relaxed.

Leg Lift with Compression

Area of Concentration: Adductor, iliopsoas, and pubococcygeal

This exercise requires extra concentration. It is a flexion exercise concentrating on the adductor and pubococcygeal area. The special nature of this exercise lies not so much in what is being done externally, but instead focuses on what you are doing internally.

The key to the effectiveness of this exercise is its Kegel-based focus. While you are squeezing the ball and lifting your knees toward your chest, keep your focus on the contraction of your pelvic floor muscle group.

Start position: Lie on the floor or a mat, facing the ceiling. With your feet flat on the ground and shoulder-width apart, flex your knees to a right-angle position. Roll your hips under to elongate your lower spine. Relax your arms and hands by your sides.

Place a small-sized Swiss or other squeezable ball between your knees and apply pressure.

Exercise: Bend from your hip joints as you lift your knees towards your chest. You should experience a flexing sensation at the point where your leg joins your core body. Be sure to keep your hips rolled under and do not allow your lower spine to arch. Hold that position, then slowly release the legs back to the straight-down position.

While completing the repetition, remember also to contract your Kegel muscles, while squeezing together with your knees. Do eight repetitions, then repeat the exercise with the squeezable ball between your ankles.

End position: Lie flat with an elongated spine and relax your abdominal muscles.

Be aware: Remember that your spine, should stay as flat as possible against the mat. Do only as many as you can while maintaining this proper form, and discontinue if you feel strain on your lower back. Each contraction of the abdomen muscles should correspond with a leg lift.

Leg Lift with Expansion Against Cord

Area of Concentration: Abductor, iliopsoas, and pubococcygeal

This flexion exercise concentrates on the abductor and pubococcygeal areas, while addressing the psoas. It provides balance and harmony to a comprehensive group of muscles such as the iliopsoas, the glutes, and those around the abdomen region.

The Leg Lift with Expansion Against Cord is a ground-based interpretation of the suspensory rack exercise done with stretch cord around the knees and ankles. You will be doing the same maneuver here, except that you will be on your back.

Start position: Lie on the floor or a mat, facing the ceiling, with your spine comfortably relaxed and touching the floor along its entire length. With your feet flat on the ground and shoulder width apart, flex your knees to a right-angle position (90 degrees, like a corner). Roll your hips under to elongate your lower spine. Relax your arms and hands on your chest, with palms facing downward below your neck. Breathe in and out comfortably. Place an expandable cord or resistance band around your knees and apply pressure.

Exercise: Bend from your hip joints as you lift your knees towards your chest. You should experience a flexing sensation at the point where your leg joins your core body. Do not allow your lower spine to arch. Hold that position, then slowly release your legs back to the straight-down position.

While completing the repetition, remember also to contract your Kegel area muscles, while expanding your knees against the restraint of the cord. Do eight repetitions.

End position: Lie flat keeping your spine elongated and your abdominal muscles relaxed.

Be aware: Remember that your spine, especially your lower spine, should stay as flat as possible against the mat. Do only as many as you can while maintaining this position, and discontinue if you feel strain on your lower back. Breathe regularly. Each contraction of the abdomen muscles should correspond with a leg lift, while each relaxation should correspond with a return to an extended leg.

Bent Knee Side Crunch

Area of concentration: Obliques

This exercise is simple and concise. It doesn't need much space or dramatic movement, but you do need to concentrate your effort.

Start position: Lie on one side of your body with your knees flexed to a 90-degree angle. Cross your hands and cover your shoulders as you straighten your spine. Keep your eyes forward.

Exercise: Contract your oblique (side muscles) to draw your upper body off the mat. Remember that you are releasing opposite side muscles to allow for your trunk to lift. Now return to start position, repeating the exercise eight times. Hold at the end of each crunch for a second, squeeze your oblique muscles, then actively release that squeeze.

End position: Lie on your side with your abdominal muscles relaxed.

Be aware: Breathe as regularly as possible throughout the exercise. It is very tempting to use the back muscles in this exercise. Be careful to isolate the area you intend to exercise.

Bent Leg Side Crunch

Area of concentration: Obliques, adductors, abductors

Once you have decided to work your obliques from your side, you might as well get your legs moving too.

Start position: Lie on one side of your body with your legs stretched straight below you. Bend your lower leg to a 90-degree angle in order to stabilize your body from rolling over. Cross your hands and cover your shoulders as you straighten your spine. Keep your eyes looking forward.

Exercise: Contract your oblique (side muscles) to draw your upper body off the mat, releasing obliques on the opposite side to allow for the lift. Simultaneously, lift your same side leg off the mat and hold. If you wish to further test your balance, try the same movement with the underlying leg straight. You may even try lifting both legs at the same time or lift the underlying leg to the upper leg.

Now release and return to the start position, repeating eight times. Hold at the end of each crunch for a second, squeeze your oblique muscles, then actively release that squeeze. Roll over and try the other side.

End position: Lie on your side with your abdominal muscles relaxed.

Be aware: Breathe as regularly as possible throughout the exercise. It is very tempting to use the back muscles in this exercise. Be careful to isolate and use the muscles you want to exercise.

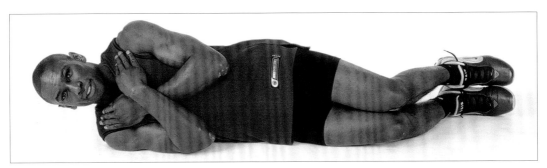

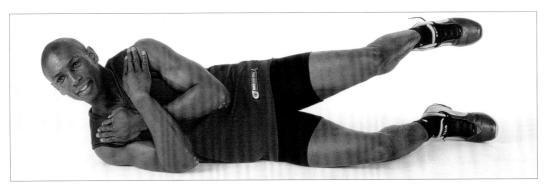

Hip Extension

Area of Concentration: Erector spinae, gluteals, psoas

The Hip Extension is a simple exercise for exploring the strength of muscles and tendons that stabilize your lower spine and help you to stand erect, and sit with good posture. You will find variations of this movement in almost any discipline, from yoga to martial arts to warm-up routines for track and field.

Start position: From the prone position, face down on the floor or mat with an elongated spine, press yourself up to a hands-and-knees "table" position still facing downward.

Maintaining balance, shift the weight to your left leg and extend the right leg straight back until you have formed one long line from your head, down your spine to your heel. Your hips remain tucked under to help maintain this straight line.

Exercise: Continue to fix your gaze at the ground, contract your gluteal and hamstring muscles, while keeping your lower back relaxed and straight. Raise the leg as high as is comfortable, then slowly lower it to 1 inch (2.5cm) above the ground. That is one repetition. Repeat the up and down motion for your desired number of repetitions, then change legs.

End position: Resume the "table" kneeling position with your weight equally distributed on all four hands and knees, breathing comfortably.

Be aware: Remember to keep your spine elongated. Those with tender knees may wish to skip the mat version of this exercise and perhaps use a Swiss Ball as a foundation and do a double leg lift. The aim is to avoid placing a "sheer load" on the knee joint, which stresses the anterior cruciate ligament. Breathe comfortably, and do not hold your breath.

Gluteal Crunch

Area of Concentration: Erector spinae, intra–vertebral muscles, gluteals

This type of exercise is sometimes known as the Superman. You may find that this exercise is more comfortable and effective, if you raise your body off the ground with one to three mats. This removes possible strain on your lower back and allows for a greater range of motion in the exercise.

Start position: Lie in a prone position with your face down on the floor or mat. Make sure your spine is elongated by tucking in your chin and rolling under your hips. Extend your arms in front of you. Your legs should lie straight back. If possible, arrange your mat so that your core is supported but your legs and arms hang off to the side.

Exercise: With your head still facing down, lift your arms, upper body and legs off the mat. Hold that position for a count of three while your back and gluteal muscles remain contracted. Slowly release to lower your arms and legs back to the mat, then repeat eight times.

End position: Resume the relaxed prone position with an elongated spine.

Be aware: Remember to keep your spine elongated. Continue breathing in a relaxed fashion, assuring that you do not hold your breath as you balance your weight on your abdominal muscles.

Alternative: Try the Uni- and Contralateral Crunch exercises on page 222.

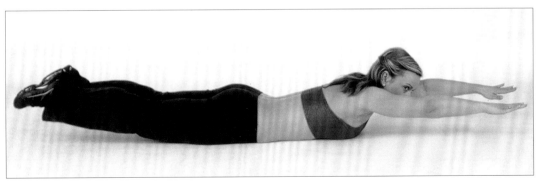

Uni- and Contralateral Gluteal Crunch

Area of concentration: Erector spinalis, gluteals

After you have mastered the Gluteal Crunch exercise, you will be ready to introduce variation to the core muscles that support your spine and hips. Rather than lift all arms and legs at once, you can practice coordination and balance.

Again, you may find that this exercise is more comfortable and effective if you raise your body off the ground with one to three mats. This allows for a greater range of motion in the exercise and possibly relieves some hyperextension in the lower lumbar region when lying in a flat prone position.

Start position: Lie in a prone position with your face down on the floor or mat. Make sure your spine is elongated by tucking in your chin and rolling under your hips. Extend your arms in front of you. Your legs should lie straight back. If possible, arrange your mat so that your core is supported but your legs and arms hang off to the side.

Exercise: To do the Unilateral Gluteal Crunch, lie with your head facing down and lift your left arm, upper body, and left leg off the mat. Hold that position for a count of three while your back and gluteal muscles remain contracted. Slowly release to lower your arm and leg back to the mat, then repeat with the right arm and right leg, eight times for each.

To do the Contralateral Gluteal Crunch, lift the left arm and upper body along with the right leg. Hold that position for a count of three. Release slowly and repeat for the right arm and left leg combination.

End position: Resume the relaxed prone position with an elongated spine.

Be aware: Remember to keep your spine elongated. Continue breathing in a relaxed fashion, assuring that you do not hold your breath as you balance your weight on your abdominal muscles.

Standing Pole

Area of concentration: All core support

The Standing Pole exercise is so simple and so deliberate that anyone can do it, yet everyone can spend a lifetime trying to master it. Standing Pole is a discipline of Yi Quan influenced by T'ai Chi.

Standing Pole encourages a quiet mind which lends itself to the task of internal reflection and introspection. This is not some passive relaxation technique, however. Standing Pole is a rigorous and challenging physical discipline that requires active participation and constant reassessment of alignment, effort, and internal feedback. The trick is actually to continue the exercise while expending less and less exertion. One of the nicest features of Standing Pole is that it is appropriate for everyone—seniors, pregnant women, those with back injuries, as well as athletes.

Start position: Wear shoes with flat soles, socks or stand in bare feet. Stand with your feet slightly wider than shoulder width apart. Bend your knees slightly, flex comfortably at hip joint, with your abdomen relaxed. Tuck your hips in for support and to elongate your spine. You will feel your weight sink down onto your feet with pressure on your heels. Press down in your armpits to extend your upper spine upward, feeling the crown or tip of your head reaching for the ceiling, while your chin stays tucked in.

Exercise: Imagine that you approach a pole and want to wrap your arms and legs around it while still standing. Keep your shoulders seated, meaning down, and reach around with your arms. Now relax as many muscles as possible and try breathing in and out from your abdomen and chest, expanding and contracting for inhalation and exhalation.

You have slight flexion at your hip joint, your knees are bouncy and flexible and your arms hug your imaginary pole at around chest height (sternum). Hold this position for as long as is comfortable, then relax.

End position: Standing comfortably with an elongated spine, gaze forward and relax your abdominal muscles while maintaining the posture described above. At the moment you weaken, relax away from the exercise and shake out your legs.

Be aware: Throughout the exercise, you must keep your hips rolled under and chin tucked in. Take note of which movements allow you greater flexibility or expansion of your core. Experiment with balance. Feel your feet and look for your weight to sink lower.

Leg Adduction / Abduction

Area of concentration: Iliopsoas, gluteals, adductors, abductors

One of the simplest ways to loosen and extend the muscles of the core is to find your adduction and abduction range of motion. Adduction of the leg is simply medial movement towards the midline of the body, whereas abduction is medial movement away from the midline of the body. Why is it important to our core capabilities? Core muscles work in harmony to provide us with stability, flexibility, posture, and locomotion. We involve the muscles of our core when we call upon the abductors and adductors to do their job. Adduction is accomplished with adductors brevis, longus and magnes, whereas abduction is accomplished with gluteus medius and minimus. However, you also must release and

lengthen your psoas in order for these muscles to work properly. If you really want to test your core balance, try these without the stabilization of a wall, chair, or bar.

Start position: Stand in front of a wall, bar, or chair with feet about shoulder width apart and one hand stabilizing you against the wall or chair. Your hips should be rolled under, your knees slightly bent, shoulders down, and your heels pressing into the ground.

Exercise: With your right leg slightly bent, make a sweeping motion across the front of your body and back. Repeat eight times and then do the same for the left leg.

End position: Stand comfortably with your spine elongated, and your feet shoulder width apart. Look forward and relax your abdominal muscles.

Be aware: For stability, be sure that you feel your weight pressing into your heel on the

standing leg. Keep your spine long and your torso relatively straight up and down during the sweep as you feel your abdominals stretch. Throughout the exercise, you must keep your hips rolled under and chin tucked in. Breathe as regularly as possible throughout the exercise.

Standard Step and Lunge

Area of concentration: Erector spinae

The step is a great piece of equipment for training your core. If you walk up a few flights of stairs in addition to fine aerobic conditioning, you also have a perfect opportunity to work your core muscles.

By keeping the discipline of tucking the hip joint and activating the iliopsoas and pubococcygeal muscles, you reinforce good posture and call upon the erector spinae and abdominals to do their work. Typically, the step platform is deployed in some sort of aerobic workout setting. Everyone can work standard step exercises in order to enhance their core. The lunge adapts particularly well to the step, offering variety and an increased degree of difficulty.

Start position: Stand with your feet about shoulder width apart, step placed in front of you at slightly longer than normal stepping distance. Your hips should be rolled under, knees slightly bent, shoulders down, and heels pressing into the ground.

Exercise: With your right foot, make a step onto the step. As you gain confidence, you may place the step further away. Allow the right leg to lower you slowly down until your upper thigh is parallel to the ground. Sink only as low as is comfortable. Your back foot, the left, should roll up on to your toes to allow this lunge step. Your left knee may tap the ground. Push back up with the right foot as you tuck the hip and feel the core muscles working for you. Raise yourself up and step back to your standing position, then repeat with the left leg leading into the lunge. Try eight on each leg.

End position: Stand comfortably with an elongated spine, feet shoulder width apart. Look forward and relax your abdominal muscles.

Be aware: For stability, be sure that you feel your weight pressing into your heel on the lunging foot. Keep your spine long and your torso relatively straight up and down during the lunge. Throughout the exercise, you must keep your hips rolled under and chin tucked in.

Pull Down Crunch with Cord

Area of concentration: Abdomen, iliopsoas

This exercise requires a little care in setting up, but it is a useful variation on the crunch and adds the dynamic of corded resistance and activation of the iliopsoas because of the standing position. Be careful not to strain the lower spine, as for any other crunch exercises working the abdomen.

Start position: Stand underneath a suspended horizontal bar, feet about shoulder width apart, legs straight. Your hips should be rolled under, shoulders down, and heels pressing into the ground. The handled stretch cord should hang over the horizontal bars. Hold each handle over your underarm/shoulder area as you bend 90 degrees at your hip joint (pelvic fold) and prepare to use your abdomen muscles.

Exercise: Contract your abdomen muscles only in order to pull down the stretch cord. By keeping your legs straight, you will experience a stretching in your hamstrings. You may also bend your knees slightly, but keep the discipline of a straight back and be sure to use only your abdominals for your range of motion.

End position: Finish with your legs bent 90 degrees at your hip, your spine straight, and breathing comfortably.

Be aware: You are working only the upper abs in this exercise, so breathe out upon contraction and inhale upon release.

Trunk Rotation

Area of concentration: Erector spinalis, obliques, transverse abdominals

When you are ready to really work the core of your body, and use the erector spinalis muscles as well as the obliques and transverse abdominis, then it is time to use a resistance band or cord. By performing the trunk rotation against the stretching resistance of the cord, you will extend and strengthen the internal muscles of the core.

Start position: Anchor your stretchable cord by looping it around a fixed exercise bar or other secure fixed device about waist high. Stand with your left side facing the anchor. Hold the two handles in your right hand and steady yourself by standing with your knees slightly flexed and feet shoulder width or a little further apart. Stand so that the resistance is engaged when you stretch the cord until your right hand is holding the handles on your right side.

You may hold your hand slightly away from your hip in a fixed position. Your hips should be rolled under, shoulders pressing down, and heels pressing into the ground.

Exercise: Breathing out, turn your trunk to the right side, feeling pressure against your left leg. Slowly allow the stretching resistance to turn you all the way back, completing one rotation. Try this eight times then switch position to your other side.

End position: Standing comfortably with an elongated spine, feet shoulder width apart, look forward with your abdominal muscles relaxed.

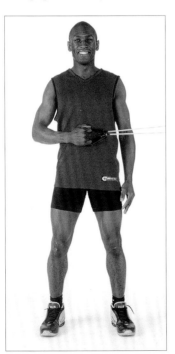 

Be aware: For stability, be sure that you feel your weight pressing into your heel on the pushing leg.

Keep your spine long and your torso relatively straight up and down during the rotation as you feel your abdominals stretch.

Throughout the exercise, you must keep your hips rolled under and chin tucked in. Breathe out on contraction and in on return.

Shallow Dead Lift

Area of concentration: Psoas, glutes, all core support muscles

The handled resistance cord is a great way to add difficulty to your core workout without progressing directly to free weights. Done in the proper fashion, this exercise creates a feeling of "groundedness" and solid core development. It may seem like a leg exercise, but don't let that fool you, you are still working your core muscles.

Again, care must be taken here not to stress the knee joint while working against the resistance of gravity and the stretchable cord. Keep your knees bent slightly and your spine straight.

Start position: Stand on top of the handled resistance cord, feet about shoulder width apart, with equal length of cord extending on each side. Your hips should be rolled under, knees slightly bent, shoulders down, and heels pressing into the ground.

Pick up the handles without slumping your back. Keep your eyes forward, and chin tucked in. Stand straight with the resistance handles pulling on the band on both sides.

You may vary this exercise by keeping your legs straight, but be very careful not to strain your lower spine and ligaments.

Exercise: Bend from your hip joints as the cord provides resistance. Be certain that your knees do not extend forward further than the vertical line rising straight up from your toes. You should experience a flexing sensation at the point where your leg joins your core body. Be sure to keep your hips rolled under and do not allow your lower spine to arch.

Next, slowly press your heels into the ground and extend your legs back up to a slightly bent knee position. Be sure your hips

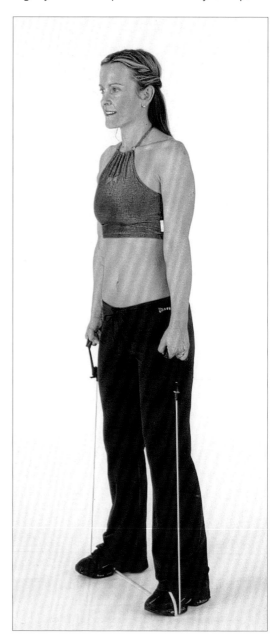

are tucked under and knees remain flexed. Try eight repetitions.

End position: Stand comfortably with an elongated spine. Look forward and keep your abdominal muscles relaxed.

Be aware: Throughout the exercise, you must keep your hips rolled under and chin tucked in.

It is often tempting to lift the chin toward the ceiling during the exercise. Resist this urge and keep your chin tucked in. Breathe as regularly as possible, inhaling on the way down and exhaling on the way up.

Alternative: You may shorten the length of the cord by doubling it, or you can pull your hands up higher.

Balanced Leg Extension

Area of concentration: Psoas

For those of you who marvel at the balance, skill, and coordination of ice skaters or roller bladers, here is your chance to give skating a try without the cold ice or hard concrete. The Balanced Leg Extension can even be done on flat ground, which may be a good way for beginners to ease into the skill.

The Bosu Ball is essentially a Swiss Ball chopped in half and mounted upon a flat board, creating a non-stable environment, good for testing balance. This exercise offers you the opportunity to explore the full range of your hip joint, activating all the support muscles between your core and your legs.

Start position: Stand in front of the Bosu Ball with your feet shoulder-width apart and hands at your side. You should feel the stability of your entire foot pressing into the ground. Keep your abdomen relaxed. Focus your eyes forward and keep your chin level with the ground.

Exercise: Continuing to fix your gaze forward, place your left foot on the crest (the top) of the Bosu Ball, or balance board, and extend your relaxed arms forward for a counterbalance as you transfer your weight over your left leg and lift your right leg behind you. You might notice that this posture resembles an ice skater pushing off one blade and gliding. Be sure that you keep your hips rolled under and feel your entire foot against the top of the ball. Your armpits should press down in order to seat your shoulders. You will notice some instability from the inherent nature of the ball, but this activates your proprioception capabilities in

your core and connective tissue. Hold this stance for 15 seconds, arms and right leg extended, then gradually return your right leg to the ground.

End position: Keeping your eyes focused forward, carefully transfer your weight from your left leg back to your right as you shift off of the Bosu Ball. You will finally return to a standing position with your weight equally distributed on both feet. Repeat the exercise with your right leg bearing your weight on the ball and your left leg elevated. Try for longer durations.

Be aware: You might be tempted to look down at your feet for a feeling of stability, but this creates the tendency to slump and defeats the purpose of the exercise.

Balanced Knee Lift

Area of concentration: Iliopsoas, gluteal, erector spinae, and abdomen

From the basic skill of balancing with one leg extended, this is a more dynamic alternative. The exercise involves moving through a range of motion and maintaining balance on an unstable environment. This exercise can also be done on flat ground, which may be a good way for beginners to ease into the skill.

The Balanced Knee Lift offers you the opportunity to explore the full range of your hip joint, activating all the support muscles that attach your core to your legs. You might imagine yourself to be a high jumper, just ready to launch over the high bar.

Start position: Stand in front of the Bosu Ball with your feet shoulder width apart and hands at your side.

Feel the stability of your entire foot pressing into the ground and keep your abdomen relaxed. Keep your eyes focused forward and your chin level with the ground, tucked in and not protruding.

Exercise: Continuing to fix your gaze forward, place your left foot on the top of the Bosu Ball and extend your relaxed arms forward for a counterbalance as you transfer your weight over your left leg and lift your right leg behind you. Be sure that you keep your entire foot against the top of the ball. You will notice some instability from the inherent nature of the ball, but this activates your proprioceptive capabilities in your core and connective tissue. Now slowly lift your right knee to a relatively comfortable position in front of you, about hip high or more if you can retain your balance. Hold this stance for 15 seconds, arms closer to

your body, then gradually return your right leg to the ground.

End position: Keeping your eyes focused forward, carefully transfer your weight from your left leg back to your right as you shift off the Bosu Ball. Finally, return to a standing position with your weight equally distributed on both feet. Repeat the exercise with your right leg bearing your weight on the ball and your left leg elevated. Try for longer durations.

Be aware: You might be tempted to look down at your feet for a feeling of stability, but this creates the tendency to slump the back.

Swiss Kegels

Area of concentration: Pubococcygeal muscles

Swiss Kegels help you establish a feeling of stability while working the pubococcygeal muscles of the pelvic floor.

Start position: Take a seated position on a Swiss Ball, bringing your upper leg roughly parallel with the ground and forming a 90-degree angle in your knees.

If you feel a little uncertain about your stability, be sure that you experiment on a soft mat and consider using a wall or attached dancer's stretch bar for added stability on your side. Be wary of slipping off or rolling into the wall, of course. If you have a partner to help

you, this may offer a better alternative. Never position a hard surface behind you.

Sit with your spine feeling elongated and your weight resting upon your sitting bones. Breathe in and out comfortably. Make sure there are no hard surfaces directly behind you; you have to protect your head.

Exercise: Feel the pubococcygeal muscles that connect your coccyx to your pubic bone directly beneath you as you sit on the ball. Squeeze them while relaxing your abdomen, hold for three seconds, then release. Repeat this eight times.

Feel your feet press into the ground to provide stability, and feel the connection of muscles working all the way up your legs to your core. You may press down into the ball and squeeze your buttocks if you feel unstable.

End position: Sit with your spine feeling elongated. Imagine your head as if it is lifting to the ceiling. Keep your eyes forward, your spine straight, and your lower spine sinking straight down into the ball.

Be aware: Be careful that you keep your spine elongated and your shoulders seated. You want your exercise effort to come from your core, so keep your chin tucked in. Breathe out as you contract and inhale as you release throughout the exercise, and press down from your armpits. Try to avoid bouncing on the ball and keep your movements smooth.

Rotations

Area of concentration: Pubococcygeal muscles, iliopsoas, erector spinae

After you have started with the basic Kegel exercise on the Swiss Ball, you can try something more dynamic. By moving slowly, you will have the opportunity to feel for and identify the elusive muscles deep inside, such as the psoas, that have such dramatic effect upon our spinal stability and alignment.

Start position: Take a seated position on a Swiss Ball, bringing your upper leg roughly parallel with the ground, and forming a 90-degree angle in your knees. Slightly lower is even better.

Sit with your spine feeling very elongated and your weight resting upon your sitting bones. Press down in your armpits. Breathe comfortably. Your arms may provide a stabilizing balance; position them away from your side with your palms facing downward. Alternatively, sit with your hands resting on your thighs. In this position, you are ready to protect yourself should you roll too far off the ball. Make sure there are no hard surfaces directly behind you.

Exercise: Begin to roll your hips in a circular clockwise direction. This is an excellent opportunity to explore your range of motion and "open" your pelvis area, by relaxing your connective tissue and encouraging flexibility. Next, try rolling your hips counter-clockwise. You may press down into the ball to accommodate your rotating hips.

You may further explore your range of motion by limiting your movements laterally (side to side) or longitudinally (front to back). Again, you are looking to relax and extend the connective tissue within the pelvis, without slumping out of a straight alignment.

End position: Sit with an elongated spine, facing forward.

Be aware: You want your exercise effort to come from your core, so keep your chin tucked in. Breathe out as you contract and inhale as you release throughout the exercise, and press down from your armpits. Try to avoid bouncing on the ball and keep your movements smooth.

Contralateral Arm / Leg Extension

Area of Concentration: Erector spinae

Once you get a feeling for balancing on the Swiss Ball, you may begin to try some prone and supine exercises that amplify those you already do on the mat. The Gluteal Crunch exercise, or "Superman," is one example where you can use a Swiss Ball to get you off the hard mat and test your stability.

Start position: From the prone position, face down on the Swiss Ball with your right arm stabilizing you against the ground. Extend the right leg straight back until you have formed one long line from your head, down your spine to your heel. Keep your hips tucked under to help maintain this straight line. Extend your left arm simultaneously to a position parallel with the ground and breathe from your abdomen.

Exercise: Continuing to fix your gaze at the ground, contract your gluteal and hamstring muscles while keeping your lower back relaxed and straight. Raise your leg as high as is comfortable, while simultaneously raising your left arm to a similar height. Allow them to

lower to below parallel in a controlled manner. That is one repetition.

You may repeat the up and down motion for your desired number of repetitions, then change to a right arm/left leg combination.

End position: Resume the prone position on the Swiss Ball, breathing comfortably.

Be aware: Remember to keep your spine elongated and breathe out with each extension, back in with each lowering/relaxation.

Full Range Crunch

Area of concentration: Abdomen, psoas, erector spinae

The Swiss Ball Crunch is an opportunity to experiment with your range of motion. Try relaxing the normal discipline of keeping a long straight spine and tucked in hips in favor of using the Swiss Ball's soft, forgiving curve to sense your lower spine's full range. You can experiment to the extent that the movement feels comfortable to you or apply the normal crunch discipline of a straight spine.

Against the bouncy ball and without the strain of a hard floor, the abdominals may enjoy a gentle elongation and stretch.

Start position: The Full Range Crunch can be completed with or without wall anchoring. Without anchoring, you simply place your feet flat on the ground while sitting on the Swiss Ball, knees at 90 degrees, and sink your lower back into the curvature of the ball. Relax your arms and hands over your chest.

Exercise: Arch your lower back into the contour of the ball gently, and allow the rest of your spine to follow this arch. Next, contract your abdomen muscles and roll your hips under, creating a feeling of contraction from both your pelvis area and your lower abdomen.

Be careful not to pull with your upper neck muscles or bounce off the ball to attain your crunch movement. Lift your chest with your contraction. The whole point of the exercise is to work the lower core muscles and explore the full range of motion.

Hold that contraction for two seconds and squeeze your muscles. Lower yourself slowly back to the curvature of the ball. Repeat this motion eight times.

End position: Lie on the ball with abdominal muscles relaxed.

Be aware: Only lift your shoulder blades as high as you can by using your abdominal muscles. Each contraction of the abdomen muscles should correspond with an exhalation, while each relaxation should correspond with inhalation.

Leg Raises

Area of concentration: Erector spinalis, glutes, psoas elongation

Leg raises can also be performed while holding onto the end of a padded exercise table. Normally, your legs would hang off the end and you would raise and lower them. Swiss Ball offers a chance to do this exercise far more comfortably. To avoid sore hips and stiff tables, it is worth giving this method a try. Using a Swiss Ball is a rather effective and forgiving method of exploring this full range of motion, using your erector spinalis, glutes and elongating your psoas.

Start position: From the prone position, face down on the Swiss Ball with your hips pressing into it. Place your hands on the ground as a steadying anchor.

Roll your hips into the ball, feeling pressure on your pubic bone as you straighten your spine. Your body should be just about horizontal, and your upper body should stay horizontal throughout the exercise.

Exercise: Breathe out as you contract the lower back and gluteal muscles and raise your legs together. Hold the upright position for three seconds, then slowly lower your legs back down. Use your hips to press into the ball as a fulcrum.

You may also try one leg at a time, which is slightly more forgiving if you feel some discomfort around your lower back.

End position: Return to a relaxed prone position and allow the curvature of the ball to induce some stretching of the upper (thoracic) vertebrae.

Be aware: Remember to keep your spine elongated. Breathe out with each extension, back in with each lowering/relaxation.

Seated Dead Lift

Area of concentration: Lower spine, psoas

There is a clever way to simulate the first movement of the Dead Lift if you are a little intimidated by using a free weight lift. The trick is to sit down and use the stacked weight machine to isolate the lower back.

One advantage of the stacked weight system is the ability to easily choose your resistance level and move up gradually as your strength and skill level dictates. Be careful not to strain your lower spine by allowing it to curve or hyperextend.

Start position: Sit in front of the row pulley associated with a stacked weight system. Your feet should be about shoulder width apart, your knees bent, and feet pressing against the frame of the weight machine. Your hips should be rolled under, shoulders down. Grasp the horizontal bar and hold it low with your arms straight.

You may vary this exercise by keeping your legs straight, but be very careful not to strain your lower spine and ligaments.

Exercise: Contract your abdomen muscles only in order to pull the row handle back. Move slowly back from about 90 degrees to 45 degrees, then slowly return to an upright position. Repeat eight times.

End position: Bend 90 degrees at your hip, spine straight. Breathe comfortably.

Be aware: Breathe out upon contraction and inhale upon release.

Crunch

Area of concentration: Abdomen, iliopsoas

In addition to the specialized machines found in gyms around the globe, there are a seemingly infinite variety of "ab workout" devices. At first glance, any machine or device that you enjoy using and will continue to use has some value. In order to determine physiological merit, however, ask yourself if the machine forces you to curve your spine unnaturally or prohibits you from keeping an elongated spine.

With any machine found in a gym, try one repetition at a very light weight. This way you may test your range of motion and determine your comfort level. Gym machines tend to have a stacked set of plate weights; a set of padded lever arms that connect to a fulcrum shaped interface and transmit the work accomplished by your body to move the weight.

Resistance can also be provided by compressed air cylinders, cords, bands, metal strips, almost anything you can think of that is hard to move, lift, bend or compress. There are gluteal and hamstring machines, hip flexors, crunch and fly extensions. Always be careful to sit squarely in the chair and watch for vulnerable joints, such as the knee, when pressing against an ankle pad. The best advice is to seek the help of a personal trainer in assuring that you are using the machine or device correctly.

The incline bench is an easily recognizable piece of equipment meant to provide some variability to resistance training. One end provides an "anchor," where you may secure a foothold or handhold that prevents you from sliding down the incline. The other end is open and the angle of inclination is adjustable.

The basic incline crunch involves exactly the same hand and body positioning and behavior as a crunch performed on the floor, along with the same exercise disciplines. The angle of inclination provides resistance, and you might feel a slight increase of blood pressure, a "rush of blood to the head," as you anchor your feet in the high position. Start with a relatively low angle of inclination. By slowly returning to the bench, you are performing a decline crunch. You can work the abdominals both ways.

Start position: Secure your feet according to the type of anchor on the bench. Most provide padded rollers, under which you slip your feet as your knees slip over another higher padded roller. Be careful not to strain your cruciate ligaments in your knees while performing any motions on the incline bench. The effort must come from the targeted area.

Roll your hips under to elongate your lower spine. Relax your arms and hands on your chest with your palms facing downward right below your neck. Breathe in and out comfortably.

Exercise: Contract your abdomen muscles until you lift your shoulder blades off the incline bench. Your lower back stays flat and you do not need to lift it off the bench. Concentrate to thrust your chest toward the ceiling, while your chin stays tucked.

Hold at the top of the movement for two seconds and squeeze your muscles. Lower yourself slowly back to the mat. Repeat this motion eight times.

If you are feeling adventurous, try the full

sit-up. Initiate the contraction in the same way that you did the crunch, but continue the motion until your chest is close to your knees. Remember to breathe out all the way up, then hold that position, then slowly inhale while lowering yourself back to the bench.

End position: Lie flat with an elongated spine and your abdominal muscles relaxed.

Be aware: It is often tempting to lift the chin toward the ceiling during the exercise. Resist this urge and only lift using your abdominal muscles. Breathe as regularly as possible throughout the exercise. Each contraction of the abdominal muscles should correspond with an exhalation, while each return to the bench should correspond with inhalation.

Leg Raise

Area of concentration: Iliopsoas, gluteals, pubococcygeals

In the free weight area of many gyms, you might find a suspensory rack. This device elevates and supports you through two padded arm rests and a padded back support. One nice feature of the rack is the lengthening effect you may experience on your iliopsoas and connective tissue in general.

There is a variety of core exercises you may perform from this platform, but it pays to be cautious. You are, after all, supporting your entire body weight upon both forearms, which can create unnatural strain in your shoulders. If you do feel stress in your rotator cuff or shoulders in general, there are plenty of mat-

based alternatives available. In the absence of a suspensory rack (as below), you may use a hanging bar to improvise the situation where your legs hang freely.

Start position: Mount the suspensory rack by resting both forearms on the pads and pressing gently with your lower spine against the padded back support. Your spine should be extended as straight as possible as your legs hang freely and feet are together.

Exercise: Bend from your hip joints as you lift your knees toward your chest. You should experience a flexing sensation at the point where your leg joins your core body. Be sure to keep your hips rolled under and do not allow your lower spine to arch. Hold that position, then slowly release the legs back to the straight-down position. While completing the repetition, remember also to contract your Kegel area muscles, the pubococcygeal group.

If you wish to add difficulty to the maneuver, twist both legs to the left and right, tapping each handle, then return them to the center, and slowly lower them down.

You may also perform a hanging jackknife by bending at your hip fold and lifting your legs in a straight position.

End position: Your spine should be relaxed and elongated with your feet hanging down.

Be aware: The most important precaution is to be sure your shoulders remain seated and down. You will have to make an effort to accomplish this, because the suspensory rack places the stress of your body weight directly upon your forearms and ultimately your shoulders. Relax your abdomen and breathe deeply to gain full benefit from the stretching effect upon your legs. Be certain not to "whip" your legs up and down; instead, make deliberate and slow movements.

Trunk Rotation

Area of Concentration: Transverse abdominals, oblique, low back

Medicine balls come in a variety of sizes and weights, depending upon the manufacturer, but they all require a degree of caution. They look innocent enough, but if you aren't ready for the weight you can strain your spine very easily. In general, hold the ball close to your trunk to avoid straining your shoulders or spine. You don't have to be an elite athlete to benefit from this training. Remember to protect your spine by keeping the correct alignment. Attention to detail is far more important than repetition. Stop before you feel discomfort, take a day of rest, then try some more.

Start position: Seat yourself comfortably upon a mat with your spine stretched long and the crest of your head reaching to the ceiling. Legs are flat against the mat and you are holding the medicine ball with two hands parallel on the side, about a forearm's length from your chest. The holding of the ball should feel as if it is originating from your solar plexus, a point in the middle of your trunk.

Exercise: Begin by twisting to the right side slowly. As you twist, roll the medicine ball so that your left hand is on top and hold that position briefly on the right before slowly twisting back to the center and bringing your hand position back to parallel on the side of the ball.

Now twist to the left hand side and slowly roll the ball so that your right hand is on top. Hold that position briefly before slowly moving back to center with hand position parallel. Repeat this eight times, slowly.

End position: The medicine ball is brought to rest in your lap as you sit with your spine straight on the mat.

Be aware: Remember to keep your shoulders in a seated position. Relax your abdomen and breathe deeply to gain full benefit from the stretching effect upon your legs.

Russian Twist

Area of Concentration: Abdominals, obliques

The trunk rotation exercises help you to develop oblique tone and power. Performing a twist under the duress of static abdominal contraction brings much more tone to the core, while encouraging flexibility in your erector spinae.

Start position: Seat yourself comfortably upon a mat with your spine elongated and the crest of head reaching to the ceiling. Bend your legs at the knee, forming a 90-degree angle, and hold the medicine ball with two hands parallel on the side about a forearm's length from your chest. Hold the ball so that it feels as if it is originating from your solar plexus, a point in the middle of your trunk. To help create this feeling, press down in your armpits and keep your shoulders pressed down and open.

Exercise: Begin by slowly lowering yourself backward to a 45-degree angle off the ground. Twist to the right while holding that position. As you twist, roll the medicine ball so that your left hand is on top. Hold that position briefly on the right before slowly twisting back to the center and bringing your hands back to a parallel position on the side of the ball.

Now twist to the left-hand side and slowly roll the ball so that your right hand is on top. Hold that position briefly before slowly moving back to center with your hands parallel. Repeat this eight times slowly. When you have mastered the exercise with your feet on the ground, try it with legs extended straight and held at 45-degree angle.

End position: The medicine ball is brought to rest in your lap as you sit with your spine straight on the mat.

Be aware: Remember that you must keep your shoulders in a seated position with your spine elongated. The slow movement is meant to impose discipline upon the strengthening action. Relax your abdomen and breathe deeply to gain full benefit from this exercise.

20-Minute Workout

Exercise Order

1 Kegels
2 Abdominal Crunch
3 Elevated Leg Rotation
4 Bent Knee Side Crunch
5 Gluteal Crunch

6 Leg Adduction / Abduction
7 Step and Lunge
8 Shallow Dead Lift
9 Full Range Crunch
10 Russian Twist

1 Kegels (See page 208)

2 Abdominal Crunch (See page 210)

3 Elevated Leg Rotation (See page 214)

4 Bent Knee Side Crunch (See page 218)

5 Gluteal Crunch (See page 221)

6 Leg Adduction / Abduction (See page 224)

7 Step and Lunge (See page 225)

8 Shallow Dead Lift (See page 228)

9 Full Range Crunch (See page 235)

10 Russian Twist (See page 245)

Pilates

Acquiring balance and equilibrium in one's body takes a little time and effort, but with the understanding that "less is more," it is achievable. Pilates offers you a gentle but powerful approach to achieving your natural potential for optimal strength, flexibility, and stamina. It could be said that Pilates is unique in its delivery as it can be personalized for specific medical conditions and posture types.

The Pilates method is a body conditioning exercise therapy, targeting the deep postural muscles to achieve core stability and strength with improved muscle balance. It involves the re-alignment of the spine to its optimum position with gentle stretching and strengthening movements. Pilates exercises are particularly recommended for those who suffer from chronic neck or back pain, postural problems, sports injuries, osteoporosis, arthritis, stress-related illnesses, M.E., and many other conditions.

It is a safe and effective way of exercising, as

you are encouraged to execute the moves slowly and within your own range of movement, so it falls within everyone's capabilities from the top athlete looking to enhance their performance and avoid the risk of injury, to clients who have never exercised much before.

Back pain is epidemic in America. It costs over $4 billion each year and, aside from the common cold, keeps more people away from work than any other single cause. Diverse evidence from many cultures show that sitting has been associated with: back pain, fatigue, varicose veins, stress, problems with the diaphragm, circulation, digestion, and colonic problems to name but a few. The answer lies in re-educating the body to move the way it was designed. Simply by using the body properly, "autonomous" sitting can be regained. Pilates can help to achieve this simple goal.

Over the years the principles associated with Pilates have been tried and tested by a variety of professions and toward the end of the twentieth century it was acknowledged by the medical profession that Pilates based exercises were extremely beneficial in the correction of spinal alignment and for joint rehabilitation. It is now practiced worldwide by osteopaths and physiotherapists. The medical profession will now, where appropriate, refer patients to a Pilates practitioner so they can learn how to integrate it into their daily life. This is because the principles can be incorporated when standing, sitting, lifting, and performing household chores. It is more than an exercise program, it is a lifestyle.

Joseph Pilates

Joseph Pilates was born in 1880 in Germany. He was a sickly child, but born with a determination to overcome his physical frailties. He studied many exercise disciplines such as yoga, gymnastics, various sports, even circus training. He subsequently became an accomplished skier, diver, gymnast, and boxer. He soon developed an exercise philosophy which combined strength, flexibility, and stamina. With his unique knowledge and understanding of the body, the series of exercises he developed are still being practiced today. There are many variations relating to the principles of Pilates ranging from those that he himself pioneered in the early 1900s to the contemporary approach that incorporates a modern understanding of fitness, anatomy, and biomechanics. The essential principles however have over the years been simplified, so that anybody of any age, aptitude, or fitness level can benefit.

Joseph Pilates concluded that if we concentrate on moving slowly and effortlessly while maintaining correct alignment, the results were profound in the improvement of core strength, flexibility, posture, and balance. The added benefits that presented themselves were that bone density remained steady, which helps to ward off increased risk of osteoporosis, and synovial fluid increased around the joints helping to fight against joint stiffness.

It appears that the only side effects from Pilates, if executed correctly, are improved posture, inner strength, toned muscles, and relief from tension and stress.

Inspiration from the East

Having studied the Eastern disciplines, Pilates incorporated the interaction of mind and body, placing great emphasis on the way we breathe and how our breathing could aid or distort movement. Because the mind is required to engage with the body to perform the movements correctly, you experience a new awareness of muscle function and control.

With the popularity of Pilates growing, classes are on the increase. Since its commercial arrival in the late 1990s, it has revolutionized the exercise and fitness industry following years of high impact, go for the burn workouts. The overall appeal of a slower more sensible approach has been welcomed by many. A program that you can look forward to, one that engages you and leaves you refreshed, alert, and with a feeling of physical and mental well-being.

Competently trained and knowledgeable practitioners are an essential element in realizing someone's potential. These practitioners have undergone many hours of training and with some many years of study, when you find one they are invaluable. There are many around now who have specialized in this field.

The exercises in this section are safe for the beginner. Books and videos are exceptionally good for reference but they cannot take the place of learning one-on-one with a qualified teacher. A postural analysis and medical questionnaire should be undertaken if you ever commence a group session.

Self-Postural Analysis

It is a good idea to take a look at your posture, which will help you when choosing a program that will benefit you most. Follow these simple guidelines to check your own posture. If you can persuade someone to help you then it will make things easier but it can be done on your own. Whatever your posture may be at this present time, you need to understand the basic language used to help get into better alignment. No matter how fit you are, understanding the basic principles are the key to the profound results Pilates can offer. Setting up your position is the most important thing when learning the basics. There is really no point in learning an exercise if your posture is out of alignment before you begin.

If you are unable to attend a class or get private tuition for a short time then please take care with the progressive exercises. The rule of thumb is, if you are struggling or tension is presenting itself then the exercise is too strong for you at that time. Remember less is more.

You will need a full-length mirror and be able to see your shape so wear something tight fitting, such as a swimsuit. Stand in front of the mirror and adopt your normal stance.

Imagine you are standing in the middle of a clock face facing 12 o'clock. Write down what you see on the self analysis sheet and come back to it in a couple of month's time to see how things have changed. Look at the analysis sheet that follows and see how you shape up.

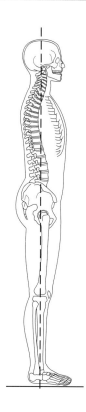

An example of optimal posture with the plumb line running through the center of the body.

Date:

Feet

Standing in the middle of your imaginary clock face, look at your feet in the mirror. Where are they pointing? Draw their position on the clock.

Knees

Where are your knees pointing?
- Level ☐
- Left higher than right/right higher than left ☐
- Facing forward ☐
- Left knee turned in/right knee turned in/both knees turned in ☐

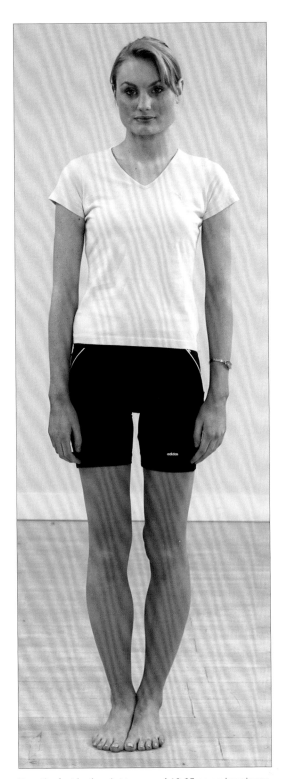

Here the feet both point to around 12:05 on an imaginary clock and the knees are noticeably turned in, especially the left.

Hip bones

Place your middle fingers on the bones at the front of your body commonly known as your hip bones.

Then look at your fingers.

Are they?

- Level ☐
- Left finger higher than right/right finger higher than left ☐

In the picture (left) notice the gap between her left arm and her body and the gap between her right arm and body. This indicates that the hips are not sitting level and that the right side is slightly higher than the left.

Look at the gaps that you have, they should be the same if you have good alignment.

Rib cage

Place your hands on your rib cage and find the bottom of the ribs with one finger. (They will be much lower than you think.) Look at your fingers in the mirror.

Are they?

- Level ☐
- Left side higher than right/right side higher than left ☐

Shoulders

Look at your shoulders to see if they sit:

- Level ☐
- Left side higher than right/right side higher than left ☐

If you look at the picture (left) you will notice that one shoulder sits higher than the other.

Head

Where does your head sit on your shoulders?

- Centrally ☐
- Tipped to the left/right ☐

If you have someone to help you, get your helper to view you from the side or ask them to take a photograph of you and place an imaginary plumb line through the body. The pictures (below) show a kyphotic/flatback posture, typically characterized by rounded shoulders.

Kyphotic/flatback posture from the side.

Kyphotic/flatback posture from the front

Side

Where does your head sit?
• Centrally ☐
• Further forward/back of the line ☐

What is your neck length?
• Short ☐
• Long ☐

Where do your arms sit?
• Centrally (middle finger down seam of your clothes at the side) ☐
• Forward ☐

Is your upper back?
• Flat ☐
• Rounded ☐

Is your lower back?
• Flat ☐
• Over arching ☐

Are your knees?
• Bent slightly forward ☐
• Hyperextended (bent backward) ☐

Back/front

Ask your helper again to view you from both the front and back or take photographs as an accurate record of your posture.

Is your head sitting on your shoulders?
• Centrally ☐
• To the left/right ☐

Are your shoulders?
• Level ☐
• Left/right higher ☐

Are the creases in the back of your knees level?
• Yes ☐
• No ☐

Are your ankles?
• Straight ☐
• Left/right toward center (dropped arches) ☐

Once you have completed your postural analysis you can then look to see what posture type you fall into. We never fall into just one, it will be a bit of a mixture but you will be able to put yourself into one or two easily.

Pilates is a Personal Thing

Everyone's posture is determined by their genetics, lifestyle, activity, and emotions. If you look at a foetus in the womb the spine is one shape; we are born with a rounded spine. The "s" shape develops during the early stages of our growth giving us our kyphotic and lordotic curves. These curves are important to maintain as they absorb impact when we walk, run, or jump. If these curves are not present then the shock waves traveling up from our feet would go straight to the head.

As we grow our muscles develop, supporting the skeleton as it moves. During childhood the number of movement patterns we performed throughout one day was great. Unfortunately as we get older, our lifestyles and recreation become more sedentary and our movement patterns are reduced even though our bodies are capable of flexibility. By the time we reach our 20s most of us have reduced our patterns to sitting, standing and lying only. In these cases the result is prolonged alteration of the natural curves of the spine and stress will be placed on the joints causing eventual pain. This is commonly described as repetitive strain syndrome. In an optimal posture the forces of gravity should be evenly distributed through the body with the muscles being at their optimal length and strength in order to support the skeleton efficiently.

If we had an ideal posture, then our skeletal system would be supported by our deep postural stabilizing muscles. We would then have our movement muscles all working at their optimum strength and flexibility in order to move us effortlessly. If all of our muscles and joints were working in harmony we would move, according to Joseph Pilates, "like the sound of a finely tuned orchestra." Every part playing efficiently and effectively for the purpose it was intended.

When you first look at changing your posture you have to look at what posture type you fall into. Unfortunately we never fall into just one type of posture as one can be the cause of another. You need to look generally at where you need to either lengthen short muscles or strengthen weak ones in order to restore optimal alignment.

If you spend your working hours seated or standing then your movement patterns will be directly affected due to sustained positions and repetitive movements. Therefore your working environment plays a huge role in how you hold yourself.

Let us look at the four main posture types:

Posture Types

Lordotic

The lordotic posture is the type you see in young gymnasts. It is also a posture seen in pregnant women and men with a beer belly due to the extra weight being carried in front. If you look at the picture below, notice that the abdominals are lengthened and the lower back is tight, which places excessive stress on the lumbar discs, causing the muscles to be over active. We often wrongly recruit the lumbar muscles when carrying or lifting heavy objects, placing more stress than is already present.

For example, when carrying heavy shopping we should be recruiting the shoulder and core stabilizers rather then relying on the lumbar extensors to support the spine. This is a common trait in those who are lordotic, creating unnecessary tension in the lower back which causes stiffness and immobility in that area. This can prove difficult to correct initially. The excessive curve which is present in a lordotic posture is there because the pelvis is being held in an anterior tilt where the hip bones are forward of the pubic bone. This position of the pelvis also causes the hip flexors to shorten and the hamstrings to be lengthened. Mobility exercises will help considerably in helping to correct these problems but care needs to be taken in executing movement in the lower back due to the probable stiffness. The spine needs to be encouraged to move slowly and gently to avoid any forced error of movement. Less is more.

Problems
- Weak gluteals (buttocks)
- Over active hamstrings
- Short hip flexors
- Weak abdominals

Solutions
- Strengthen abdominals and gluteals (buttocks)
- Increase segmental control of the spine to reduce lordosis and increase mobility
- Lengthen hip flexors
- Stretch back extensors

Exercises
- Hamstring stretch
- Shoulder bridge
- Abdominal preparation
- Seated "c" curve
- All fours, cat's tail
- Shell stretch
- Arm floats
- Monkey squat

Kyphotic

Kyphosis is the posture that has the round-shouldered appearance. It is seen mainly in those who have sedentary jobs, such as office workers and those who sit all day at a computer or drive for a living. Sitting causes major postural imbalances in the spine and affects the length, strength, and stamina in certain muscles.

For example, when your body is sitting in a chair all day, the muscles that should be supporting you are actually inhibited. The buttocks, our biggest muscle in the body, can very often be our weakest. The leg muscles are also inhibited when sitting as they too are being supported but they are also being kept in a bent position for long periods which can cause the hamstrings in the back of the legs to shorten and the quads at the front of the legs to lengthen. All are inactive while sitting so have a tendency to be weak. We then have to accept that the muscles in the ankles and feet are not taking any weight all day so they too become weaker. Lastly the position of the head is never at its optimal position when sitting especially at a computer if you're constantly looking down at the keyboard then up at the screen.

Slumping is common when sitting and this is contributory to many digestive problems as well as muscular imbalances. When we slump the lumbar spine is forced out causing us to lose our natural lordosis. The result is a double imbalance of kyphosis and flatback.

Kyphosis and flatback don't always come together. A person can suffer with kyphosis but not sit all day, a nurse for example who is bending over regularly.

Problems

- Short/tight pecs (chest muscle)
- Lengthened trapezius muscle in the upper and middle fibers (causing round shoulders)
- Weak abdominals
- Weak gluteals (buttocks)
- Tension in neck and shoulders

Solutions

- Stretch chest muscle
- Strengthen postural fibers in middle and lower trapezius
- Strengthen abdominals and gluteals (buttocks)
- Lengthen neck extensors, strengthen neck flexors

Exercises

- Standing heel raises
- Arm floats
- Shoulder squeeze
- All fours
- Shell stretch
- Breast stroke preparation
- Side lying open door
- Skull rock
- Hamstring stretch
- Shoulder bridge
- Monkey squat

This posture shows a double imbalance of kyphosis and flatback.

Sway Back

The sway back posture is often known as the lazy posture. It is commonly adopted by teenagers and those who stoop because they are conscious of their height. It is also the posture that most catwalk models adopt which becomes an occupational posture.

The noticeable features of a sway back are sitting into the hip and favoring one leg when standing, allowing the abdominals to relax and lengthen. The head is usually held to one side rather than being central and the arms hang forward.

It gets the name lazy because those who have this posture can sometimes very easily correct it by standing tall and distributing their weight evenly through the legs. If the posture is long standing then there are considerable differences in the strength on one side of the body to the other. By favoring one leg, the muscles on one side will be shortening while on the other side they will be lengthening. The abdominal tone in sway backs is lax so all of the abdominal family will need conditioning to help correct this posture. It is the only posture where the hip flexors are likely to be lengthened and in need of strengthening, whereas in all the other postures the hip flexors need to be lengthened in order to release tension at the top of the legs.

Problems
- Favors one leg when standing
- Lengthened hip flexors
- Tight hamstrings
- Lengthened abs/obliques
- Head slant

Solutions
- Strengthen all the abdominal group
- Strengthen the hip flexors
- Stretch the hamstrings
- Re-align neck position

Exercises
- Standing set position
- Heel raises
- Arm floats
- All fours, cat's tail
- Breast stroke preparation
- Shell stretch
- Side lying open door
- Skull rock
- Single leg stretch
- Obliques
- Hamstring stretch
- Shoulder bridge
- Shoulder squeeze
- Monkey squat

Flat Back

The flat back posture is just as it suggests—the back is flat, having lost the lordotic curve. It is seen in those who sit for prolonged periods especially if sitting in a slumped position, such as the couch potato or someone slouching in an office chair while making a phone call. The muscles in the lumbar spine can become fixed quite quickly, resulting in an inability to bend forward or backward freely. Due to this stiffness, mobility exercises need to be taken slowly and gently to encourage the spine to move and to regain its natural curve. When a flat back posture is identified, the pelvis is in a posterior tilt where the hip bones sit behind the level of the pubic bone causing the lumbar spine to lengthen. Those with flat backs will complain that they cannot get up and move well after sitting or sleeping but are fine once they have been up for a while. The flat back posture very often accompanies the kyphotic posture, so you may have identified your own posture falling into these two groups.

Problems
- Spine is fixed
- Lack of mobility, especially in extension
- Gluteal inhibition (weak buttocks)

Solutions
- Strengthen gluteals and abdominals
- Increase mobility and range of movement in area that is fixed
- Increase lordosis

Exercises
- Arm floats
- Standing heel raises
- Seated "c" curve
- Hamstring stretch
- Shoulder bridge
- Hip roll
- Abdominal preparation
- Side lying open door
- Swimming legs and arms
- Breast stroke preparation
- Swan dive
- All fours, cat's tail
- Shell stretch
- Monkey squat

The Five Basic Principles of Pilates

The five basic principles of Pilates educate you in how to hold the spine correctly during movement and will help to correct any imbalances that have been identified in your postural analysis.

These five principles are listed below:
1 Lateral (thoracic) breathing
2 Neutral pelvis
3 Rib cage placement
4 Scapula placement
5 Neck alignment

Lateral (Thoracic) Breathing

The power of breath

Breathing is one of our automatic functions that many take for granted and yet it is our primary source of energy. The way we breathe is mirrored in the way we live. Negative emotions can affect our breathing patterns and this has a knock-on effect on our posture. You may have noticed when you are stressed or worried that your chest begins to tighten and your breath becomes shallow and faster, increasing your heart rate. If we are calm, the breathing and the heart rate is slower as we take the air deeper toward the abdomen using the diaphragm. Focusing on your breathing helps to increase the oxygen flow and rids us of the carbon dioxide in the blood. It increases our lung capacity and circulation. If our breathing is impeded then the flow of oxygen slows down allowing toxins to build, gathering bacteria and causing congestion. Joseph Pilates realized the powerful connection between the mind and body and though we accept that the Eastern disciplines of yoga and t'ai chi use this in their own practice and have done for thousands of years, it was quite profound for a westerner to address this at the beginning of

the twentieth century for general exercise prescription. It is now becoming widely accepted that breathing exercises have profound results in improving our physiological and psychological well being.

When the breath is calm, your moves are smooth and the body is relaxed and free of tension.

Mastering lateral breathing

Lateral breathing in Pilates is probably the most difficult to master and you will hear people comment on this, that they just can't get it right, but it is really quite easy if you allow your breath to become natural. Most of the moves follow the natural rhythm of the body so it becomes logical to breathe in if we want to extend the spine and to breathe out when the body wants to flex.

Take a deep breath in and see what your body does. You will lift up when you breathe in and when you breathe out you relax.

As the principles of Pilates are on core stability we are using the deep lower abdomen muscles which prevent the breath from traveling down into the stomach. We are also

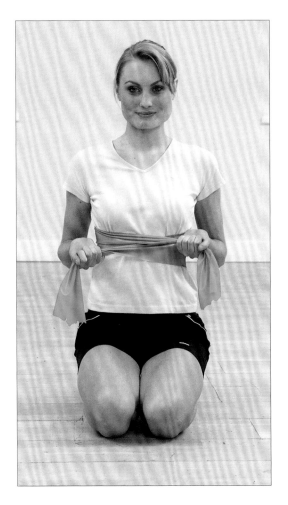
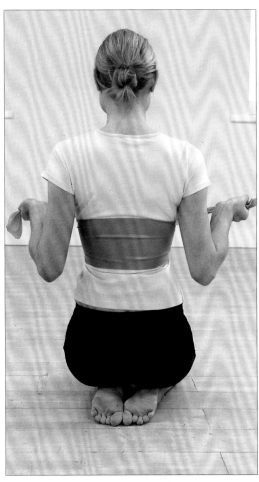

1   Place an exercise band or scarf around the rib cage as seen in the picture and cross it over in front. Have it wide across your back so you can feel it.

2   As you take a full breath in, take the breath into the band and feel it expand. The hands will come closer together as the band expands.

3   As you breathe out pull the band. You will feel the ribs close down and your hands will go further apart.

concentrating on shoulder stability, which prevents the breath from staying high in the chest. So if it can't go down and it can't stay up, where does it go? It has to go out, laterally using the expansion of the rib cage. Should that area of the body be a little stiff then it can take some time for the intercostals to regain their elasticity so don't despair if you find this part difficult to begin with, persevere and you will achieve results.

Opening up the ribs is essential for full and healthy breathing. Do this in front of the mirror and watch your shoulders. When you breathe in don't allow the shoulders to rise up. Direct the breath into the rib cage and let them expand like bellows.

Neutral Pelvis

Assessing the alignment of your pelvis used to be down to the expertise of a doctor or a gynaecologist. We are now able to assess this ourselves. If you look at the diagram below it

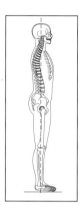

Neutral Posture

shows the neutral position where the hip bones, A.S.I.S. (anterior superior iliac spine) and the pubic bone are in a parallel line to one another. This means you will have a natural lordotic curve.

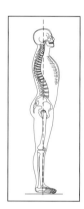

Anterior Tilt or Lordotic Posture

If however the pelvis is in an anterior tilt and the hip bones are forward of the pubic bone, this will increase the lordotic curve of the spine, placing pressure on the lumbar discs. If the hip bones are sitting

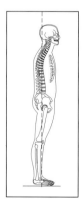

Posterior Tilt or Kyphotic Posture

behind the pubic bone in a posterior tilt, the curve is lost and this puts strain on the lumbar discs. So in order to maintain a healthy back it is imperative that we try to restore neutral alignment.

Finding a neutral pelvis

This can be done in a number of ways, but here are two ways to find a neutral pelvis.

Finding a neutral pelvis in a standing position

1 Stand with your feet parallel and hip width apart.
2 Keep your knees soft, not bent or locked out.
3 Keep your hands placed at the waist on top of the hip bones as if resting on top of a bucket of water.
4 Draw the shoulders down and keep the upper body still and stable.
5 Tilt the "bucket" to pour the water out of the front. You will feel your back arch creating an increase in the lordotic curve.
6 Now tilt the bucket back to pour the water out of the back so you now loosen the lordotic curve.
7 Continue with this a few times to feel the movement. You may be surprised at how small the move is when you don't allow the upper body to move. Shoulders stay still.
8 Bring the bucket to where you consider level. This will be your neutral pelvis.

Finding a Neutral Pelvis when Lying Down (supine)

In Pilates we are aiming all the time to isolate the area we are working. If we have tight or weak muscles anywhere then the body is very clever at cheating. It will recruit other muscles to assist, so by making the movement less we are able to focus on that area and determine whether we are cheating or not. It's ok to cheat as long as you know you're doing it. Then you can start learning how not to.

So ask yourself during this exercise: "Can I roll the marble forward and back without moving my head or shoulders?" If the answer is "Yes," then you're not cheating. If the answer is "No," make the move smaller until the answer becomes "Yes."

You may be surprised at how little movement you have when not cheating.

1 Lie with your feet parallel.
2 Keep your knees bent in line with your hip bones.
3 Place the heel of your hands on your hip bones, your fingers toward the pubic bone and thumbs toward the navel, forming the shape of a triangle.
4 Place an imaginary marble into the triangle and roll it toward the fingers, arching the back.
5 Now roll toward your thumbs and feel your back press into the mat. This is called imprinting.
6 Continue through those two ranges of movement.
7 Notice how much movement is going on in the upper body.
8 Bring your marble to the center of your triangle now. You should not be arching or imprinting. From the side, your hands should look level to the floor.

Rib Cage Placement

When we breathe, the ribs should move laterally like bellows which massage the internal organs. Unfortunately, more often than not when we breathe the breath goes either down into the abdomen or it stays high in the chest raising the shoulders. If our ribs are stiff, they will rise rather than expand causing the spine to extend. This in turn causes the pelvis to tilt placing pressure on the lumbar discs. Correct placement of the rib cage is therefore an essential element to the stability of the spine and correct alignment.

Rib cage placement while standing

1 Stand with your feet hip width apart.
2 Keep your knees soft and in line with your hip bones.
3 Your pelvis is in neutral.
4 Place your thumbs on your bottom rib.
5 Place your middle finger on your hip bone.
6 Draw your thumbs and ribs down toward your hips and fingers. (Your body will bend or flex forward.)
7 Open the distance between your thumbs and fingers. (Your body will extend and the back arch.)
8 Feel the movement coming from the rib cage.
9 Now stand upright and find a neutral pelvis. Find the gap between your ribs and hips and stay there for the correct rib cage placement.

Rib cage placement when lying down (supine)

1 Lie on your back with your knees bent.
2 Your feet are parallel in line with your knees and in line with the hips.
3 Keep your pelvis in neutral.
4 Place your hands on your ribs, your fingers touching.
5 Imagine your ribs are like butterfly wings. When you breathe in the wings open and when you breathe out the wings close.
6 If you find your bottom rib with your thumbs and your hip bones with your fingers, you will have a gap of about 4 inches (10cm).
7 Draw the ribs closer to the hips so the thumbs come closer to the fingers and your shoulders will want to lift off the floor. You are closing the gap and the body is beginning to flex.
8 If you expand the distance between your thumb and finger, the back will arch away from the floor and your ribs will flare.
9 Bring yourself back into a neutral pelvis position and just allow the ribs to soften down so the back is not over-arching nor imprinting.

Scapula Placement

The shoulder blades (scapula) should ideally lie flat against the rib cage. They move quite freely upward/downward/outward/inward and rotate and the muscles that are attached to them are key players in shoulder stabilization.

If you look at the numerous muscles listed below that directly effect the position of the scapula, you will appreciate the complexity of diagnosis when a shoulder problem occurs.

Mid fibers of Trapezius adduct and slightly elevate the scapula. Rhomboids also adduct the scapula. The Levator Scapulae works with the Trapezius to elevate and adduct. Serratus Anterior draws the scapula forward to sit against the ribs. The Deltoids abduct the shoulder. The Supraspinatus is attached to the spine too, which helps the Deltoid in abducting the arm, also attached to the spine of the scapula. Teres Major adducts and medially rotates the Humerus. It is attached to the bottom edge of the scapula. Subscapularis originates inside the surface of the scapula. Teres Minor originates at the edge of the scapula and it laterally rotates the Humerus.

In the event of any of these muscles becoming tight, short, or lengthened the scapula will be displaced.

Aligning the scapula

1 Stand in front of a mirror, feet hip-width apart.
2 Keep knees soft in line with hip bones.
3 Keep your pelvis in neutral.
4 Keep your arms by your side.
5 Shrug the shoulders up to the ears.
6 Draw shoulders down and away from the ears.
7 Repeat a couple of times to focus on the shoulder blades rather than the shoulders. Feel them move up in your back when you shrug and move down when you release.
8 Visualize the scapula moving down your back.

Look in the mirror and see where the arms are. Press the middle finger into your leg gently. Now draw the shoulder blades together as tightly as possible and you will notice your fingers will shift around the leg. This shows you that the position and movement of the scapula affects the position of the arms.

Draw the shoulder blades toward one another again but only slightly, and release. Keeping your shoulder blades moving down your back helps with shoulder stability and corrects faulty movement patterns in the upper body.

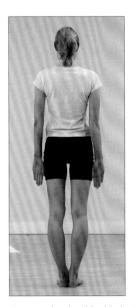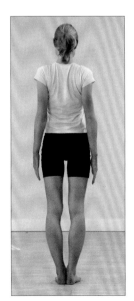

Squeeze the shoulder blades together.

Neck Alignment

The position of the head on top of the spine is extremely important. When correct the natural lordotic curve in the neck is present. The head weighs approximately 10–15lb (5kg), so if it is not centrally placed, the distribution through the first few vertebrae is doubled, sometimes tripled, causing overload and tension.

Ideally the head should sit centrally on top of the atlas, the first vertebrae, so the load can be evenly distributed down the spine.

Aligning the neck

1   Lie on your back with your knees bent.
2   Keep your feet in line with your knees and your knees in line with your hip bones.
3   Your pelvis is in neutral.
4   Your rib cage and scapula should be in correct alignment.
5   With your head resting on floor nod your chin toward your chest to create a double chin.
6   Slide your head back to look behind you.
7   Go through these two ranges of movement and stop where you feel the center is. Are you looking directly at the ceiling, or can you see more ceiling in front than behind or vice versa?
8   Use a towel or block under the head if you are looking at more ceiling behind than in front.
9   Think of holding a small peach under the chin to keep the alignment.
10   These learning procedures in alignment are exercises in their own right, so take your time to learn them.

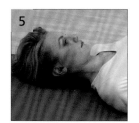

Head too far back.

Head too high.

Head in alignment.

Abdominal Muscles and Core Stability

Our abdominal muscles are made up of four groups. The Rectus Abdominus, the External Obliques, the Internal Obliques, and the Transverse Abdominus (TA). Out of those muscles, the ones we focus on in Pilates are the deep stabilizing muscles, which are the Transverse Abdominus and Internal Obliques. The Rectus Abdominus and External Obliques form the superficial muscles which sit on top.

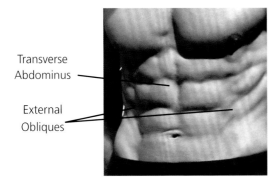

Transverse Abdominus

External Obliques

The Rectus Abdominus, when defined, gives the appearance of a "six pack" and the External Obliques allow us to twist and turn. Although these two superficial muscles are engaged when we perform any abdominal activity, the emphasis is concentrated on strengthening the Transverse Abdominus and the Internal Obliques. These two muscles form part of our internal corset along with the Multifidus muscles which sit close to the spine and our pelvic floor muscles, which are at the base of the torso and are explained in more detail a little further on.

The Transverse Abdominus working with other muscles to create an internal girdle, along with the movement of the diaphragm. These muscles when working optimally create a cylinder inside the body holding the organs and spine in place. This is known as abdominal hollowing. To learn how to do abdominal hollowing follow the exercises listed below. This can take time to master so look at doing this on a daily basis to begin with before starting your program.

Abdominal hollowing (standing)

1   Stand with your feet hip-width apart.
2   Keep your knees in line with the hip bones.
3   Take hold of the waist band of your shorts and pull them out in front of you.
4   Pull your abdominals in as tightly as you can, creating a big gap between yourself and your shorts. If you are pulling in as tightly as possible then it will be at 100 percent.
5   You will not be able to sustain this for very long so let it go.
6   Now pull in about 50 percent.
7   Now pull in at 25 percent. You know the muscle is switched on. Let go.
8   Now pull in again to 25 percent and continue breathing normally. Check every time you breathe out that you still have 25 percent engaged.

Initially try to do this up to 5 breaths until it becomes easier. Try this when standing, sitting, lying on your front, and on your back as you will be asked to do this when you come to learn the exercises. This is referred to throughout as tensing the Transverse Abdominus.

The Pelvic Floor Muscles

We all have pelvic floor muscles. They are attached to the inside of the pelvis and form a sling between the legs supporting our internal organs. The strength of these muscles is reduced in pregnancy and in obese individuals. The tone of the muscle also reduces as we get older. When the muscle is weak we can even experience incontinence when coughing or jumping. It is therefore important to regain control of the pelvic floor muscle and there is no age limit when this can be started. In Pilates we focus on this muscle while re-educating the other core stability muscles which form the internal corset.

Pelvic floor exercises

Learning how to use the pelvic floor again is an exercise in itself and should be performed as often as possible. Due to the fact it is an internal exercise, there should be no visible sign of you using it. To check the strength of your pelvic floor, next time you go to the bathroom, try and stop the flow of urine half way. The muscle you use to do this is the pelvic floor muscle. Try this exercise:

1 Lie on your back with your knees bent.
2 Relax the buttocks and the leg muscles.
3 Begin to tighten the muscle around the back passage as if you wanted to prevent flatulence.
4 Don't squeeze the buttocks, though.
5 Try to take this feeling now toward the front, the muscle you rely on when you need to prevent passing urine and there is no bathroom for miles.
6 Hold this for two breaths then relax.

The pelvic elevator

Think of the pelvic floor muscle as an elevator inside the body. When you engage the muscle the elevator comes up to the first floor. Hold it for at least one breath before relaxing back to the ground floor. As it gets stronger it will feel as if it is coming up to the second floor. Try not to let it drop back down, release it slowly.

Importance of working the pelvic floor

The exercise above helps us to work the pelvic floor slowly and with control—by doing this we are increasing the fibers known as slow twitch. These fibers increase the stamina within the muscle and help to sustain its strength. As we get older we are fighting against gravity and our internal organs are not exempt, they rely on the pelvic floor and core stabilizers to keep them in place.

If the muscle weakens the organs begin to drop and in severe cases cause prolapse and incontinence. The exercise above helps to strengthen the slow twitch fibers and assists in core strength.

We also have fast twitch fibers which we rely on in cases of emergency. For example, when we cough, sneeze, slip, or jump, the fast twitch fibres switch on to prevent us from passing urine or wind involuntarily. Therefore they too need conditioning.

To increase our fast twitch fibers we do the same kind of exercise as the pelvic elevator but quickly. Like a light switch, switching on, off, on, off.

The Ten Commandments of Set-up Positions

When starting any of the exercises you need to be in correct alignment. It is pointless executing an exercise if the body is incorrectly placed. You need to go through the ten command-ments listed below before you start an exercise in a new position. You will also find these instructions within the routines listed in the next section. This will become very automatic in time but it is important to follow the ten commandments every time you change position.

You can sit on a block with your knees bent to make sure the spine is neutrally aligned.

Alternatively you can cross your legs. The importance is that the spine is in its neutral position.

1 Keep your feet apart in line with your knees.
2 Keep your knees in line with your hip bones.
3 Your pelvis should be in its neutral position.
4 Engage the Transverse Abdominus.
5 Your rib cage is soft and down.
6 Keep your shoulders away from your ears, arms by your side. (When on "all fours" keep your hands directly under your shoulders and when on your side keep your arms at shoulder level.)
7 Your shoulder blades are down.
8 Keep your chin in and neck long.
9 Breathe in to prepare. Breathe out to move.
10 Your pelvic floor is engaged.

All these positions follow the ten commandments. These are your set positions before starting an exercise.

This is the full, seated set position.

Standing set position.

Side lying set 1 position.

Side lying set 2 position.

Prone set position.

Supine set position.

All fours set position.

Before You Start

You need to know before starting a new program if it is suitable for you. If you have any concerns regarding your medical condition, you need to consult your doctor and ask advice.

If you follow the guidelines and you are careful with any progressions then you will see great results.

Take time to read the basic principles and try them one by one initially as they are exercises in their own right. The workouts themselves won't work as effectively if the five basic principles are not in place.

Try to pick a time when you know you will not be disturbed. Maybe turn off your cell phone so you have no distractions. Ideally we want to work and learn in a peaceful environment where you can concentrate on what you're doing and more importantly what you're feeling.

Equipment Needed

You don't need a lot of equipment but having some basic essentials will make things easier for you.

Firstly, you need enough space to be able to lie on your back and have room to outstretch your legs. You also need room to extend your arms over your head and out to the side without having any obstacles in your way.

- A large bath towel or exercise mat to lie on. If using a towel, fold it over so you have some cushioning to support the whole back.
- A small towel to use under the head when needed.
- A long scarf or exercise band.

- A small soft ball or cushion.
- A yoga block or phone directory to sit on.
- Some peace and quiet. Take the phone off the hook and turn your cell phone to silent.
- Wear something comfortable so as not to restrict your movements as any tight clothing will be uncomfortable.
- It is nice to have some background music playing. Choose something relaxing and avoid having any music with vocals or a hard beat. Quiet music playing does help relax both the mind and the body.

Put aside a place for your equipment so it is handy each time you come to practice. If you put stuff away it is a great excuse not to do your routine but if it's out it reminds you. There are a variety of exercises and a number of ways to perform them. Although all of the exercises shown are at a beginners level, make sure to use them with discretion according to your condition.

20-Minute Workout – Ideal for Sway Back Posture Types

This routine is good for people who stand all day, such as shop assistants or hairdressers. It is good for those who are conscious of their height and slump and teenagers and models will also benefit from this routine.

This routine is as follows:

- Standing set position
- Standing heel raises
- Foot pedals
- Standing balance
- Arm floats
- All fours cat
- Breast stroke preparation
- Prone squeeze
- Shell stretch
- Hip roll
- Skull rock
- Abdominal preparation
- Single leg stretch
- Obliques
- Shoulder bridge
- Shoulder squeeze
- Monkey squat

Standing Set Position

Objectives: To develop good standing alignment and strengthen the trunk stabilizers to maintain good posture.

Start Position

- Standing set position.
- Feet apart in line with your knees.
- Knees in line with your hip bones.
- Pelvis in its neutral position.
- Transverse Abdominus slightly tensed.
- Rib cage soft and down.
- Shoulders away from the ears, arms by your side.
- Shoulder blades down and engaged.
- Chin down, neck long.
- Breathing in and out.
- Pelvic floor engaged.

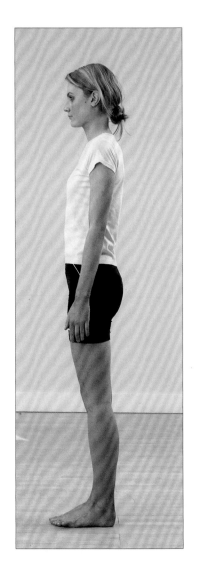

Standing Heel Raises

Objectives: To strengthen the Gluteal Medius muscle to help prevent the pelvis from tilting involuntarily when walking or climbing stairs. To strengthen and mobilize the ankles. To strengthen the core stabilizers. To prepare for the foot pedals and balance exercises.

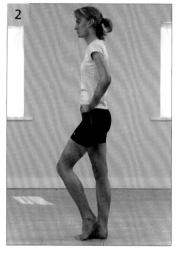

Start Position

- Standing set position.
- Feet apart in line with your knees.
- Knees in line with your hip bones.
- Pelvis in its neutral position.
- Transverse Abdominus slightly tensed.
- Rib cage soft and down.
- Shoulders away from the ears, arms by your side.
- Shoulder blades down and engaged.
- Chin down, neck long.
- Breathing in and out.
- Pelvic floor engaged.

Technique

1 Breathe in to prepare.
2 Breathe out to engage Transverse Abdominus and pelvic floor and raise the left heel away from the floor.
3 Breathe in to replace the foot down.
4 Breathe out to engage Transverse Abdominus and pelvic floor while you raise the right heel. To detect any involuntary movement in the pelvis, place the hands on the hips while you execute the moves. Your aim is to move without the pelvis rocking from side to side.
5 Breathing in to replace the foot down.

Repetitions

- 5–10 times

Hints & Tips

- Watch you don't shift your weight from one hip onto the other.
- Your weight distribution through the legs shouldn't change even as you lift the heels because the weight should just transfer into the ball of the foot.
- If you watch yourself in the mirror, you are aiming to see no movement within the body, just the legs.

Foot Pedals

Objectives: To strengthen the ankles and develop mobility. To strengthen the stability of the hips. To increase strength of the Gluteal Medius muscle, which helps to stabilize the pelvis.

Start Position

- Standing set position with arms either by your side or resting on the hips.

Technique

1 Breathe in to prepare.
2 Breathe out to engage the Transverse Abdominus and pelvic floor and raise the left heel.
3 Breathe in to engage the Transverse Abdominus and pelvic floor and raise the right heel to balance.
4 Breathe out to lower the left heel and bend the right knee, keeping the right heel up.
5 Breathe in to raise both heels to balance.
6 Breathe out to lower, keeping the left heel up.

Repetitions

- 5–10 times depending on the strength of the ankles.

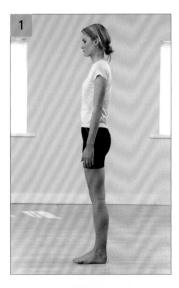

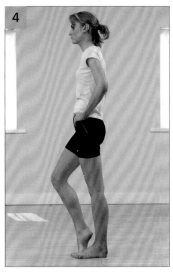

Hints & Tips

- Aim to go straight up and down rather than shifting from side to side.
- When the hands are resting on the hips, keep the shoulders relaxed and down.

Standing Balance

Objectives: To strengthen the ankles and develop mobility. To strengthen the stability of the hips. To increase strength of the Gluteal Medius muscle which helps to stabilize the pelvis.

Start Position
- Standing set position.

Technique
1 Breathe in to prepare.
2 Breathe out, engage Transverse Abdominus and pelvic floor and bring one foot off the floor, raising the knee toward 90 degrees.
3 Breathe in to replace the foot down.
4 Breathe out to engage Transverse Abdominus and pelvic floor and bring the other foot off the floor, raising knee toward 90 degrees.

Repetitions
- 5–10 times.

Hints & Tips
- Keep lifted out of the hip so as not to sink or slump into opposite side.
- Keep abdominals tight to prevent leaning back.
- Place hands on hips to check stability.

Arm Floats

Objectives: To strengthen shoulder stability. To mobilize the shoulder joint.

Start Position
- Standing set position.

Technique
1 Breathe in to prepare.
2 Breathe out to engage Transverse Abdominus and pelvic floor. Stabilize the shoulders and raise the arms, leading with the thumbs to shoulder level. Imagine you have helium balloons attached to the thumbs, so the arms float up and float down effortlessly.
3 Breathe in to return the arms down by your side.

Repetitions
- 5–10 times.

Hints & Tips
- Keep the shoulders down as the arms raise.
- Don't allow the ribs to flare or rise when lifting the arms.
- Keep the weight central in the feet and equally distributed.

All Fours Cat

Objectives: To strengthen all trunk stabilizers focusing mainly on shoulder stability. To develop core strength and to bone load the upper body, strengthen the spinal extensors, and encourage balance and strength.

Start Position

- All fours set position.
- Feet apart in line with your knees.
- Knees in line with your hip bones.
- Pelvis in its neutral position.
- Transverse Abdominus slightly tensed.
- Rib cage soft and down.
- Shoulders away from the ears, hands directly under the shoulders.
- Shoulder blades down and engaged.
- Chin down, neck long.
- Breathing in and out.
- Pelvic floor engaged.

Technique

1 Breathe in to prepare.
2 Breathe out to engage Transverse Abdominus and pelvic floor, tuck the tail bone down and drop the head to lift up from your center, tightening the abdominals.
3 Breathe in to send tail bone toward the ceiling, allowing the back to arch gently, keeping the shoulder blades down.
4 Breathe out to engage Transverse Abdominus and pelvic floor. Stabilize shoulders and return to the all fours set position.

Repetitions

- 5–10 times.

Shell Stretch

1 This helps to stretch out after the All Fours Cat. Breathe in to sit back toward the heels.
2 Breathe out to relax and release. Give the hands a shake out.

Breast Stroke Preparation

Objectives: To develop correct scapula stabilization by strengthening the postural muscles in the upper back. To strengthen postural fibers and develop thoracic extension. To lengthen the chest muscles and to strengthen the deep neck flexors.

Hints & Tips

- Keep the buttocks and legs relaxed throughout.
- Don't be tempted to just raise the head, initiate the movement from the shoulder blades.

Start Position

- Prone set position.
- Feet apart in line with your knees.
- Knees in line with your hip bones.
- Pelvis in its neutral position.
- Transverse Abdominus slightly tensed.
- Rib cage soft and down.
- Shoulders away from the ears, arms by your side.
- Shoulder blades down and engaged.
- Chin down, neck long.
- Breathing in and out.
- Pelvic floor engaged.

Technique

1 Breathe in to prepare. Watch that head alignment is correct when prone.
2 Breathe out, engage Transverse Abdominus and pelvic floor and draw the shoulder blades down into the back pockets. Lift the breast bone off the floor.
3 Breathe in.
4 Breathe out to release back to the floor.

Repetitions

- 5–10 times.

Note:

Pigeon toes (see below) can help to relax the gluteals (buttocks) and it can also help to eliminate the feeling of pinching in the lower back.

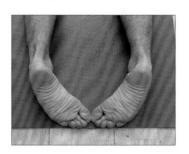

Prone Squeeze

Objectives: To strengthen the gluteal muscles (buttocks) and hamstrings. To strengthen core stability and develop hip mobility.

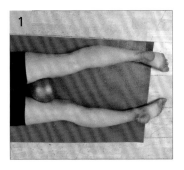

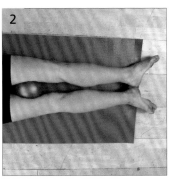

Start Position

- Prone with feet turned in (pigeon toes) and hands resting under forehead, shoulders stable.
- Place a soft ball or cushion between the top of the legs.

Technique

1 Breathe in to prepare.
2 Breathe out to engage Transverse Abdominus and pelvic floor. Bring heels together and squeeze ball between thighs.
3 Breathe in and allow heels to drop apart.

Repetitions

- 5–10 times

Hints & Tips

- The hip bones and the pubic bone stay down on the floor during the movement.
- The back stays stable and in neutral.
- Keep the shoulders relaxed and down.
- Maintain the pelvic floor lift on the squeeze.

Shell Stretch

Objectives: To stretch and release back extensors.

Technique

1 Breathe in and out while in this position, keeping the body relaxed.

Hints & Tips

- Knees can be quite far apart in order to get chest close to thighs.
- If you have any knee problems, roll onto back or side and hug knees into chest.

Hip Roll 1

Objectives: To mobilize the lumbar rotators of the spine. To strengthen the trunk stabilizers and the internal and external obliques. To develop core strength.

Start Position

- Supine set position with knees and feet together.

Technique

1 Breathe in to prepare.
2 Breathe out to engage Transverse Abdominus and pelvic floor.
3 Take the knees toward the right, turning the head toward the left.
4 Turn the left palm toward the floor to create stability in the shoulder leaving the right hand facing the ceiling.
5 Breathe in.
6 Breathe out to engage Transverse Abdominus and pelvic floor and bring the knees and head back to center. Focus on using the obliques in the waist when returning to center.
7 Repeat to the other side.

Repetitions

- 5–10 times.

Hints & Tips

- Keep shoulders down on the floor throughout.
- Don't take the legs too far to the side or the back will overextend causing the ribs to rise.

Hip Roll 2

Objectives: To lengthen and strengthen the obliques. To develop good rotation of the spine with segmental control. To promote awareness of the shoulder blades and to strengthen the shoulder stabilizers.

Start Position
- Supine set position.

Technique
1 Breathe in to prepare.
2 Breathe out to engage Transverse Abdominus and pelvic floor and raise one leg off the floor.
3 Breathe in to imprint the spine by pressing the low back gently toward the floor.
4 Breathe out to engage Transverse Abdominus and pelvic floor and raise the second leg without moving the spine.
5 Breathe in.
6 Breathe out, engage Transverse Abdominus and pelvic floor, and take knees to left and turn head to right.
7 Breathe in.
8 Breathe out to engage Transverse Abdominus and pelvic floor and return legs and head to center, focusing on using the obliques.

Hints & Tips
- You have to be careful that your alignment is kept in the spine and in the neck. This picture shows correct head alignment.
- Keep the awareness in the waist muscles which are initiating the movement on the return.

Repetitions
- 5 times on each side.

279

Skull Rock

Objectives: To lengthen the neck extensors (nape of neck) and strengthen the neck flexors (throat). Also relaxes fibers in Upper Trapezius around the neck and shoulders.

Start Position
- Supine set position.

Technique
1 Breathe in to prepare.
2 Breathe out to engage Transverse Abdominus and pelvic floor. Drop chin toward the chest.
3 Breathe in.
4 Breathe out to release head back to its natural placement.

Repetitions
- 5–10 times.

Hints & Tips
- Don't force the chin down—this is a small movement.
- Keep shoulders relaxed.

Abdominal Preparation

Objectives: To strengthen the Transverse Abdominus by maintaining abdominal hollowing while lifting the head. This exercise also strengthens the core, the shoulder stabilizers, and the deep neck flexors.

Modification

- If you suffer with neck or shoulder problems, do not lift head off the floor. Continue with everything else just omit the lifting of the head and shoulders.

Start Position

- Supine set position.

Technique

1. Breathe in to prepare.
2. Breathe out to engage Transverse Abdominus and pelvic floor.
3. Breathe in for skull rock.
4. Breathe out to slide the ribs toward the hips, hands toward the ankles. Raise the head and the shoulders and look toward the knees.
5. Breathe in to return.
6. Breathe out to release and relax.

Repetitions

- Start with 5 and build up to 10 as it can be very tiring on the neck muscles.

Hints & Tips

- Use the modification if you have any neck or shoulder problems.
- Don't raise the head and shoulders if the abdominals are doming.
- Buttocks stay relaxed.
- Pelvis stays in neutral.
- Don't forget to do the skull rock before lifting the head.

Single Leg Stretch 1

Objectives: To develop core strength. To strengthen trunk stabilizers and increase coordination skills.

Start Position

- Supine set position.

Techniques

1 Breathe in to prepare. Do skull rock.
2 Breathe out to engage Transverse Abdominus and pelvic floor. Raise one leg off the floor.
3 Breathe in.
4 Breathe out to engage Transverse Abdominus and pelvic floor. Raise the other leg.
5 Breathe in and take hold of the left leg gently.
6 Breathe out to engage Transverse Abdominus and pelvic floor as you extend the right leg away.
7 Breathe in as the leg returns toward the chest and you swap the hands over.
8 Breathe out to engage Transverse Abdominus and pelvic floor as you extend the left leg away.

Repetitions

- 5–10 times on each leg.

Hints & Tips

- The spine remains still and stable throughout the movement.
- Neck remains long and relaxed on the mat or your head support if using one.
- The abdominals are not to dome when the leg extends.
- The back stays down on the floor.

Single Leg Stretch 2

Start Position

- Supine set position.

Technique

1 Breathe in to prepare.
2 Breathe out to engage Transverse Abdominus and pelvic floor. Slide ribs to hips and raise head and shoulders to look toward the knees.
3 Breathe in to raise one leg off the floor.
4 Breathe out, engage Transverse Abdominus and pelvic floor and raise the other leg.
5 Breathe in to hold the left leg gently.
6 Breathe out to engage the Transverse Abdominus and pelvic floor as you extend the right leg away.
7 Breathe in as the leg returns toward the chest and swap the hands over.
8 Breathe out, engage Transverse Abdominus and pelvic floor as the right leg extends.

Repetitions

- 5–10 on each leg.

Hints & Tips

- Maintain neutral pelvis so the back does not arch or press down.
- If the neck begins to ache during the repetitions put it down but continue with the legs.

Obliques

Objectives: To strengthen the abdominals, focusing on the obliques (waist muscles). To develop core strength and strengthen trunk stabilizers.

Start Position
- Supine set position.

Technique
1 Breathe in to prepare.
2 Breathe in, taking the hands behind the head.
3 Breath out to engage Transverse Abdominus and pelvic floor. Rotate the body taking the left elbow toward the ceiling, with the right elbow toward the floor. The left shoulder comes toward the right hip, raising the shoulder blade away from the floor.

4 Breathe in to return to center.
5 Breathe out to engage Transverse Abdominus and pelvic floor. Rotate the body taking the right elbow toward the ceiling, with the left elbow toward the floor. The right shoulder comes toward the left hip, raising the right shoulder blade away from the floor.

6 Breathe in to return to center.

Repetitions
- 5–10 on each side.

Hints & Tips
- The elbows stay wide, chest open.
- The movement is initiated in the obliques.
- Keep it small so the internal obliques are targeted rather than the external ones.

Obliques with Single Leg Stretch

Objectives: To increase coordination and strength in the abdominals while maintaining pelvic stability.

Start Position

• Supine set position

Technique

1 Breathe in to prepare for skull rock.
2 Breathe out to engage Transverse Abdominus and pelvic floor. Slide ribs to hips and raise head off the floor to look toward the knees.
3 Breathe in to raise one leg off the floor.
4 Breathe out to maintain tension in Transverse Abdominus and pelvic floor and raise other leg off the floor.
5 Breathe in and take both hands behind the head.
6 Breathe out maintain Transverse Abdominus and pelvic floor as you extend the left leg away and rotate the left shoulder toward the right knee, maintaining neutral pelvis.
7 Breathe in to return to center, both knees in.
8 Breathe out to maintain Transverse Abdominus and pelvic floor. Extend the right leg away and rotate the right shoulder toward the left knee.
9 Breathe in to center.

Repetitions

• 5–10 times on each leg.

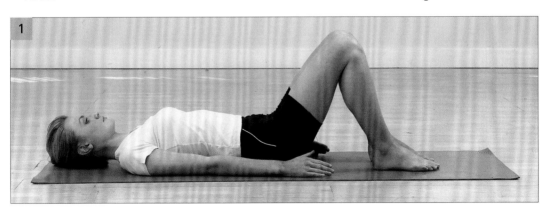

Hints & Tips

- Don't rock in the pelvis while rotating from one side to the other.
- Abdominals stay hollowed—no doming.
- Elbows stay wide, chest open.
- Don't pull on head or neck.

Note:

This exercise requires strong abdominals in order for it to be executed correctly.

Shoulder Bridge

Objectives: To improve segmental control of the spine to increase mobility. To develop core, strengthen gluteals and hamstrings, improve trunk stability, and lengthen hip flexors.

Start Position

- Supine set position. Feet a little closer to the buttocks than you would have them normally. If you have been using a block under your head in this position, take it away for this exercise only.

Technique

1 Breathe in to prepare.
2 Breathe out to engage Transverse Abdominus and pelvic floor. Tilt the pelvis.
3 Breathe in.
4 Breathe out to maintain Transverse Abdominus and pelvic floor. Squeeze the buttocks and lift off the floor, peeling one vertebra off at a time, lifting toward the shoulder blades.
5 Breathe in.
6 Breathe out to engage Transverse Abdominus and pelvic floor. Go down to the floor sequentially, returning the spine to neutral.

Repetitions

- Start with 5 and increase to 10.

Hints & Tips

- It is a slow exercise so take as many breaths as you need.
- Keep checking that the abdominals are hollowed and the pelvic floor engaged.
- Check the weight distribution between your feet to see if you are favoring one side at any time.
- Only ever go up as high as comfortable.
- Don't allow the ribs to flare as you get higher off the floor.

Shoulder Squeeze

Objectives: This exercise strengthens the middle fibers of the Trapezius to encourage scapula retraction. This helps to strengthen shoulder stability and the external rotators which help to keep good upper body posture and lengthen the chest muscles.

Start Position

- Standing set position.
- Feet apart in line with your knees.
- Knees in line with your hip bones.
- Pelvis in its neutral position.
- Transverse Abdominus slightly tensed.
- Rib cage soft and down.
- Shoulders away from the ears, arms by your side.
- Shoulder blades down and engaged.
- Chin down, neck long.
- Breathe in and out.
- Pelvic floor engaged.

Technique

1 Breathe in to prepare.
2 Breathe out to engage Transverse Abdominus and pelvic floor. Squeeze the shoulder blades toward one another and the arms and hands will rotate out.
3 Breathe in to relax the shoulder blades, allowing the arms to relax and hands face the body again.

Repetitions

- 5–10 times.

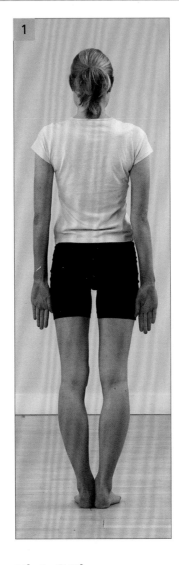
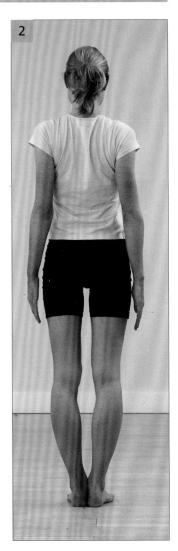

Hints & Tips

- Initiate the movement from the shoulder blades, don't just move the arms.
- Keep the rib cage down during the squeeze.
- Keep a good gap between ear and shoulder.

Monkey Squat

Objectives: To develop correct lifting skills by strengthening trunk stabilizers whilst bending. To strengthen the gluteal, legs, and ankles.

Start Position

• Standing set position.

Technique

1 Breathe in to prepare.
2 Breathe out to engage Transverse Abdominus and pelvic floor. Stabilize the shoulders. Hinge from the hips and bend the knees, taking the bottom back and hands toward the knees.
3 Raise the arms toward shoulder level.
4 Breathe in to return to standing.

Repetitions

• Start with 5 and progress to 10.

Hints & Tips

• Spine stays neutral.
• Bend at the knees not the waist.
• Keep shoulders in line with the hip.
• Keep arches lifted in feet.

20-Minute Workout – Ideal for Flat Backs

The exercises in this routine are designed for a flat back but can be beneficial if you sit for prolonged periods during the day or know that you tend to slouch when sitting. Stiffness in the low back is a problem with flat back postures and therefore extra care needs to be taken when trying to mobilize areas that are fixed.

This routine is as follows:
- Arm floats
- Standing heel raises
- Roll down
- Seated "c" curve
- Hamstring stretch
- Shoulder bridge
- Hip roll
- Abdominal preparation
- Side lying open door
- Swimming legs
- Swimming arms
- Breast stroke
- Swan dive
- Cat's tail

Arm Floats
See page 274.

Standing Heel Raises
See page 271.

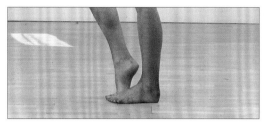

Roll Down 1

Objectives: The emphasis in this exercise is to increase the mobility of the spine in areas where it is fixed. It also strengthens the trunk stabilizers.

Start Position
- Standing set position.

Technique
1 Breathe in to prepare.
2 Breathe out to engage the Transverse Abdominus and pelvic floor. Drop the chin toward the chest.
3 Take the head and shoulders a little further down toward the shoulder blades.
4 Breathe in.
5 Breathe out to engage Transverse Abdominus and pelvic floor and start to restack the

spine back to standing.

Repetitions
- 5–10 times.

Hints & Tips
- At this level watch you don't hinge from the hips when taking the head and shoulders forward.
- Don't take it any further if you feel tension in the back.

Roll Down 2

Objectives: To increase the mobility of the spine in areas where it is fixed.

Start Position

• Standing set position.

Technique

1 Taking the roll down a little further, bending at the knees as you get further toward the floor, maintaining abdominal hollowing to support the lower back.
2 Position yourself chest to thigh, head to knee, and hands to the floor.
3 Breathe in.
4 Breathe out to start restacking the spine.
5 Move from the tail bone, sending it toward the floor as you stand.
6 Come back up to a full standing position.
7 Breathe in.

Repetitions

• 5–10 times.

Hints & Tips

• Don't hinge at the hips on roll down, bend the knees.
• Keep knees soft not locked out at any time.

Seated "C" Curve

Objectives: To strengthen the abdominals and develop core strength. To mobilize and strengthen the spinal muscles. To strengthen the shoulder stabilizers while sitting.

Start Position

- Seated set position.
- If slumping use a block.
- Legs crossed or knees bent and apart.
- Knees in line with your hip bones unless crossed.
- Pelvis in its neutral position.
- Transverse Abdominus slightly tensed.
- Rib cage soft and down.
- Shoulders away from the ears, hands resting on the knees.
- Shoulder blades down and engaged.
- Chin down, neck long.
- Breathing in and out.
- Pelvic floor engaged.

Hints & Tips

- Initiate the movement from the pelvis not the shoulders.
- The shoulders stay over the hips during the movement (ask someone to check or watch yourself side on in the mirror). There should be an imaginary line from the shoulder to side of hip when sitting upright and when in "c" curve.

Technique

1 Breathe in to prepare.
2 Breathe out to engage the Transverse Abdominus and pelvic floor, tilting the pelvis to create a "c" curve in the spine.
3 Breathe in to lift and return to neutral spine.

Repetitions

• Start with 5 and build up to 10 as this can be tiring on the hip flexors and spinal muscles.

Hamstring Stretch

Objectives: To lengthen the hamstrings, to develop core stability, and to strengthen trunk stability.

Start Position

- Supine position with one leg extended. Use an exercise band or long scarf around the extended leg.
- Shoulders relaxed and elbows down.

Technique

1 Breathe in to prepare.
2 Breathe out to engage Transverse Abdominus and pelvic floor and raise the leg slowly off the floor, maintaining neutral alignment in the spine and pelvis.
3 Breathe in and out for 3–5 breaths.
4 Breathe in.
5 Breathe out to engage Transverse Abdominus and pelvic floor and lower the leg to the floor.

Repetitions

- 3-5 on each leg.

Hints & Tips

- Keep the pelvis in its neutral position.
- Keep the buttocks on the floor.
- Shoulders relaxed.
- Chin tucked slightly in to keep length in the back of the neck.

Shoulder Bridge

Objectives: Segmental control of the spine to increase mobility. To develop core strength. To strengthen gluteals and hamstrings. To strengthen trunk stability.

Start Position

- Supine set position—feet a little closer to the buttocks than you would normally.
- If you have been using a block under your head in this position, take it away for this exercise only.

Technique

1 Breathe in to prepare.
2 Breathe out, engage Transverse Abdominus and pelvic floor, and tilt the pelvis into imprint.
3 Breathe in.
4 Breathe out, maintain Transverse Abdominus and pelvic floor. Squeeze the buttocks and lift off the floor, peeling one vertebrae off at a time, lifting toward the shoulder blades.

5 Breathe in.
6 Breathe out, maintain Transverse Abdominus and pelvic floor as you come down vertebrae by vertebrae, keeping the buttocks tight until they come back to the floor.

Repetitions

- Start with 5 and increase to 10.

Hints & Tips

- Keep checking that the abdominals are hollowed and the pelvic floor engaged.
- Check the weight distribution between your feet to see if you are favoring one side at any time.
- Only ever go up as high as comfortable.
- Keep knees in line during the lift.

Hip Roll 1

See page 278.

Abdominal Preparation

See page 281.

Side Lying Open Door 1

Objectives: To develop thoracic rotation. To strengthen shoulder stability. To stretch the chest muscle. To strengthen internal and external obliques.

Start Position

- Start in the side lying set position.
- Your feet are in line with your knees.
- Your knees in line with your hips.
- Your pelvis in its neutral position.
- Your rib cage is soft and down.
- Your shoulders are away from your ears.
- Your arms are out in front in line with your shoulders.
- Your shoulder blades are down.
- Tuck your chin in and keep your neck long.
- Breathe in and breathe out.
- Keep your pelvic floor engaged.

Technique

1 Breathe in to prepare.
2 Breathe out and engage the Transverse Abdominus and pelvic floor muscles and raise the arm toward the ceiling turning the head to follow the hand.
3 Breathe in to stay.
4 Breathe out to engage the Transverse Abdominus and pelvic floor muscles and close the arm following the hand with the head. The movement is in just the shoulder and head, and not the trunk.

Side Lying Open Door 2

Start Position
- The side lying set position.

Technique
1 Breathe in to prepare.
2 Breathe out, engage the Transverse Abdominus and pelvic floor muscles and raise the arm toward the ceiling, turning the head to follow the hand.
3 Breathe in, hold the position, and stabilize the shoulder by dropping it toward the floor.
4 Breathe out, maintain the engagement in the Transverse Abdominus and pelvic floor muscles, and twist from the waist to open the chest. Follow the hand with the head, keeping the knees together and the hips stacked.
5 Breathe in and hold the position.
6 Breathe out, engage the Transverse Abdominus and pelvic floor muscles, and twist from the waist to return the body to its side position and point the arm toward the ceiling.
7 Continue to close the arm up.

Repetitions
- 5 is all that is required if done correctly. Repeat the movement on the other side.

Hints & Tips
- Keep your hips and knees together during the movement to keep the pelvis in alignment.
- If you have stiffness in the neck watch you only go as far as you can, keeping the nose in line.
- Initiate the twist from the waist (oblique muscle) in both directions, not from the shoulders.

Swimming Legs

Objectives: To strengthen the gluteals and hamstrings. To develop core strength. To lengthen the hip flexors.

Start Position

- Start in the prone set position, supporting your head with your hands.
- Keep your feet apart in line with your knees.
- Your knees are in line with your hips.
- Your pelvis is in a neutral position.
- Engage the Transverse Abdominus muscles.
- Your rib cage is soft and down.
- Your shoulders are away from the ears, hands under the forehead.
- Your shoulder blades are down and engaged.
- Tuck your chin in to keep the neck long.
- Breathe in and breathe out.
- Engage the pelvic floor muscles.

Technique

1 Breathe in to prepare.
2 Breathe out, engage the Transverse Abdominus and pelvic floor muscles, lengthen the legs, and raise one leg off the floor keeping the legs long.
3 Breathe in to return the leg to the floor.
4 Breathe out to engage the Transverse Abdominus and pelvic floor muscles, lengthen the legs and raise the other leg off the floor.
5 Breathe in to return the leg to the floor.

Repetitions

- 5 times with each leg.

Hints & Tips

- Keep both hip bones and the pubic bone on the floor as you lift the legs.
- Watch you don't tense up in the shoulders
- Don't bend the knees, keep lengthening away.

Swimming Arms

Objectives: To develop coordination of upper and lower body. To strengthen shoulder stabilizers. To develop good scapula placement.

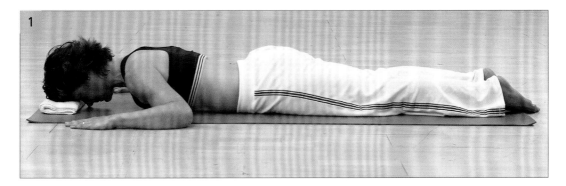

Start Position

- Start in the prone set position, with your arms in the "W" position (or with your arms by your side if the "W" causes tension in the shoulders).

Technique

1 Breathe in to prepare.
2 Breathe out, engage the Transverse Abdominus and pelvic floor muscles, and raise one leg off the floor, at the same time raising the opposite arm just off the floor, but not too high.
3 Breathe in to lower the leg and arm.
4 Breathe out, maintaining the engagement in the Transverse Abdominus and pelvic floor muscles, and raise the opposite arm to leg.
5 Breathe in to return.

Repetitions

- 5 times on each side.

Hints & Tips

- The movement of the arms is initiated by moving the spine.
- Bring the elbows back to the floor each time.
- If your elbows do not come to the floor, place the arms by your side.

Breast Stroke

Objectives: To strengthen the postural muscles in the mid back for thoracic extension. To educate the scapula to fall into the correct placement. To strengthen the deep neck flexors.

Start Position

- Start in the prone set position. If you try this exercise and find you have an increase of pain or discomfort then do the first three steps of the exercise only and omit the lift of the breast bone.

Technique

1 Breathe in to prepare.
2 Breathe out, engage the Transverse Abdominus and pelvic floor muscles, and draw the shoulder blades down and together. Raise the arms just off the floor externally rotating at the shoulder so the palms face one another. At this stage the head stays down.
3 If you have decided not to take this any further then release the shoulders back to the floor on an in breath, raising and stabilizing the arms in an out breath and repeating this 5–10 times. Make it an effortless movement.

4 Breathe in to slide the shoulder blades further down the back, raising the breast bone just off the floor, keeping the head in alignment with the shoulders, and maintain the engagement in the Transverse Abdominus muscles.
5 Breathe out to lower the breast bone to the floor.

Hints & Tips

- Watch that the head rest is not too high or too low. Your nose needs to be pointing down.
- Don't lift too high; the essence is on thoracic extension not lumbar.
- Keep the buttocks and legs relaxed. If you can't relax them, try placing the feet in the pigeon-toed position, which helps to disengage the activity in those areas.

Repetitions

- 5-10 times.

Swan Dive

Objectives: To develop full spinal extension, to mobilize the lumbar spine, and to develop strength and stability in the shoulders.

Start Position

- Start in the prone set position, with the arms in the "W" position.

Technique

1 Breathe in to prepare.
2 Breathe out, engage the Transverse Abdominus and pelvic floor muscles, slide the shoulder blades down the back, and raise the breast bone off the floor, keeping the elbows down.
3 Breathe in to lift a little higher off the floor, raising the elbows, lengthening the arms, and extending the spine.
4 Breathe out, maintaining the engagement in the Transverse Abdominus and pelvic floor muscles, return onto the elbows. Keep your head up.
5 Breathe in, draw the shoulder blades down the back, and lift up through the spine.

Repetitions

- 5–10 times.

(*Continued on page 304*)

Hints & Tips

- Your elbows stay in toward the body and do not flare out.
- Your shoulders stay down away from the ears.
- Don't over extend or push higher than is comfortable.
- Keep your pubic bone down on the floor. The pictures actually show the pubic bone off the floor, which can happen easily if you have upper body strength but are inflexible in the lumbar spine. This is typical of the flatback posture, where the lower back is stiff.

Cat's Tail

Objectives: To strengthen all trunk stabilizers focusing mainly on shoulder stability. To develop core strength. To strengthen the spinal extensors. To develop balance and strength.

Technique

1 Breathe in to prepare.
2 Breathe out to engage the Transverse Abdominus and pelvic floor muscles, tucking the tail bone under (like a cat's tail going between its legs), and keeping the upper back stable and still.
3 Breathe in to return to the all fours set position.

Repetitions

- 5–10 times.

Hints & Tips

- Maybe do this one alongside a mirror and watch your upper back.
- Placing a small ball on your upper back can help with the awareness of the movement. It will focus your attention straight away.
- Breathe in to sit back toward the heels into a shell stretch, after the movement (as below).
- Breathe out to relax and release. Give the hands a shake out.

Start Position

- Start in the all fours set position.
- Your feet are apart in line with your knees.
- Your knees are in line with your hip bones.
- Your pelvis is in its neutral position.
- Engage the Transverse Abdominus muscles.
- Your rib cage is soft and down.
- Your shoulders are away from the ears and your hands are under the shoulders.
- Move your shoulder blades down your back.
- Tuck your chin in to keep the neck long.
- Breathe in and breathe out.
- The pelvic floor is engaged.

Yoga

Mental attitude

Approach your yoga practice with a smile. You know you are going to feel better the moment you start. Remember it's fun and makes you feel good.

The practice of yama and niyama (physical and mental conduct) enable us to approach our practice with grace and equanimity. Think of practicing as a time to pamper yourself physically and mentally.

Be gentle, kind, and patient with yourself as you learn new ways of thinking and responding.

Praise yourself. Criticism breaks down our inner spirit, praise builds it up. Tell yourself how well you are doing. Accept yourself as you are. Refuse to criticize yourself. Everybody changes. When you criticize yourself, your changes are negative, when you approve of yourself, your changes are positive.

Do not terrorize yourself with your thoughts, it is a terrible way to live. Find a mental picture that gives you pleasure and immediately switch your scary thought to a pleasurable thought. Plant your own garden and cultivate your soul, instead of waiting for someone to bring you flowers. As you progress, you will find the practice of yoga begins to take you away from the body image or how fat or thin you are. Your attitude changes to "How do I feel?" not "How do I look?"

As we become accustomed to feeling toned from the inside, we consciously choose foods and a lifestyle that promote this feeling of well-being. Yoga produces a feeling of lightness and vitality. This is experienced in the mind also. As we learn to let go and release physical and psychosomatic tension, we recognize that our thoughts and attitudes make our life what it is. As the Buddha said:

We are our thoughts.
Everything we do arises with our thoughts.
With our thoughts
We make our world.

So if you want to change yourself and your world, change your thoughts. Think of light. Think of love.

Breathing

It has been said that a man counts his life in years, a yogi in the amount of breaths he takes. The breath, postures, and emotions are linked. Listen to your breathing. Is it smooth, deep, and rhythmic? Or is it short, shallow, and ragged? Deep, rhythmic breathing produces vitality and the ability to think clearly. Short, shallow breathing brings tension, anxiety, and irritability. With practice we learn to observe our breath and the changes that occur in breathing; whether we are active or still, tense or relaxed, happy or sad.

Recognizing these feelings, emotions, and tensions, we learn to consciously relax and let go of negative emotions and embrace a positive approach to life. The breath, its rhythm and depth, is the focus of our attention. No complicated routines are necessary for this. Listening to your breath automatically detaches you from the worries and the anxieties of your mind. When your breath is calm, your mind is calm also. When your mind is calm, your body responds by moving gracefully.

Sit cross-legged for breathing exercises.

When we first start listening to the breath, we become aware of the sound and quality of our breath. Then we become aware of the rise of the chest as we inhale, the fall of our chest as we exhale. We can imagine our lungs to be like a pair of balloons; when we breathe in the lungs expand and fill, when we breathe out, the lungs contract and empty.

Our breathing becomes quieter as we realize that listening to the breath is in reality an internal listening. It's not about how quiet or noisy our breath is. It's more a connection made to how you really are at this moment in time. Not how you look or how you feel.

Sometimes, when looking introspectively, we experience feelings of sadness, frustration, and anger. This is normal. The trick is not to hang on to these feelings. Breathe these negative anxieties out.

Preparation for Practice

The yoga postures can be modified and adapted to suit your needs and environment. The postures teach us to know ourselves, our limitations, our strengths, and our weaknesses. Recognizing these traits, learning to accept them, instead of fighting them, helps us to achieve perfect equilibrium and to be at peace with ourselves and our environment.

However you must find an experienced teacher who will guide you. It is important that you always inform your teacher of any injuries, illness, or disabilities. It is a good idea to commit your medical history to paper, so you can give your teacher the information needed to help you. Writing things down in a letter can avoid embarrassment in a class. Not everyone wants the whole class to know of their problems.

If you have any type of health issue, including pregnancy, you must seek your medical practitioner's consent before trying out the postures. If your doctor is unsure about yoga movements, take this book with you, emphasizing there is no strain or stress and you will be moving at your own pace. The most important things to remember are:

- Yoga should be practiced on an empty stomach, with a three-hour break from eating food. Early morning is an ideal time.
- Clothing should be loose, comfortable, and lightweight.
- You will need a yoga mat to practice on. You can use a towel or blanket, but a sticky yoga mat is best.
- Find the optimum place to practice. The room should be warm, light, and quiet.
- Make sure you will not be disturbed. Your family and friends need to get used to the idea that when you are practicing, it's time out.

It's important to remember that yoga is for all ages and all sizes, endomorphs and ectomorphs alike.

Yoga can be practiced during most weeks of pregnancy, but ask your doctor for advice.

- Try and practice at the same time every day so you can get into a routine.
- Approach yoga with grace and ease.

Mothers with young children may find it difficult to practice without distractions, but you have to find the time and place to make it happen. Many people prefer to practice in the evening. In which case you must make sure your evening meal is completely digested (three hours). Include a good relaxation (at least ten minutes) at the end of the practice so you can sleep well and you are not fired up, as if you had been doing an aerobic activity.

Whatever time of day you choose to practice, it is paramount that you begin with the Complete Breath and finish with the Closing Breath. This gives us a very definite feeling of beginning and ending.

Follow instructions carefully, especially as a beginner. Know your sequence before you begin, even if it means having these written down nearby. Do not start your practice and make it up as you go along. Follow the instructions in this section and then practice and make perfect.

How to use this section

Read the instructions carefully until you are familiar with them. You may like to practice with a friend who can read the instructions out to you.

Following the breath is paramount. As you read the instructions, follow the breath and imagine yourself performing the pose. This is a great way to prepare for practice.

In time you will find you want to know more and more about yoga. On first reading this section you may find some parts too heavy or irrelevant to your needs. But with time you will be looking for more information. What may have passed you by as relatively meaningless six months ago could now be an integral part of your practice.

Practice, enjoy, and be at peace.

Before you begin

Make sure:
- The room you are practicing in is warm and light.
- You have not eaten for at least three hours.
- You have a yoga mat, or towel to practice on.
- You are wearing loose, comfortable clothing.
- You will not be disturbed.
- You have a chair or strong table near, for the modified poses.
- You are committed to a minimum of twenty minutes practice.
- You decide which sequence or postures you are going to practice.

The Postures

Mountain Pose (tadasana)

Standing still as a mountain, steady and secure. Encourages an energizing breathing pattern.

Method

1 Stand with your feet hip width apart.
2 Keep your eyes forward, spine erect, and arms by your sides.

3 Distribute your weight evenly along the length of your feet.
4 Listen to your breathing.
5 Breathe in, fill, and expand your lungs.
6 Breathe out, contract, and empty your lungs.
7 Make at least four complete breaths, until your breathing becomes smooth and rhythmic.
8 Tune into the rhythm of your breath. Focus your attention on your breath.
9 Become aware of the rise of your chest as you breathe in, the fall of your chest as you breathe out.

Benefits

- Masters the art of standing correctly, in correct alignment.
- Develops stability and awareness of posture.
- Provides a foundation from which other postures are developed.
- Corrects imbalances in the posture, breath, and flow of energy.
- Calms the breath.

Precautions

- Don't tense your spine. The knees should be soft, not locked.

Complete Breath

Helps to harmonize the breath and movement. Energizes the body and mind.

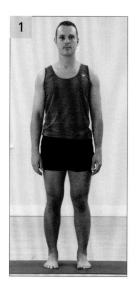

Method

1 Stand in Mountain Pose.
2 Breathe in and out.
3 Breathe in, raise your arms to shoulder level.
4 Breathe out, turn your palms to the sky.
5 Breathe in, raise your arms above your head, palms facing each other.
6 Breathe out, lower you arms to your sides.
7 Allow your breath to guide your movements.
8 Repeat four times.

Benefits

• Energizes the entire system, overcoming fatigue.
• Increases the intake of oxygen, resulting in clarity of mind and a healthy, glowing complexion.

Precautions

• Don't force your breath.
• Remember, the movement follows your breath.

Refresher Breath/Moon Pose

Encourages the mind and body to relax.

Method

1 Stand in Mountain Pose.
2 Breathe in and out.
3 Breathe in.
4 Breathe out, bend your knees.
5 Breathe in.

6 Breathe out. Let your chin fall toward your chest.

7 Breathe in.

8 Breathe out and let your body fold forward, bending at the hips, and relaxing toward the floor.

9 Breathe in. Look between your thighs.

10 Breathe out.

11 Breathe in and out.

12 Breathe in. Slowly uncurl, vertebra by vertebra. Come up to standing. Your head comes up last.

13 Breathe out. Keep your eyes forward.

14 Repeat four times.

15 The movement follows your breath.

Benefits

- Gently stretches the lower back and the back of the legs.
- Relaxes the neck, shoulders, arms, and hands.
- Blood flows into the head to refresh and revitalize.

Precautions

- Only relax forward as far as you comfortably can. There should be no pain.
- Avoid this pose if you suffer from high blood pressure, heart disease, glaucoma, detached retina, or back pain.

Abdominal Lift

Drawing the belly towards your spine. Slims and tones the whole of the abdominal area. Stimulates the fire energy.

Method

1 Stand in Mountain Pose
2 Breathe in and out.
3 Breathe in.
4 Breathe out. Bend your knees.
5 Breathe in.

6 Breathe out. Lean forwards, place your palms onto your thighs.
7 Gently rounding your back, keep your elbows away from your sides.
8 Breathe in and fill your lungs.

14

9 Breathe out. Draw your belly towards your spine.
10 Squeeze your ribs together.
11 Draw your belly inward and upward.
12 Look between your thighs.
13 Hold the pose, then relax your belly.
14 Come up to standing with your spine erect and eyes forward. Breathe in.
15 Breathe out and bring your arms to your sides.
16 Repeat four times, then breathe easy.

Benefits

- Tones and slims the abdominal area. The waist becomes slimmer.
- Helps to tighten up the pelvic floor.
- Increases strength and flexibility in the abdomen.
- Helps eliminate toxins in the digestive tract.
- Increases awareness of the movement of the diaphragm as we breathe in and out.
- Increases the quality of the breath.

Precautions

- Don't force your breath.
- Avoid this posture if you are menstruating, have inflammation in the abdominal areas, or high blood pressure.

Sun Salutation Standing

Opens energy centers and improves the posture. A harmony in breath and movement.

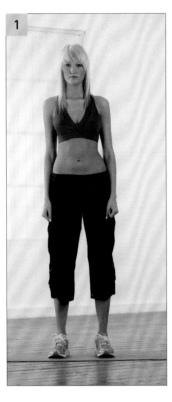

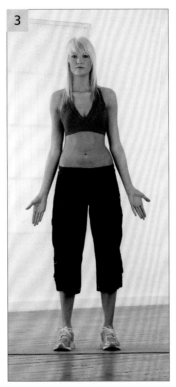

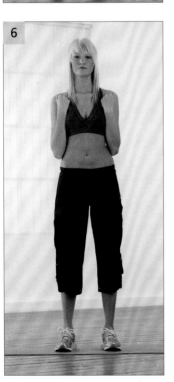

Method

1 Stand in Mountain Pose.
2 Breathe in and out.
3 Breathe in. Turn your palms to face the front.
4 Breathe out.
5 Breathe in. Lightly clench your hands into fists.
6 Breathe out. Raise your fists to your shoulders.
7 Breathe in. Raise your elbows.
8 Breathe out and stretch out your arms in front of you, keeping them at shoulder level.
9 Breathe in. Raise your hands, keeping your elbows at shoulder level.
10 Breathe out. Turn your palms to face each other.
11 Breathe in and turn your palms to face forward.
12 Breathe out. Turn your palms to face each other.

13 Breathe in and lightly clench your hands.
14 Breathe out and stretch out your arms in front of you, keeping them at shoulder level.
15 Breathe in. Bring your fists in to your shoulders.
16 Breathe out. Lower your elbows.
17 Breathe in. Lower your arms.
18 Breathe out. Open your palms.
19 Breathe normally in Mountain Pose.

Benefits

- Encourages a deep, rhythmic breathing pattern.
- Opens and stimulates energy centers that are connected to the healthy functioning of the internal organs.
- Increases vitality and aids concentration.
- Helps calm the emotions.

Precautions

- Take your time and do not rush this posture. Keep your shoulders away from your ears (i.e. not hunched up).
- Follow the natural rhythm of your breath.

Standing Forward Bend

A pose where you bring your hands to your feet or ankles. It helps clear and calm the mind.

Method

1. Stand in Mountain Pose.
2. Breathe in and out.
3. Breathe in. Raise your arms to shoulder level.
4. Breathe out. Place your hands on your hips.
5. Breathe in. Lift up through your waist.

6 Breathe out. Relax forwards, bending and rolling over the hips. Leading out with the chest, then chin, nose, eyes, forehead, and the top of your head toward the floor. Look between your thighs.

7 Breathe in.

8 Breathe out. Slide your hands down your legs, elbows bent, resting your hands on your legs, where you can hold the pose comfortably. Hold the pose.

9 Breathe in and out three times.

10 Breathe in. Look forward.

11 Breathe out. Place your hands onto your hips.

12 Breathe in. Lift up through your waist.

13 Come up to standing with your eyes forward and spine erect.

14 Breathe out and bring your arms to your sides.

15 Repeat four times.

16 Breathe normally.

Benefits

- Slims and firms the arms, waist, abdomen, buttocks, and legs.
- Promotes a youthful vigor.
- Lengthens the spine, increasing its flexibility.
- Stretches all the muscles of the back of the body.
- Creates a foundation from which other forward bends are developed.
- Can correct a small imbalance in the length of the legs.
- Aids concentration.
- Invigorates the entire nervous system.
- Increases the circulation to the legs, torso, and brain.
- Massages the internal organs.

Precautions

- Avoid this posture if you suffer from high blood pressure.
- If your hamstrings are tight, do not cause yourself discomfort or pain.
- If you have a slipped disk, do not do it. Accept your body's limitations.
- Keep your weight in the front of your feet, do not push into your heels.

Standing Back Bend

By arching your spine in the opposite direction this posture acts as a contrapose to the forward bends described earlier.

Method

1 Stand in Mountain Pose.
2 Breathe in and out.
3 Breathe in. Raise your arms at your sides to shoulder level.

4 Breathe out. Place your hands on your hips.

5 Breathe in. Lift up through your waist.

6 Breathe out. Gently arch your spine. Raising your chest to the ceiling, eyes to the ceiling also.

7 Breathe in and out three times.

8 Breathe in.

9 Breathe out. Lower your chest, face, and eyes.

10 Breathe in. Keep your eyes forward and your spine erect.

11 Breathe out. Lower your arms to your sides.

12 Breathe normally. Be aware of tension, release it and let it go.

Benefits

- Releases tension in the lower back.
- Helps to slim the waist.
- Tones and stretches the neck and refreshes the face.
- Strengthens the spine and increases the flexibility of the spine.

Precautions

- Only go as far as is comfortable. If in doubt, leave it out.

Triangle Pose (trikonasana)

Extend to the right and left in this pose. Triangle Pose helps to tone, slim, and shape the waist and legs. It builds strength and flexibility in the legs.

Method

1 Stand in Mountain Pose.
2 Breathe normally.
3 Walk your feet, double hip width apart. Keep your feet parallel and your eyes forward.
4 Breathe in and out.
5 Breathe in. Raise your arms to shoulder level.
6 Breathe out. Turn your left foot inward 45 degrees. Your left big toe points toward your right big toe.
7 Breathe in. Turn your right foot 90 degrees to the right.

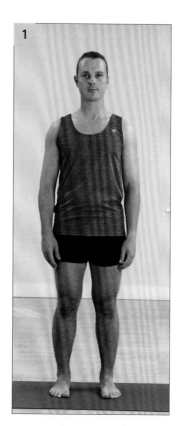

8   Breathe out. Relax. Check your pose for comfort and ease.

9   Breathe in. Lift up through the waist. Reach out to the right.

10 Breathe out. Bend to the right, placing your hand on the outside of your lower leg.

11 Breathe in. Look up toward your raised hand.

12 Breathe out. Extend your raised arm to the sky. Hold the pose.

13 Breathe in and out three times.

14 Breathe in. Lift up through your waist, come up to standing, keeping your arms parallel to the floor and your spine erect.

15 Breathe out and move your arms to your sides. Breathe in. Turn your feet back to face the front.
16 Breathe out. Keep your eyes forward.
17 Breathe in and out
18 Repeat to the opposite side.
19 Walk your feet back to hip width apart.
20 Stand in Mountain Pose.
21 Breathe normally.

Benefits

- Stretches, slims, and tones the waist, hips, and thighs.
- An invigorating stretch which makes the whole body feel lighter.
- Stimulates the circulation.
- Opens and develops the chest, building strength and stamina.
- Increases flexibility.
- Aids digestion and helps regulate the appetite.

Precautions

- Only go as far as you comfortably can. If you have back problems, place your hand on your thigh and not on your lower leg.
- If you have neck problems, do not turn your head to look at your raised hand and keep your eyes looking forward.
- Do not overstretch, it will work against you.
- Do not bend your raised arm.
- Distribute your weight evenly, between each leg and foot.
- Do not sink into your hips.

Legs Wide Forward Bend (prasarita padottanasana)

This pose will significantly stretch the legs and is expanding, extending, and rejuvenating.

Method

1 Stand in Mountain Pose.
2 Breathe easy.
3 Walk your feet to double hip width apart.
4 Keep your feet parallel and your eyes forward.
5 Breathe in and out.
6 Breathe in. Raise your arms to shoulder level.
7 Breathe out. Place your hands on your hips.
8 Breathe in. Lift up through your waist.
9 Breathe out. Bend at your hips. Reach forward and relax downward with the top of your head toward the floor. Look between your thighs.
10 Breathe in. Place your palms flat on the floor with your fingers parallel to your toes.
11 Breathe out. Let the top of your head relax toward the floor. Breathe in and out three times.
12 Breathe in. Look forward.
13 Breathe out. Move your hands onto your hips.
14 Breathe in. Lift up through your waist, come up to standing with your eyes forward and spine erect.
15 Breathe out and bring your arms to your sides.
16 Breathe normally.

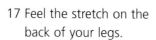

17 Feel the stretch on the back of your legs.
18 Walk your feet back to hip width apart.
19 Stand in Mountain Pose.

Benefits

- Tones and firms the back of the legs and especially the thighs
- Increases the flow of blood to the brain.
- Relieves headaches, anxiety, irritability, and insomnia
- Aids the digestive process.

Precautions

- For those with back problems, keep your knees bent.
- Not suitable for those with a heart condition, high blood pressure, detached retina, or glaucoma.
- Keep legs firm and backs of knees soft.

Warrior Pose (virabhadrasana)

This is a very dynamic posture that tones, slims, and strengthens nearly all parts of the body. It cultivates a strong body and healthy mind.

Method

1 Stand in Mountain Pose.
2 Breathe normally.

3 Walk your feet double hip width apart, with your feet parallel and your eyes forward.

4 Breathe in and out.
5 Breathe in. Raise your arms to shoulder level.
6 Breathe out. Imagine your arms resting on clouds.
7 Breathe in. Turn your right foot 90 degrees away from you.
8 Breathe out. Bend your right knee, so that the knee is directly above your toes.
9 Breathe in. Look along the fingertips of your right hand.
10 Open your chest.
11 Extend out through your fingertips.
12 Breathe out. Press the outside edge of your back foot flat to the floor.
13 Breathe in and out three times.
14 Breathe in. Straighten your right leg.
15 Breathe out. Turn your right foot back to face the front.
16 Move your arms to your sides.
17 Breathe normally.
18 Repeat to your left side.
19 Feel your inner strength and balance.
20 Walk your feet back to hip width apart. Stand in Mountain Pose.

Closing Breath

This posture helps to finish the sequence by closing down the energy centers.

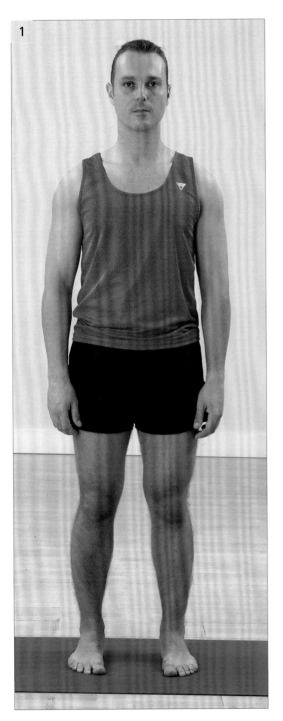

Method

1 Start from Mountain Pose.
2 Breathe in and out.
3 Breathe in. Raise your arms above your head. Arms straight, elbows soft.
4 Place your palms together above your head.

5 Breathe out. Lower your palms to your chest.
6 Then move your arms to your sides.
7 Breathe in. Raise your arms above your head. Palms together.
8 Breathe out. Lower your palms to your chest, breathing out with a big sigh.
9 Move your arms to your sides.
10 Breathe in. Raise your arms above your head.
11 Place your palms together.

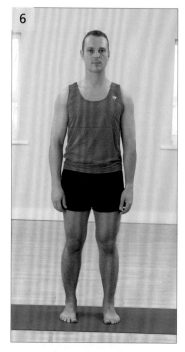

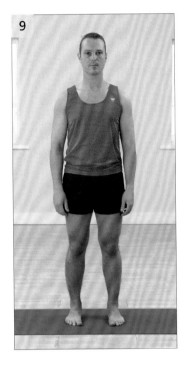

12 Breathe out. Lower your palms to your chest.

13 Breathe in. Bring your feet together.

14 Breathe out. Look forward, take a small bow.

15 Breathe in. Take your feet back to hip width apart.

16 Breathe out. Bring your arms to your sides and keep your eyes forward. Keep your spine erect.

17 Stand in Mountain Pose.

18 Breathe calmly.

Benefits.

- Closes down the energy centers. Energy is within us, stored for when we need it.
- Gives a feeling of closure to the sequence.
- Creates a feeling of calm and well-being.

Precautions

- Do not overstretch.
- Keep your focus and don't rush.

20-Minute Sequences

Sequence 1

1 Mountain Pose (4 breaths)

(See page 310)

2 Complete Breath (x1)

(See page 311)

3 Refresher Breath (x1)

(See page 313)

4 Abdominal Lift (x1)

(See page 316)

5 Sun Salutation (x1)

(See page 319)

6 Standing Forward Bend (x2)

(See page 324)

7 Standing Back Bend (x1)
(See page 328)

8 Triangle Pose, both sides (x1)
(See page 331)

9 Wide Legs Forward Bend (x2)
(See page 335)

10 Standing Back Bend (x1)
(See page 328)

11 Mountain Pose (4 breaths)
(See page 310)

12 Closing Breath
(See page 340)

Sequence 2

1 Mountain Pose (4 breaths)

(See page 310)

2 Complete Breath (x1)

(See page 311)

3 Refresher Breath (x1)

(See page 313)

4 Abdominal Lift (x1)

(See page 316)

5 Sun Salutation (x1)

(See page 319)

6 Standing Forward Bend (x2)

(See page 324)

7 Standing Back Bend (x1)

(See page 328)

8 Triangle Pose, both sides (x1)

(See page 331)

9 Wide Legs Forward Bend (x2)

(See page 335)

10 Standing Back Bend (x1)

(See page 328)

11 Warrior Pose (x1)

(See page 338)

12 Mountain Pose

(4 breaths)

(See page 310)

13 Closing Breath

(See page 340)

Massage

Exercise is one way to use the body to calm a stressed-out mind. Massage is another. Essentially, massage refers to a wide variety of techniques that involve stroking, kneading, or otherwise manipulating the muscles and soft tissues. The soothing power of touch has long been recognized, and it comes as second nature to most of us. Think of the way a mother instinctively comforts her baby by patting and rubbing the infant's back. Massage has simply taken this natural instinct and codified it into a therapeutic system.

Almost every culture has a tradition of using the hands as healing tools. In Eastern Asia, these traditions include acupressure and shiatsu. In the Western world, the most familiar method is Swedish massage, which uses long strokes, kneading, and friction on the top layers of the muscles. It's a full-body treatment in which oils or lotions are often used. Swedish massage can be gentle and soothing, or it can be vigorous and stimulating, depending on the speed and firmness of the strokes. This helps explain why it can have different effects on different people. Some feel drowsy after getting a Swedish massage, while others feel invigorated. In either case, the pleasure that a massage gives is usually enough to make the recipient feel like a new person afterward.

Beyond that, massage can stretch tight muscles, releasing the tension there. Studies have found that it can also promote feelings of relaxation and wellness, and alleviate feelings of anxiety and depression. Some research has also suggested that it may reduce blood pressure and promote better sleep.

The exact means by which massage exerts its positive effects is still unknown. However, there's evidence that it stimulates the nervous system, increases the flow of blood and oxygen to the cells, and enhances circulation in the lymph system—a network of organs, nodes,

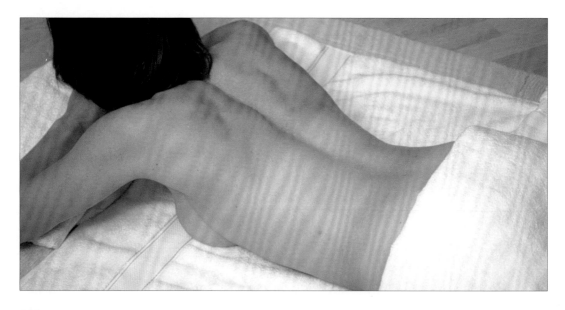

ducts, and vessels that is a major component of the body's immune response. Of course, the exact effects on a particular individual will depend on the technique used, the skill of the person giving the massage, and the mental and physical state of the person receiving it. For the best possible results, you may need to see a professional massage therapist. Nevertheless, even a basic massage that a partner gives you at home is a great way to untie the knots in tense muscles and promote relaxation.

The gentler Swedish massage techniques are generally safe and fine for most people to try on their own. If you're pregnant, ill, or injured, however, ask your doctor if there are any specific techniques you should avoid. Don't massage any part of your body that is painful or inflamed, or where the skin is broken. Let the person giving the massage know if something hurts or feels unpleasant. Also, keep in mind that different people have different comfort levels when it comes to being touched. Listen to your own feelings about what's right for you. If you feel more stressed rather than less so after a massage, try another approach next time. For a full-body massage at home, you'll need a willing partner with whom to take turns.

The nice thing about massage is that it's almost as pleasurable to give as to receive. To set the stage for relaxation, pick a quiet spot. Dim the lights, and perhaps turn on some slow, soft music.

Head lines

To see why head massage is so relaxing, try this simple experiment: Think of something annoying that has happened to you recently. Concentrate on how irritated you felt at the time. Then imagine yourself getting more and more upset, until you're really furious. Now notice how the muscles in your face feel. Is your forehead furrowed? Is your jaw clenched? It's little wonder that tension headaches and jaw pain are two very common symptoms of stress. By releasing all that tension from your face and scalp, you can often turn down the heat on your stress response, too. These two mini-massages can help.

Brow smoother

Place your index fingers side by side in the center of your partner's forehead (see below left). As one moves up, the other moves down. Continue doing this as you walk your fingers apart to your hairline (see below right). Then walk them back together again in the middle of your forehead. Repeat two times. This, and the following massages, can be done with a partner or on your own.

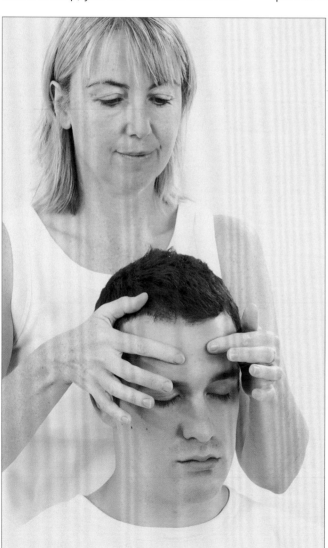

Jaw dropper

Place the four fingers of each hand next to each other on the chin (see right). Massage the muscles there in little circles. Then move the hands about half an inch apart, and massage some more (see below). Continue moving along the jawline this way until you reach the bottom of your ears. Then massage your way back to the chin again. Repeat two times.

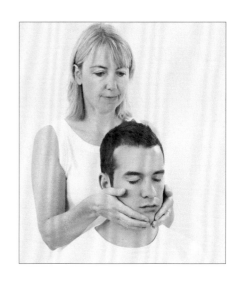

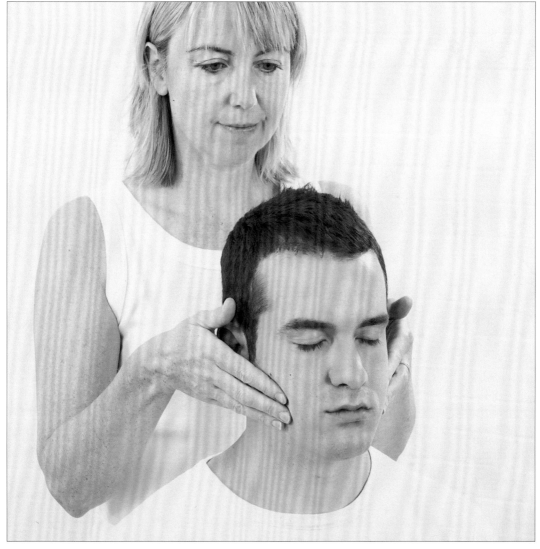

Back Massage

Time required:	About 20 minutes
What you'll need:	A large bath towel for your partner to lie on, a towel to cover their legs and a small towel to act as a head rest.
Caution:	Don't massage the neck or back if the person receiving the massage has an injury, infection, or pain in the area. Check with a doctor first if the person has a chronic medical condition. If a massage stroke causes pain, stop it immediately.

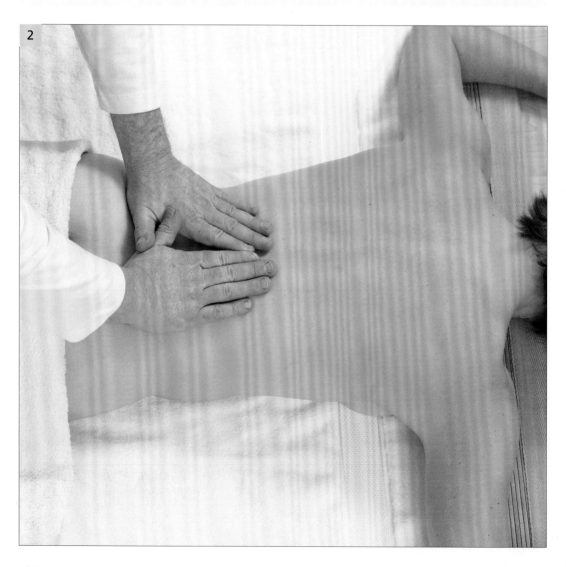

2

Back Preparation

This sequence helps loosen the tissue around the back and helps to stimulate blood flow and relieve tension. To aid the stroke, lightly oil your palms. This is a good stroke to use to spread oil on your partner's back at the start of a massage. An interesting substitute for oil, if your partner is averse to it, is talcum powder.

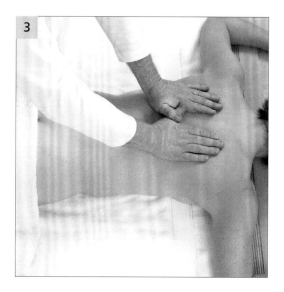

1. Kneel level with the buttocks facing the head so that you can lean into the stroke. Take up a position so that you can complete the movement and reach the shoulder blades without putting an undue strain on your back. So, if necessary, sit closer to the head and start the movement further up the back.

2. Place both hands on the lower back around the base of the spine and then with fingers pointing towards the head, sweep them forward together. Interlock your thumbs to give a more continuous stroke.

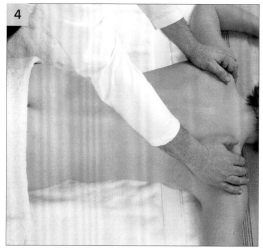

3. Move your hands forward on either side of the spine to a point on the shoulder blades just below the base of the neck and then begin to split them apart.

4. Bring them out around the shoulder blades.

5. Return them to the waist with a smooth, flowing action. Slide them upward to the base of the spine and start this effleurage stroke again.

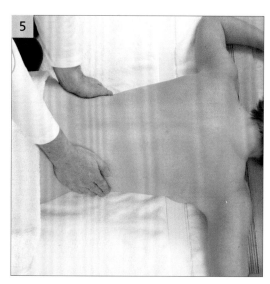

Shoulders

1. With your hands either side of the spine, start this stroke level with the shoulder blades. Press firmly into the muscles with a circular motion of the thumbs, moving your hands slowly up to the spine.

2. Continue the stroke forward until your thumbs reach the top of the neck.

3. To facilitate massage of the shoulder area move your partner's arm back (be careful, the sudden removal of the arm as a prop can make the position uncomfortable for some). Continue to make firm, circular movements with the thumb across the shoulder blade.When you have finished one shoulder blade, repeat on the other side.

4/5. Double up your hands to give more pressure and rotate around the shoulder blade.

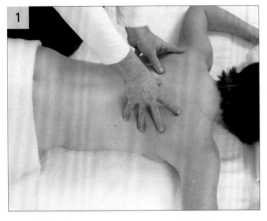

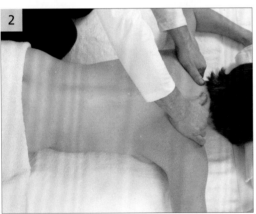

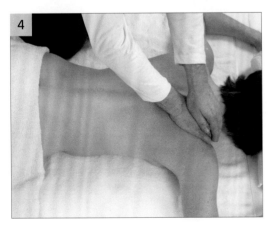

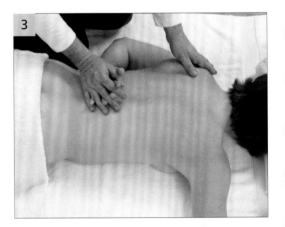

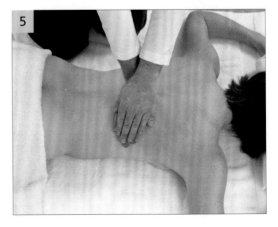

Back

1. Using your hands in concert, knead the area on your partner's side, squeezing the flesh between each hand, but taking care not to pinch. Start at the shoulder and move to the waist and then repeat on the other side.

2. With hands unclenched, execute a chopping motion on the fleshier areas with a brisk action. Avoid the spine and boney areas. Cover as much of the back as you can.

3. Now use a cupping technique. Cup your hands and clap them on the back with a brisk motion, bringing them down alternately and not simultaneously.

4. After all the vigorous activity of cupping and chopping, now use the soothing effleurage stoke described in Back Preparation.

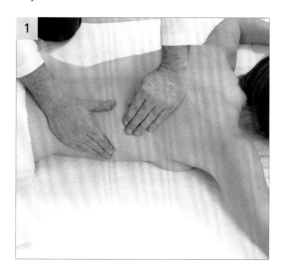

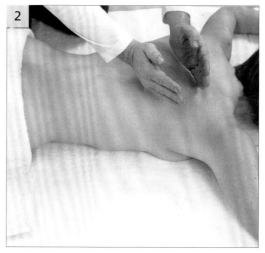

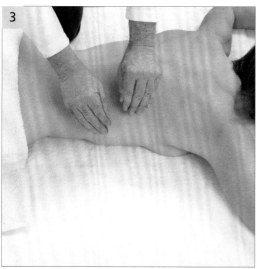

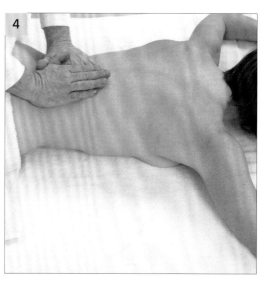

Head and Neck Massage

Time required:	About 20 minutes
What you'll need:	A partner and a firm chair
Caution:	Don't massage the head or neck if the person receiving the massage has an injury, infection, or pain in the area. Check with a doctor first if the person has a chronic medical condition, such as osteoporosis or blood pressure problems, that might make head or neck massage risky. If a massage stroke causes pain, stop it immediately.

1. Give the massage to a partner first. This both familiarizes you with the technique and demonstrates it to your partner. Later, you can take your turn as the recipient. Have the other person sit in a firm chair. If the person has long hair, clip it up while you work on her neck. Ask the person to sit up comfortably straight. Stand directly behind them and rest your hands gently on their head. Take a few minutes to allow your breathing to synchronize with the other person's.

2. Place one hand on the person's forehead. Have them tilt their head forward slightly, resting the weight of their head in your hand. With the fingertips of your other hand, make a series of firm, smooth, gliding strokes down the sides and back of their neck to warm and relax the tissues there.

3. Release the person's head. Place both of your hands on their shoulders with your thumbs on either side of the spine at the base of the neck. Apply steady pressure with the thumbs while rotating them in little circles at that spot. Let the person's comfort level guide how firmly you press. Then move your thumbs up about half an

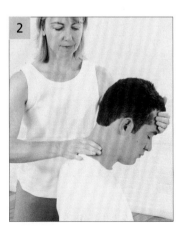

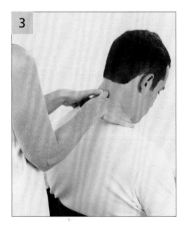

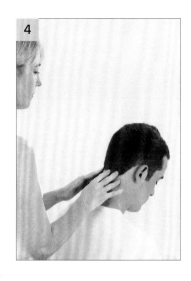

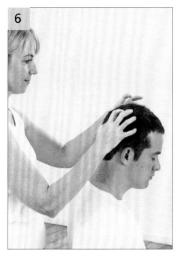

inch. Press the thumbs into the muscles on the sides of the spine, and rotate. Keep working your way up the neck until you reach the base of the skull. Repeat the whole process two times, each time slightly farther from the spine.

4. Stroke your fingertips down the sides and back of the person's neck again, much like in Step 1. This time, however, keep your strokes very light and feathery. Continue for a couple of minutes. If they start to get goosebumps, then keep up the light strokes until the goosebumps subside.

5. Unclip the person's hair, if it's up. Place both hands on top of their head and take a few moments to allow your breathing to

synchronize again. Then, pressing with the palms of your hands, make circular movements. You should feel the scalp moving over the skull. Reposition your hands and repeat. Keep this up until you've covered the entire scalp, but check to make sure this is comfortable.

6. Place your fingertips on the person's front hairline. Rotate your fingertips in little circles, as if you were shampooing the person's hair. Reposition your hands slightly, and repeat. Keep this up until you've covered the entire scalp.

7. Hold both hands above the scalp. Use your fingertips to gently pat all over the scalp in a steady rhythm. Keep your wrists loose, and let your fingers rebound off the scalp, like

raindrops bouncing off the sidewalk.

8. Comb lightly through the person's hair with your fingers, separating the hair but not touching the scalp. Continue for a couple of minutes.

Foot Self-Massage

Time required: About 20 minutes

What you'll need: Nothing

Caution: Don't massage an injured, infected, or painful foot, or press on an area with varicose veins. Check with your doctor first if you have a chronic medical condition that might affect your feet, such as foot and toe problems, diabetes, or arthritis. If massaging a spot causes pain, stop immediately.

1. Sit on a chair. Plant one foot on the ground, and lift the other one, crossing it comfortably over the opposite thigh.

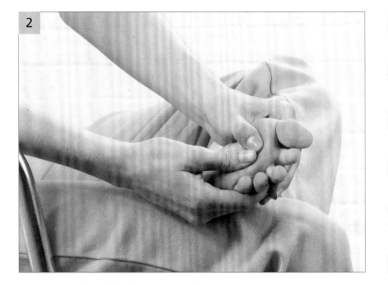

2. Grasp the inside of your foot. Place both hands side by side just below the toes. The thumbs should be on the sole of the foot, and the fingers should be on the top of the foot. With the hand closer to the toes, gently turn the foot away from you. Keep the hand closer to the ankle stationary. Then, with the hand near the toes, gently turn the foot toward you, still keeping the hand near the ankle static. Repeat this back-and-forth motion several times.

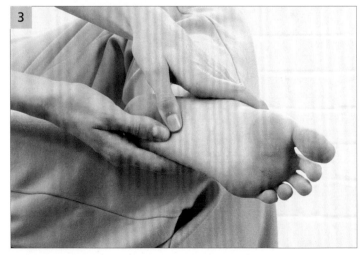

3. Reposition both hands slightly closer to the ankle.

Repeat Step 1. Continue moving your hands down the foot this way until the hands are just above the ankle.

4. Grasp the ball of your foot with both hands. One hand should be holding the inside of the foot, and the other hand, the outside. Place the thumbs on the sole of the foot a little below the big toe

and second toe. Place the fingertips on the corresponding area on the top of the foot. Gently push the foot down and away from you with the right hand, and up and toward you with the left hand. Reverse. Try a figure of eight motion. Repeat this several times.

5. Reposition your hands on the second and third toes.

Repeat Step 3. Do the same on the third and fourth toes, and the fourth and fifth toes.

6. Cup the back of your heel loosely with the hand on the same side of the body, placing your thumb below the ankle bone. With your other hand, grasp the ball of the foot just below the toes. Using the hand by the toes, slowly and gently rotate the foot in a clockwise direction several times. Repeat in a counterclockwise direction.

7. Grasp the ball of your foot with the hand on the same side of the body, placing your fingers on top and your thumb on the sole. With your other hand, grasp the big toe. Slowly and gently rotate the toe in a clockwise direction several times. Repeat in a counterclockwise direction.

8. Apply Step 7 to each of the toes in turn.

9. Repeat all of the above steps on the other foot.

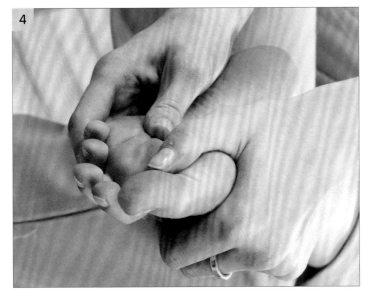

4

6

Hand Self-Massage

Time required:	About 20 minutes
What you'll need:	Nothing
Caution:	Don't massage an injured, infected, or painful hand, or press on an area with varicose veins. Check with your doctor first if you have a chronic medical condition that might affect your hands, such as arthritis, diabetes, or carpal tunnel syndrome. If massaging a spot causes pain, let up immediately.

1. Grasp your left thumb, and pull slowly and gently outward. Take three long, deep breaths. Repeat on each of the fingers of your left hand.

2. Press your right thumb into the palm of your left hand. Rotate the thumb in little circles on that spot. Continue for several seconds. Then move to another spot and repeat. Keep this up until you've covered the whole palm.

3. Place your left hand on your lap or a table, palm down. Press your right forefinger against the outside base of your left thumb. As you take a long, deep breath in, slowly trace up the outside of the thumb to the thumb tip.

4. As you let the breath out, slowly trace down the inside of the thumb to the inside base. As you take a deep breath in, slowly trace up the side of the index finger to the

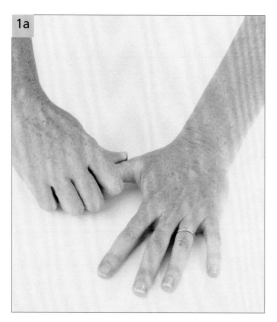

1a

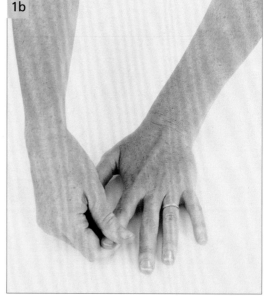

1b

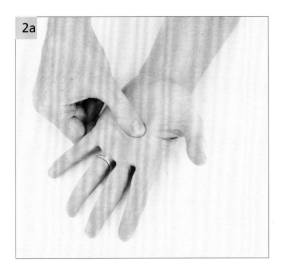

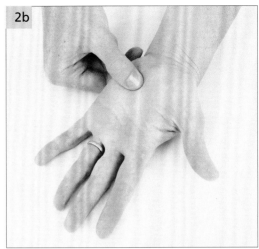

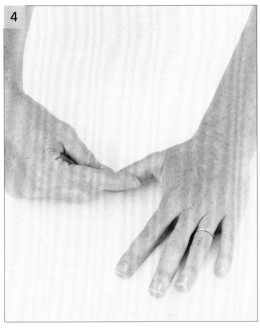

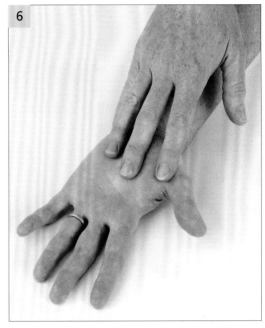

tip. Continue this way along all of the fingers. Then reverse direction, until you get back to your starting point.

5. Turn your left hand over, palm up. Loosely interlace the tips of your right fingers with those on your left hand.

6. Slowly drag your right fingertips down your left fingers, palm, and wrist in a very light, feathery motion. Repeat for a minute

or two. At first, this may tickle a bit, but soon it should feel very soothing.

7. Repeat all of the above steps on the other hand.

Index